I0709739

Into the White

Into the White

The Renaissance Arctic and the End of the Image

Christopher P. Heuer

ZONE BOOKS · NEW YORK

2019

ZONE BOOKS
633 Vanderbilt Street
Brooklyn, NY 11218

Printed in the United States of America.

Distributed by The MIT Press,
Cambridge, Massachusetts, and London, England

Library of Congress Cataloging-in-Publication Data
Names: Heuer, Christopher P., author.
Title: Into the white : the Renaissance Arctic, the end of the image /
    Christopher P. Heuer.
Description: Brooklyn, NY : Zone Books New York, 2019. |
    Includes bibliographical references.
Identifiers: LCCN 2018045506 | ISBN 9781942130147
Subjects: LCSH: Arctic regions — In art. | Arts, Renaissance —
    Themes, motives.
Classification: LCC NX653.A68 H48 2019 | DDC 709.02/4 — dc23
LC record available at https://lccn.loc.gov/2018045506

I like places . . . where, if you make a mistake, you die.

— Lawrence Weiner, on the Arctic

Contents

We Could Not See Out of Our Eyes

In June of 1578, the English privateer Martin Frobisher launched the last of three doomed voyages in search of a Northwest Passage to Asia. His fifteen ships left Plymouth one month later than planned, headed for eastern Greenland. Weeks into the trip, Frobisher's fleet encountered a colossal storm of fog, snow, and ice. The expedition's chronicler, a sailor named Thomas Ellis, described what happened next: "The storm increased, the ice enclosed us . . . so we could see neither land, nor Sea . . . the rigorousness of the tempest was such and the force of the ice so great that [the ice] raced the sides of the shippes . . . thus continued we all that dismall and lamentable night plunged in this perplexitie, looking for instant death."[1]

One of the ships sunk, and at least two others were put so far off course that they ended up backtracking by weeks. Three vessels were eventually able to make landfall near Baffin Island. They succeeded in filling their holds with 1,350 tons of a mysterious ore that Frobisher had discovered on a previous voyage, which he believed to be gold. Setting off for England, more storms set in, with twenty sailors lost. When at last the haul of Frobisher's ore was unloaded back in Bristol that August, it was melted down in Dartford, and the result, as one investor put it, "wrought far from the riches looked for."[2] The stuff, it turned out, was pyrite — fool's gold — and entirely worthless.[3] It was eventually dispatched as brickwork, still visible today in walls around Portsmouth and southern Ireland.

But after the ships drifted home, a remarkable little booklet was published to document (and partially defray the costs of) the disastrous voyage. Appearing in late 1578, it contained, among other things, the world's first visual description of an iceberg (Figure 1.1). Made, supposedly, after drawings by Ellis himself, the print combined four separate views of an ice mass from a distance. Ellis apologized that the iceberg could not be "shewn" as a totality but could be envisioned only from various angles. As he wrote: "1. At the first sight of this great and monstrous peece of yce, it appeared in this shape. 2. In coming neare unto it, it shewed after this shape. 3. Approaching right against it, it opened in shape like unto this, shewing hollow within. 4. In departing from it, it appeared in this shape."[4] Muddled visual relationships between water and air, "land and Sea," became, in Ellis's ink lines, proffered as a sequence of views on a revolving, ever-changing hulk. Allegorized, here, was not just Ellis's "perplexitie," but also a confrontation with conditions that simply did not fit into European schemes of pictorial composition, space, selfhood, and communication.

As elsewhere in New World travel writing and art — as Tzvetan Todorov long ago claimed — pictorial description emerges as inadequate in Ellis's text.[5] And this breakdown itself emerges as a rhetorical convention. Yet as with other accounts of the early modern Arctic, here such inadequacy meant something different than it did in those reports written by adventurers in balmier climes, a development that has yet to be fully examined. Icy, unpopulated, commodity poor, visually and temporally "abstract," the Far North — a different kind of terra incognita for the Renaissance imagination than the sun-drenched Indies — offered no clear *stuff* to be seen, mapped, or plundered. With this, the following book argues, the Arctic quietly, yet powerfully challenged older understandings of image-making in the early modern period. Not a continent, or an ocean, or a meteorological circumstance, the Arctic forced explorers, writers, and early artists from England, the Netherlands, and Germany to grapple with a different kind of "wonder." Here, there were virtually no exotic animals, teeming forests, or enchanting civilizations to study or to loot. In the frigid North, that is, the idea of description as a kind of accumulative endeavor of "representation"

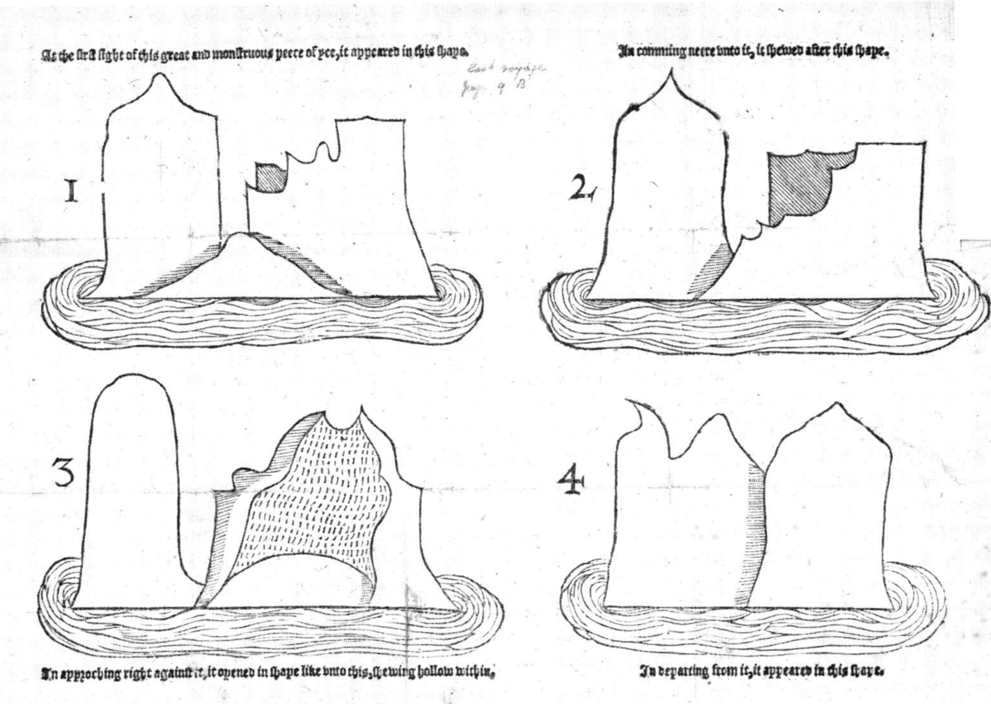

Figure 1.1. *Thomas Ellis, A true report of the third and last voyage into Meta incognita: achieued by the worthie Capteine, M. Martine Frobisher Esquire* (London: Thomas Dawson, 1578), sheet before fol. A1r., Huntington Library and Gardens, San Marino.

was thrown into question. The North was unsettling not because of dazzling difference, but because of monotonous sameness. Rather than an Eden, to Renaissance travelers the Arctic was something like the moon.

The following chapters track a sequence of episodes and objects from European and American Arctic experience between 1500 and 1650. Meshing art history, the history of science, and the study of literature, the book introduces a largely unstudied body of early modern culture and thought. For a few obscure artists, travelers, and natural philosophers, it argues, the Arctic prompted fascinating aesthetic questions about perception, matter, time, and vision, about what, exactly, seeing, resources, and discovery might be. What follows is, broadly, not some awestruck paean to topographic extremes or another prehistory of the modern *informe*. Rather, it is an attempt to reckon with the historical relation between environment and "art" in an era when both concepts were still new.

The Arctic was (and is) a physically dark and blindingly bright place; early visitors commonly described how it demotivated normal means of sight, of recognition. In 1579, an anonymous English pamphleteer spoke of a "penetrating cold that, boring out the inhabitants eyes, giues them the sauce of hunger."[6] Or as a Danish sailor simply said of Greenland in 1607: "We could never see."[7] The Far North of America was not settled in the early years of European expansion the way the South was, and northern Asia was all but unknown to the West. Travelers' accounts almost uniformly thematized blindness, obstruction, and disorientation: "We could not scarce see one another . . . nor open our eyes," wrote one Arctic sailor in 1578.[8] This was a poetics that (at least in later English cases) paralleled Elizabethan arts and letters. (We know that Shakespeare read descriptions of Siberia and the Scandinavian Arctic and lifted parts of them for *Twelfth Night* and *Hamlet*.) But being *like* nothing else, the Arctic regions confounded literary strategies of analogy. The ability to contrast and compare had been employed in more southerly voyages and other pilgrimages, of course. It was a move found in works such as Oviedo's *Historia general de las Indias* (compiled in Mexico in the 1530s) or Hans van Staden's *Warhaftige Historia* (1557) about Brazil. Yet in the polar narratives, it was singularity and inaccess that became a trope: "Walls, mountains, and bulwarkes of yse, choaked uppe the passage, and denied us entrance," wrote Frobisher's lieutenant George Best of Hudson Bay in 1578. For both the straits and their recounting, there was simply, as Best put it, "no waye to passe further in."[9]

Yet this is not just geographical determinism. What separates this early modern Arctic moment from the (better-studied) nineteenth-century age of polar expeditions and photography is simple: the Reformation. We often historicize the pictorial imagination of the poles in terms of the paintings of William Bradford, the photography of John L. Dunmore and George P. Critcherson, and the landscapes of Frederic Church (Figure 1.2).[10] Eleanor Anne Porden's 1818 poem "The Arctic Expeditions" captures this aesthetic: "Sail, sail, adventurous Barks! go fearless forth / Storm on his glacier seat this misty North." Such obsessions with the Arctic were not just responses to, but crucial forces in the creation of global capitalism and the Romantic sublime, as Angela Byrne has noted.[11] Yet long before Kant and Burke had provided the aesthetic scaffolding *of* that sublime, before Mary Shelley set *Frankenstein* at the North Pole, Arctic works appeared in the world of Luther and Shakespeare, of iconoclasm and plague, during a moment when traditional Christian conceptions of the image itself were under pressure. And unlike (say) the Spanish and Portuguese narrators, Dutch and British explorers came out of what one writer has called a "defiantly Protestant polemics."[12] That is, they were extremely sensitive to illusion or the appearance of illusion. It was a moment when the veracity or efficacy of representations in general — the idea of what images were supposed to do — was being fervently debated along confessional lines. Arngrímur Jónsson published his 1571 description of Iceland, *Brevis commentaries de Islania*, for example, as a deliberately Lutheran riposte to "papist" image policies and what he called "church" mystifications about the barbarous Far North.

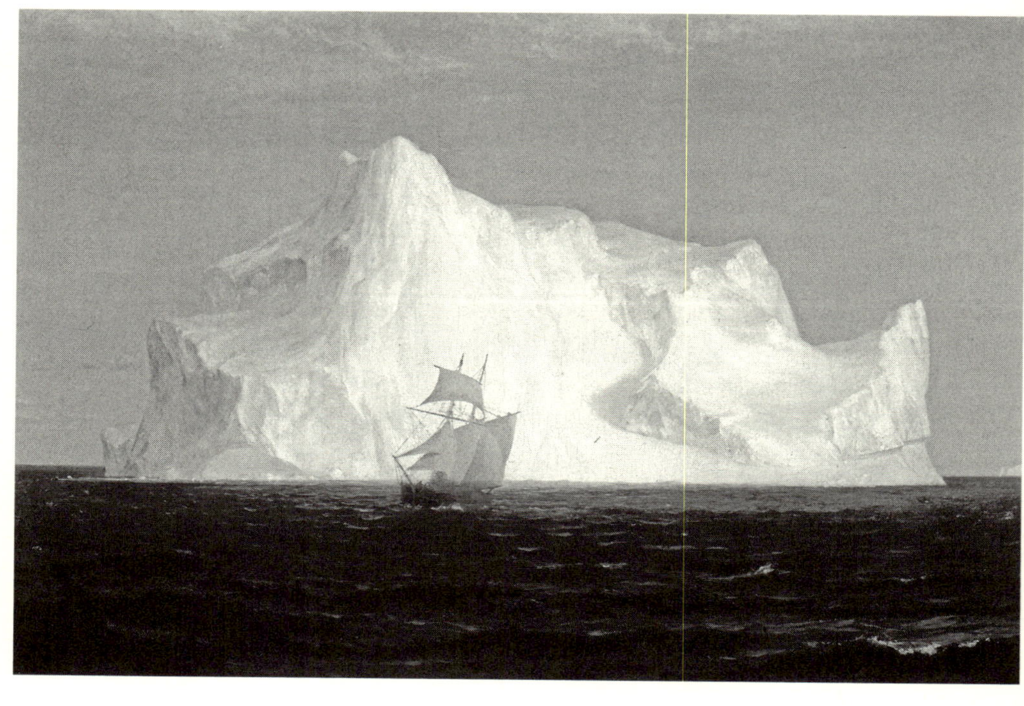

Figure 1.2. Frederic Edwin Church, *The Iceberg*, 1891, oil on canvas, 50.8 x 76.2 cm, Carnegie Museum of Art, Pittsburgh, Howard N. Eavenson Memorial Fund for the Howard N. Eavenson Americana Collection, 72.7.3.

Protestant discussions bespoke a very complex set of anxieties about, on the one hand, worldly things and sensory experience, and on the other, the unreliability of visual imagery as a whole. For in an object-averse milieu, the very idea of scarcity often took on favorable status. The barren and visually impoverished lands of the Arctic bred terror, worry, and fright, but also the physical and imaginative possibility of new and alternative realities.

This is a connection that has been only furtively explored within the humanities. Some of the most inventive describers of specifically Northern phenomena were concretely involved with Reformation image debate, and not always on the side of iconoclasm. The Swedish bishop Olaus Magnus, a subject of the chapters to follow, authored a fascinating and lavishly illustrated tract in 1555 entitled *The History of the Northern Peoples* — all while participating in the Council of Trent.

But art? It is important to stress that *Into the White* is not — directly — about the rich indigenous visual traditions of the North: the Inuit and the Norse, for example (although it does summon them at points). Nor does this little book seek to claim some hitherto-unnoticed icy "influence" upon mainstream European artistic production of the sixteenth century. What the Arctic *did* supply, I want to suggest, is what Stephen Greenblatt once termed "imaginative energies" to European cultural production.[13] All early modern travel writing assumed different standards of believability, of reference.[14] And at the same time, artists' encounters with the printed and illustrated reports on new lands often clashed with home-grown notions of picture making as a self-consciously artificial act.[15] In early reports of (say) steamy Virginia or Mexico, one often sees epistemological difficulty overcome in this vein by authors' assimilating new people and things into old narratives of monstrous races or Arcadian utopias, topics understood as wondrous presentations.

Yet the Arctic, as the literary historian Eric Wilson puts it, was "a negative geography."[16] There was almost nothing at which even to wonder. The Far North was a world away from courts, cities, and riches: it was everything the rest of Renaissance Europe was not. Then, as now, the idea of the Arctic as a featureless, immeasurable expanse, an abstraction that is all but invisible, spoke to the language of both colonization and corporate resource exploitation (with Frobisher's ore a premonition of modern-day oil drilling in the Arctic Sea). I do not intend (just) to pose the Arctic as another bizarre geography prompting curious pictures or writings. Rather, at issue here is the question of what to image when your subject is, pseudomorphically, like a "nonsite" — a terrain present, but physically and ontologically unmoored. Unlike the far South, the extreme North was never a continent — it was a labyrinth of islands and sea.[17] And more than one scholar has pointed to the drastic drop in year-long average temperature in Europe during the period from 1540 to 1620 — the so-called "Little Ice Age" — as a very real force in the art history of transalpine regions.[18] The interrelationship of the environment and the arts — the fetish issue of our late-capitalist artworld — might find precedent with certain cases that follow here.

This is not to say, of course, that early impressions of the Arctic simply resonated with then-present European conditions or staged some premodern destabilization of perception correspondingly registered in art. Unexpected precedents *do* lurk in the sixteenth century, I argue, for both contemporary art's present fascination with (Ant)Arctic landscapes, and current ecocriticism's questioning of Enlightenment distinctions between nature and culture. What follows will not track some facile Arctic teleology of modern painting or claim some Northern provenance for twentieth-century art's obsession with the white void.[19] The book, instead, hopes to trace the roots of the current environmental mode back before industrialization, to the years after the discovery of America. The nineteenth century undoubtedly changed the way the Arctic was represented. But the visual culture of a more familiar "Arctic sublime,"[20] an aesthetic "on the side of enterprise, rivalry and individuation ... a phallic swelling arising from our confrontation with danger"[21] in which the human remains the privileged narrative center for (say) a forbidding snowscape (Figure 1.3), is only one part of the story of art and ecology in the West. And where an "environmental" aesthetic

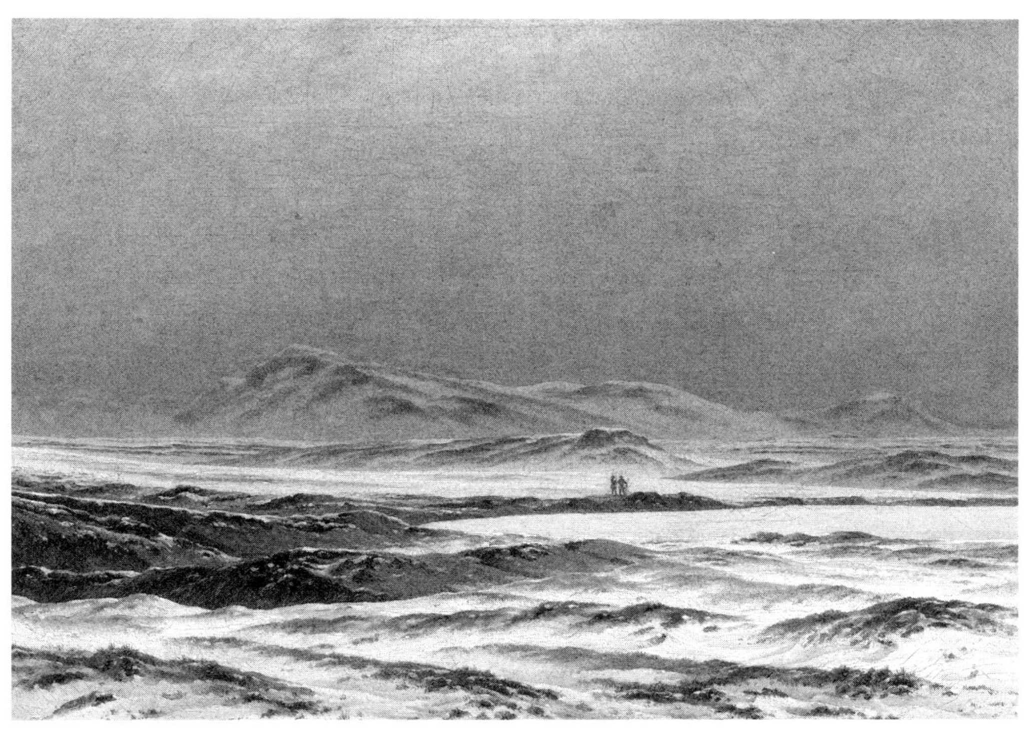

Figure 1.3. Caspar David Friedrich, *Northern Landscape, Spring,* c. 1825, oil on canvas, 35.3 x 49.1 cm, National Gallery of Art, Washington D.C., Patrons' Permanent Fund, 2004.113.1.

is concerned, to ignore what developed in late medieval Europe is almost to mirror the presentist move of linking capitalism and industrialization, imparting the early modern a misleading coherence, even an innocence.[22]

The early explorers' motivations were quite different from each other, but their responses shared skepticism about place's "natural" link to some fixed identity, whether topographical, confessional, or political. During the Renaissance, the Arctic, as a different kind of desert, often recalled biblical ideas of both banishment and contemplation. It was not so much a finite "place" as a condition.

This book's focus, then, is upon what might be called the visual poetics of the Far North: the codes, strategies, and operations of the region's construction, interpretation, and representation by early artists, writers, and natural historians. While centered on older practices, it frequently admixes the new. This is because the temporally and materially disquietous nature of the Arctic landscape here surveyed (at once land, sea, and air, as we will explore) mandates, I submit, a different kind of approach. Historians of early American literature and technology such as Mary C. Fuller, Jeffrey Knapp, and Peter Mancall have provided crucial readings of Arctic voyage literature, isolating its distinctness from — and dialogues with — other species of New World narratives.[23] (In fact, it has been argued somewhat convincingly that before Columbus sailed for the West Indies in 1492, he actually visited Iceland as a young sailor on a Portuguese fishing craft.)[24] Critical Arctic scholarship, for all its richness, has often focused on ethnographic or cartographic questions, on dematerializing narratives of cultural "exchange." The present study hopes to offer a different, if adjacent story, attending in a theoretically informed way to objects, to the material specificity of drawings, texts, maps, prints, and paintings of and from the Arctic from approximately 1480 to 1620. In this, the book draws from literature on Reformation aesthetics. Yet it also seeks to reconfigure the relation between vision and exotic "encounters" in terms of natural history and anthropology.

The book, then, relies upon a slightly different position than many cognate studies of the Far North: namely, that early European articulations of the Arctic were endeavors actually ambivalent about the visual. That is to say: along the lines proposed in a book such as Michael Gaudio's *Engraving the Savage*, the dynamic within early modern Arctic encounters (a largely Protestant phenomenon) was not so much between "self" and "other" as between seen and unseen.[25]

The Arctic put pressure on the notion of New World information transmitted back home. It put pressure, that is, on a perspectival model of encounter and subjectivity, the model for much writing about exoticism in the early modern period, a model in which the other is glimpsed from without or seen *through*, as in Alberti's construction of perspective. Hilltop surveys of New World plentitude are familiar enough: Arthur Barlowe in 1584 described Virginia: "Under the banke or hill where we stoode, we beheld the vallies replenished with goodly Cedar trees . . . the island had many goodly woods, full of Deere, Conies, Fowle, even in the middest of summer, an incredible abundance."[26] Seen from a stable viewpoint, this warm new world opened itself up (so it seemed to Barlowe) as a wealth of discernable *things*. Ellis's iceberg (see Figure 1.1), meanwhile, suggested a murkier encounter. Its object was perhaps water, perhaps land, perhaps frozen air. Its vista was glimpsed fleetingly, unsurely (if at all) from below, in "hideous fogge and mist."[27] Its description was visually decentered, even filmic. As we will see, so many other artworks from this ambit also were prints and were astonishingly self-conscious about their status as mediated messages. They recurrently noted their own capacity for misreading, misinterpretation, or outright failure.

Ultimately, Ellis's remarkable iceberg woodcut summons *Into the White*'s humbler concern: how early modern aesthetic responses to, and constructions of, the Arctic upend and complicate some categories that are blithely applied to histories of Renaissance exoticism in art and science: categories such as wonder, identity, and curiosity. These were modes of encounter present in the Far North, to be sure. Yet they were not the only ones. As Ellis's report made clear, the Arctic experience subsisted not just in *what* is seen, but in a productive anxiety about *how* the act of seeing itself is transformed or even cancelled by a terrain that resisted — in a very real sense — some stable humanist contingency between subject, object, and image. And this was often a literally and figuratively dark process. While nineteenth-century explorers, writers, and photographers often conceptualized the Far North as a site of conquest, heroism, and sublimity, the dominant experience of the Renaissance Arctic was of the intractability, strangeness, and the "perplexitie" of matter. And this resonated (and shaped) new scientific discoveries back in Europe (Robert Boyle's *New experiments and observations touching cold* [1665] would rely heavily on Arctic accounts).[28] Recovering that experience, in historical terms, is one of the modest aims of this book.

In the texts and scant images surviving from Northern voyages, we find explorers frequently doubting their own abilities or their technologies. This is a *directed* doubt, however, not some elegiac breakdown of truth, one that wrought some astonishing pictorial experiments: as Joyce Chaplin brilliantly puts it, "voyages to the north blended creativity with desperation."[29] What follows pivots around a sequence of case studies, but is interleaved with episodes from the now.

After a chapter about the Arctic in antique thought and Atlantic humanism, my analysis in Chapter 3, "'A Strange Quantity of Ice,'" turns to Arctic measurement and specifically the metric of *scale*. As both a concrete gauging rubric (maps) and a more general way of understanding human relations to space, scale engaged explorers in very real ways. That unfamiliar spatiovisual experience, for example, might trouble any sorties to the Far North became a documented concern in the sixteenth century. Well into Frobisher's time, great curiosity stirred around a lost book known as the *Inventio fortunata* (Fortune-making discovery), written by an anonymous Franciscan friar, allegedly at sea (the tract, known through glosses of a Dutch-language summary from the 1490s, narrated an icy voyage heading as far northwest as the Canadian archipelago, even detailing encounters with inhabitants the Norse called

"Skraelings," ancestors of the modern Inuit). The *Inventio* also told of a magnetic rock at the North Pole. The account circulated in manuscript form and became the basis for the first-ever maps of the Arctic Circle.

For cartographers, the Arctic was a region that literally redefined the boundaries of the world.[30] A chart of the North Pole issued by Gerardus Mercator in Antwerp in 1569 offered a means to introduce a new graphic system for representing the world, the projection that still bears his name. His map formally reimagined the globe as a cylinder — as an abstraction. But true North remained a plural (and literally captioned as such) relational concept. Rather than admit the ambiguity of precise location determination, Mercator left the landscape unresolved: he laid out the Arctic as a site of geographical questions.[31]

Chapter 4, "The Savage Episteme," turns to the human, with the case of kidnapped Inuit depicted on woodcuts from Frankfurt and Augsburg in 1566. The taking of living people as expeditionary trophies from the North was grimly common in New World voyages in 1570s, as was, more surprisingly, their portraiture. The Flemish expatriate Cornelis Ketel, who lived in London, was paid for making six pictures of a "tartar man" (likely an Inuit hunter) in 1576. As captives from "Terra Nova," these unfortunates were wondrous exotica for European audiences, but their depiction presented problems for the broadsheet form, itself an unsteady medium for the authority of eyewitness testimony. In Reformation Europe, both Calvinist and Catholic propagandists mobilized images of the Inuit to decry confessional savagery back home. But I argue that the "wild man" paradigm that had been previously used to represent earlier captives from (say) New Spain — a paradigm assuming a clean break between civil and other — buckled in the Arctic prints. The appearance of the Inuit was coincident with specific outbreaks of iconoclasm in Antwerp in 1566, as well as with half-heard reports of other Northern *naturalia* such as narwhals and walruses — phenomena that had been sketched by Albrecht Dürer and were being studied by Swiss natural historians such as Conrad Gessner (1516–1565) at this same time. The prints of the captives, thus, do not just stage the tension between the authority of words and images in visual descriptions of the non-European. Rather, designers were trying to delineate an alternative sphere of New World "indigenous" life, one that was to culminate (as we will see) in the famous watercolors (and subsequent prints) of John White.

Chapter 5 begins in Lapland, then moves to Rome. It was there that the exiled Uppsala bishop Olaus Magnus (1490–1557) composed his monumental *Historia de gentibus septentrionalibus* (History of the people who live under the seven stars), printed in 1555, a book eventually translated into six languages. Its more than four hundred individual woodcuts offered content on folklore and customs, with expositions of history and religion and three separate chapters on snow. Long famed as a key work of "ethnography," the book, I argue, actually uses Northern realms and climate as the basis for a lengthy defense of images. In this, Olaus diverges from histories of the extreme North common among scholarly audiences in his own day: Tacitus's *Germania*, Norse and Celtic folklore, and humanist myths of the primeval forest.

Chapter 6, "Arctic Ink," moves to the deathly voyage of the Netherlandish navigator William Barents (1550–1597). Barents's sixteen-man crew, searching for the Northeast passage, was forced to over-winter on Nova Zembla (in what is now northern Russia) in 1596. Most of the crew, amazingly, survived. An officer on board, Gerrit de Veer, kept a diary of the journey, telling tales of polar bears, Arctic foxes, aurorae borealis, frostbite, and scurvy, an account that, published in 1600 as an illustrated book, became one of the first adventure bestsellers. What is perhaps most remarkable, however, is the physical archaeological evidence of that ordeal that survives today in the form of 200 different objects now in Amsterdam. Apart from clothing, tools, and a mechanical clock that stopped because of the cold, there is a collection of Flemish engravings. The latter were intended to serve as merchandise in the Far East. Frozen in the Siberian permafrost for more than three centuries, these now-recovered sheets represent one of the strangest cultural displacements — of objects, as well as of people — during the century's exploration.

The Barents chapter, then, along with Chapter 7, "'There Are No Fortresses,'" takes up the idea of advanced art *in* the Arctic, rather than of it, a phenomenon that has hugely expanded in our own centuries. Alongside the reality of a year-round Northwest Passage (a development actually welcomed by many impoverished Far Northern communities)[32] and the broadened availability of commercial travel to the North, the region has become accessible — and relevant to contemporary art as never before. But it still remains an empty realm, which has left it open both to neoliberal aesthetic spectacle and to social creativity. The Soviet Union's hope-filled obsession with Northern settlement in the 1920s and 1930s, I argue, supplies a surprising return — perhaps modernity's *only* return — to the poetics of material Arctic possibility (and terror) that the sixteenth century engaged. While fashioning its own mythologies of Northern heroism (ones, that, we will see, looked precisely to Muscovy in the Renaissance), the Stalinist USSR looked *past* the nineteenth-century colonialist sublime. It instead nourished the idea of an unspectacular, bureaucratic Arctic of camps and technology, a place at once futuristic and murderous. Here I discuss a specific case of Soviet Arctic photomontage — the 1933–34 work of El Lissitzky and Sophie Küppers for the periodical *SSSR na stroike* (USSR in construction). Then, turning to more contemporary work by Olafur Eliasson and, differently, the Center for Land Use Interpretation in Greenland, this chapter probes contemporary art's reconfiguration of an aesthetic of Northern dullness, slowness, and, as Adorno once put it, "coldness."[33] Against the idea that recent works represent some neo-Romantic abstract recoil into deaccelerated nature, I argue that certain art practices are in fact probing the opposite: a heterogeneous interest in information technologies and posthuman or prehuman histories. These engagements remain at once contingent upon and questioning of media's capacities to "reveal" — just as Ellis's iceberg woodcut had been.

What follows is not a lament, or necessarily a polemic, but a sustained and historical critique of early modern theories of representation that uses Arctic material as a fulcrum. If anything, it seeks to temper the breezier accounts of how images matter to studies of the Renaissance's "global" character or the relation between art and ecology.[34] In so doing, the book means to shed light on materials that are little known to all but specialists, yet turn out to be surprisingly relevant to some of art history's compelling and often problematic revisitings: the neopoetics of matter,[35] messaging and miscommunication,[36] or even geohistory's relation to advanced art practice.[37] The book is not a prehistory of earth art, but, perhaps, a posthistory of Renaissance landscape: an exploration of a milieu where a stably humanist "point of view" did not apply.

CHAPTER TWO

The Stars Down to Earth

To the ancient Greeks, the Arctic was a cosmological situation, rather than a place. Their word *artici* designated those earthly regions that lay beneath the stars in the constellation *arktos* (arctic, from αρκτικός, or, "near the bear"). It signaled a zone of stars in the night sky that, unlike others, moved only in tight circles around a seemingly fixed point — "ever-visible" bodies, wrote Euclid.[1] Stars within this Arctic Circle (at least when seen from mainland Greece) did not move across the horizon over the course of weeks and months, as did other constellations. Inaugurated was the idea of an earthly Arctic as a zone on the globe where the "permanent" stars were directly overhead and where, as Gemnius of Rhodes wrote in the first century BCE, it was dark for half of the year.[2] Ptolemy would fix this Arctic Circle, an imaginary line, at around 63 degrees north of the equator.[3]

What exactly did the ancients offer the early moderns regarding the Far North? For Greek cartographers, the concept of an Arctic Circle was from its inception problematic: it was, in essence, a varying cosmological value. The celestial arctic — the visible part of, say, the star Polaris — varied depending on from where on the surface of the earth one was observing it. This was an issue noticed early on; even today, the Arctic Circle is not fixed, but a constantly shifting zone that is based on celestial movement. The geographer Posidonius (d. 51 BCE), for example, identifying the Arctic as a relative quantity, was quoted by Strabo as asking, "How one could determine the limits of the temperate zones, which are non-variable, by means of the 'arctic circles,' which are neither visible among all men nor the same everywhere?"[4] This mismatch with universal determination became woven into the idea of the Arctic at its roots.

Cold Breathing

Posidonius, in fact, spoke mockingly of Pytheas of Massalia, who very possibly sailed to the sub-Arctic regions, likely Iceland, around 320 BCE.[5] Pytheas's lost book, *On the Ocean*, described the terrestrial conditions of the Far North as a haunting "sea lung" (*pleumōn thalattios*) at the ends of the earth, in which "the earth and the sea and everything else are suspended. This substance is like a fusion of them all; and can neither be trod upon not sailed upon."[6] He called the region "Thule."[7] Herodotus had spoken only of a vague *erēmos alēthōs*, a land of desolation, "where no nation of man lives."[8] Not water, solid, or air (but somehow all three), the region's very being did not fit into clear taxonomies of matter. It was a terminal space, one of, as Herodotus went on to claim, "the furthest things that can be mentioned."[9] The idea of the Arctic as a suspension without distinctions between earth and air harkens back to Plato of the *Phaedo*, who speaks of sites where mud, steam, water, and air all flow and mingle together, with "no bottom and no foundation."[10] Such a prelapsarian state rooted in cold, rather than warmth, would later animate the thought of Walter Benjamin—avid collector of snow globes—about precivilization beginnings. Benjamin metaphorized words as a miasmic "snow flurry" with the ability to upset the arrangement of the world.[11]

Pytheas, in fact, remained a uniquely charged figure. His earliest mention appears in Dicaearchus of Messina, a student of Aristotle and the philosopher Eratosthenes. The writers Timaeus and Hipparchus both took him at his word.[12] Strabo, far more hostile, dismissed Pytheas as a fabulist—one who "had claimed to have surveyed the entire Northern coast of Europe as far as the bounds of the kosmos," but remained, in this, the "lyingest man" (*anēr pseudodistatos*), "a showman of the marvelous."[13] In fact, the associations gradually attached to Pytheas—and with him, Thule—continually surface as ones of ever-shifting truth and falsity. And self-conscious commentary *upon* that shifting. Antonius Diogenes's fragmentary novel, *Incredible Things Beyond Thule* (second century CE), sets a ludic comedy in and around actually recorded places and people, citing authors such as Pytheas and his tales as a parody of the "natural history" writing genre. For Antonius, to speak of Thule was to rehearse marvels.[14] His narrator, the traveler Denias, relays these wonders in the first person, thus transforming the drama of the story from some encyclopedic listing of geographical strangenesses to the personal experience *of* those geographical strangenesses—a far from unique antique strategy. Yet what seems to have been different about Diogenes's book (based on the inordinate number of medieval commentaries about the novel that survive) is the way his "Thule" seemed to signal not just an imaginary place, but a literary conceit generative of *further* imaginary places, presented as if seen.

Here, for example, is Synesius, bishop of Cyrene (370–413), in a letter to a Christian friend: "Whenever we listen to tales of the world beyond Thule, whatever Thule may be, [it] gives to those who have crossed it freedom to lie."[15] "Visiting" the Far North, it seems, here is synonymous with reading. Which was precisely what further explorers did. To an anonymous ninth-century reader writing in marginalia, Thule recalled those places in Lucian's *True History* (itself self-consciously presented as a fabulation) where inhabitants "do not have bodies but are invisible (αφανει) and without flesh, showing only a form and a shape," where "there is no nighttime there, nor is the day ever very bright."[16]

Thule, thus, could serve as a blatantly imaginary, satiric place such as Aristophanes's Cloudcuckooland, but also part of the earth known and viewed. Tacitus, meanwhile, would lump all lands above the North Sea together as a place "one might call antipodal" (*utque sic dixerim Oceanus*).[17] His main subject was far more southern: Germany. Thule, however, was a world apart; and in the *Agricola*, Tacitus actually focused by name on the conditions of the Arctic seas, as Pytheas had done: "The sea was sluggish and hard to row against, and was barely stirred by the winds."[18] Islands in such ice could not be reached. This was a different kind of wilderness than the German forest.

The poetic and ideological value of "Thule" began to take on new visibility in the sixteenth century.[19] Commentaries on Pliny by Joachim Vadianus (1522) and Antoine du Pinet (1562) equated Thule with Iceland; the Brabantine physician and linguist Johannes Goropius Becanus, writing in 1569, actually mentioned Pytheas by name.[20] Astronomers, rediscovering Ptolemy, could fix the terrestrial Arctic Circle at 63.5 degrees from the equator with precision: the region's indefinability now migrated from cartography into the realm of history.[21] Humanists enlisted Thule as a general image of extremes, a semilegendary place with an antique pedigree; Felix Faber, Conrad Celtis, Ronsard, and others invoked Thule as a rhetorical catch-all for the wild edges of the world.[22] An even more elusive account is that of the Byzantine merchant Laskaris Kananos, who traveled from Constantinople to, it seems, Iceland sometime before 1438.[23] In a manuscript that survives now in Vienna, Laskaris describes staying in the land of the "fish eaters," where "the day consisted of six months, from the beginning of the spring to the autumnal equinox."[24] Only after the century's later voyages would specifics of the North's physical conditions (such as cold) surface in Thule's poetic profile. In 1600, Thomas Weelkes, an English composer, actually set an anonymous love poem about the Far North ("Thule: The Period of Cosmography") to a madrigal.[25]

What was most jarring to many Renaissance writers was the strange *lack* of Arctic descriptions in ancient sources. In the humanist imagination, the Arctic was not just a designation of empty earth, but a place resistant to mapping, where the elements blurred. It was, as Aristotle put it, one of the ζώνες (zones or bands) literally *outside* the realm of habitation. "Thule" was one more speculation about what lay at the edges of the *oikoumenē*, the habitable earth. Yet as a realm cut off from communication with civilization (so readers thought), the Far North represented not just an extremity, but possibly another world (*alii orbes*).[26] In translations of a thirteenth-century astronomy text by Johannes de Sacrobosco, *De sphaera mundi* (On the sphere of the world), the extreme North and South of the earth were illustrated as cracked striations (Figure 2.1). These were contrasted with bands of towns and cities in the more temperate zones, marked off by the chords of a circle.[27] Habitability was possible only in those places protected from extremes.

Such bands strayed into published adaptations of Ptolemy. The Saxon mathematician Peter Apian (Latinized to Petrus Apianus) published the extremely popular *Cosmographia* in 1524, a small book that later went through forty-five editions in four languages. In a rare 1532–33 abridgement of the *Cosmographia* printed in Antwerp, Apianus tied global bands to the five fingers of the left hand in a woodcut (Figure 2.2), distributing them, as he wrote, "grammatically."[28] Even at the antipodes, the body was literally the measure of the earth. As he explained, "Where the thumb is, there is the Arctic, which is called the North, and we understand that it is much too severe and uninhabitable."[29] Aristotle's microcosm / macrocosm analogism remains in place. But Apianus offers a model for readers to understand the Arctic by thinking about how their own bodies are located in relation to other spaces.[30] The digit-based analogy — a throwback to medieval memory systems — connects even the vast, uninhabited *zona frigida* to a kind of manual intimacy. Such mapping is still reliant upon the sturdy idea of the body as measure, the framework of "feet" and "palms." And yet the strain on this scale wrought by both discoveries and a reconceptualization of the Far North is evident, as Apianus explains in a tacked-on section about the geographical discoveries in the Indies.[31] Important here is the realization that the poles were the parts of the earth most subject to change with these alterations to ancient notions of zones.

Of course, lines (Arctic or not) were not only cartographic modes of representation in Europe in the sixteenth century. South Atlantic mapping and Italian linear perspective were processes roughly contemporaneous with each other in development. Both were interested in the construction of arenas for action. In the *Della pittura* of 1435, Alberti ascribed to the term *prospettiva* a double meaning: it could designate a process for creating the illusion of depth on a flat

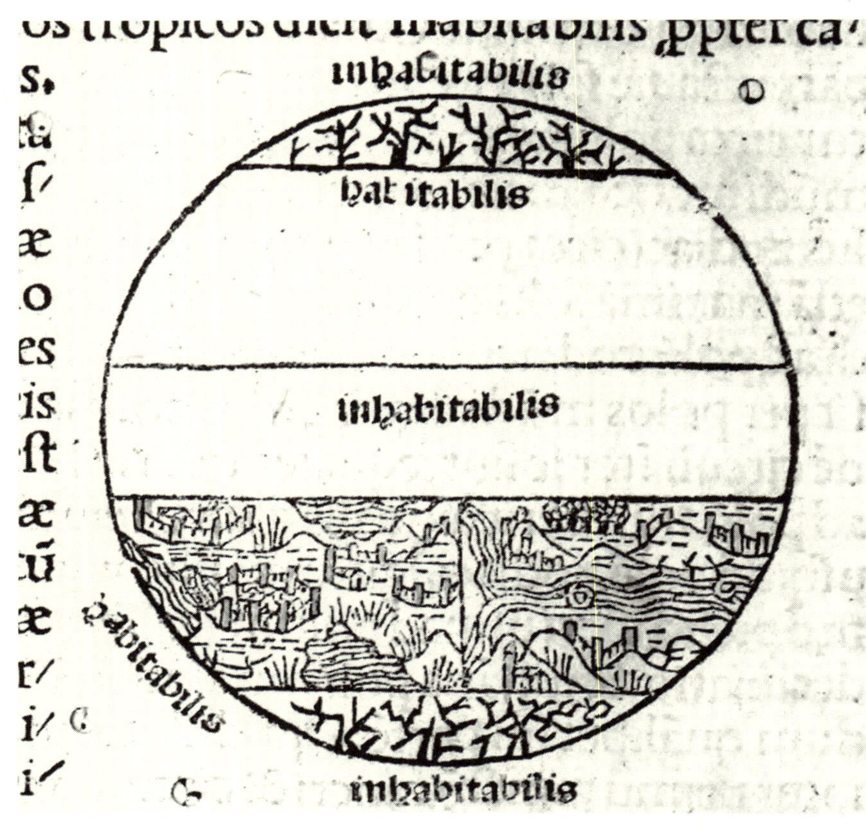

Figure 2.1. Johannes de Sacrobosco, *De sphaera mundi* (Venice: Octavianus Scotus, 1490), fol. 5v., Thomas Fisher Rare Book Library, University of Toronto.

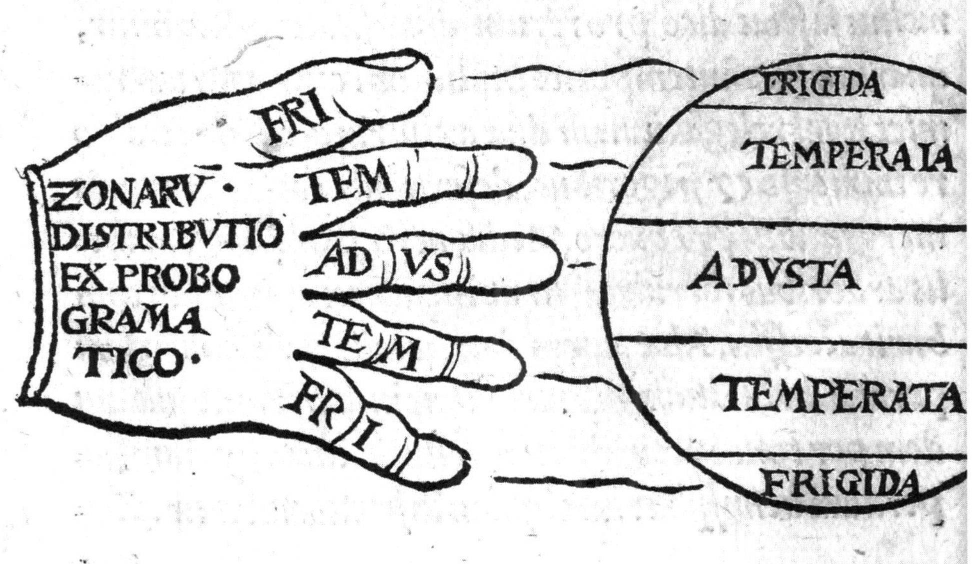

Figure 2.2. Petrus Apianus, *Cosmographiae introductio: cum quibusdam geometriae ac astronomiae principiis ad eam rem necessarijs* (Ingolstadt: Apianus, 1533), fol. 14v., John Carter Brown Library, Brown University, Providence.

surface or for ordering and controlling structural information from a single point of view.[32] In either case, it assumed a fixed relationship between an observer and sets of objects, a screen between work and world. *Perspectiva artificialis* — as a drawing system, a symbol — was meant to collapse the experience of lived space to serve geometric ends.

And after Alberti's moment, perspective (like cartography) had become a myriad of pictorial practices. Quattrocento ideas about perspective had begun to travel and fragment once art tracts in North Europe appeared, often turning away from "spaces" to investigate the problematics of bodies and shapes. Artists used it to decorate jewelry and furniture — to play optical games. Albrecht Dürer in 1525 called perspective a *Durchsehung* — a seeing through — thus transforming itself away from a means to simulate stages for stories and toward the creation of otherworldy patterns. Protestant questioning of the patly optical played a part. With Dürer's pupil Erhard Schön (Figure 2.3), for example, the 1530s were a time to produce both *Vexierbilder* (puzzle pictures) and pro-Lutheran propaganda.[33] It was as if perspective, in a Reformed context, could surrender to refraction and secrets.

For art history, of course, perspective remains a famously transhistorical phenomenon. It is tiresome to rehearse the many ways perspective compositions in the Quattrocento are traditionally paired with an epochal point of modernity — the beholder, rather than the guild or the Catholic Church — as determinant of the "world picture," the rationalization of space and the reorganization of the artwork surface itself as the potential subject of a painting. Art-historical recuperations of these moments, most famously the work of Erwin Panofsky, have followed the model of a perspectival picture itself, looking back upon the past from an artificially stable point. Panofsky invoked Dürer's language to describe perspective as a model of "exactness and predictability" that staged the self in relation to a controlled nature. This "central" perspective spoke to a single viewer while claiming, like a map, to offer a universalized "fully rational — that is, infinite, unchanging, and homogeneous — space,"

Panofsky claimed.[34] Hubert Damisch and others have attended to the wildness suppressed by such a system. In all cases, however, perspective empowered a subjective "I" anterior to its own linear framework, as thinkers from Merleau-Ponty to Lacan have discussed. And in this, Renaissance perspective actually bespoke a schizophrenic poetics of subjectivity. It is a framework that collapses seeing and knowing by "showing" neither.

Across objects and spaces, that is, the classic story of perspective remains that of a subject-centered address, one that a cartographic conceit like the Arctic seemed to refute.[35] Like the later Kantian sublime, perspective thus entered European art as a way of thinking about reason via reason's unpresentability. And like that sublime, traditional perspective pivoted upon the free individual. It offered a way to arrange virtual spaces and a means to define the self based upon orderly epistemological distance. "Thule"'s material reality tolerated no such order. If perspective promised early moderns *access* to the world, access granted in a flash from a single consoling viewpoint, the Far North suggested an imaginary where "the furthest things" forever resisted visual capture.

The Arctic as Movement

In many sixteenth-century contexts, this new perspectival thinking affected understandings of the sea. No longer regarded as a limit or obstruction, the oceans became (as in Alberti's picture plane) a passageway. In Tudor England, the Far North suggested a commercial foil to Iberian dominions in the South: "There is left one way to discover, which is into the North," wrote a courtier to Henry VIII in 1527.[36] In Britain, pamphlets began to appear that touted the viability of such enterprises, dubiously asserting the preferability of its frigid temperatures to the "intemperate Climats" found in the tropics.[37] Colonies, argued investors, would be the solution to the growing problem of poverty in London, which was a direct result of the century's increased defeudalization of large estates. Land enclosure, combined with Henry VIII's early dissolution of the monasteries, flooded English cities with migrants during the 1560s.[38]

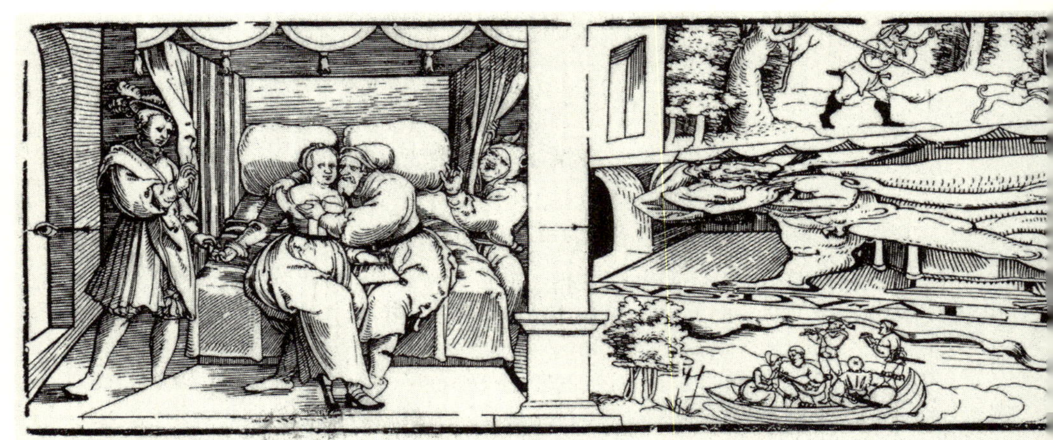

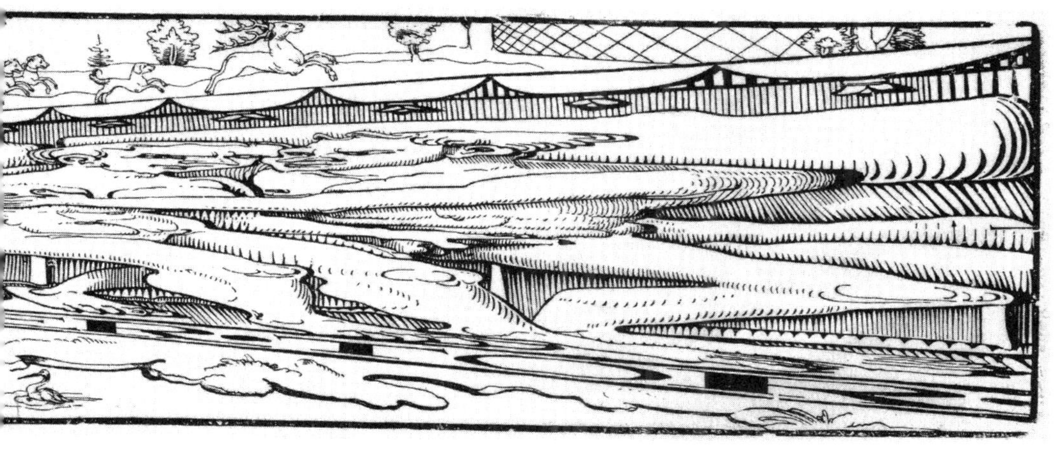

Figure 2.3. Erhard Schön, *Aus Du Alter Tor!*, 1530s, woodblock print, 5.5 x 76.6 x 2.9 cm, Kupferstichkabinett, Staatliche Museen, Berlin, Inv. Derschau 297.

English explorers of the Arctic were proceeding under astonishing levels of confidence that everything known about the Far North since the ancients was wrong: that it was devoid of resources, perennially dark, uninhabitable. The English Arctic, they convinced themselves, could be charted, measured, and described — even if it was only partially visible. The century's great forays into what would become northern America all depended upon this belief.

Such is the vision secreted within Hans Holbein the Younger's 1533 double portrait of Jean de Dinteville and Georges de Selve (Figure 2.4). It is a painting known for its mimetic extravagance, its assemblage of devices dependent upon number. Yet the panel is centered, unexpectedly, on the Far North. On the bottom shelf of the depicted table, Holbein rests a terrestrial sphere, tilted to show Europe and the North Pole; it is a model of the earth unmounted in a stand (the globe was meant to be hand held),[39] based on an actual orb fashioned in Nuremberg around 1530.[40] At the time of the painting, Holbein was working for the Tudor court, and the globe is shown with England's potential dominions given visual prominence. While the Western Hemisphere is mostly in shadow, one section of the orb is starkly and dramatically lit: the Arctic (Figure 2.5). Holbein shows an open sea just above what is now Hudson Bay. This specific latitude is tipped toward an unseen light source to reveal details of the polar cap as a white void atop a sea channel in extreme North America, ringed by an Arctic Circle painted in red. This is just below the simple label "DESERTII" (desolation). Set, hopefully, tantalizingly close to mainland Europe, this Arctic is lashed by a meridian that distinguishes Spanish and Portuguese dominions (the Tordesillas Treaty of 1494 had split the known earth into Occidental and Oriental realms) to show a wished-for Northwest Passage near Labrador, visible just astride a shadow.

This dream of an open polar sea would motivate English financiers to fantasize about larger speculative enterprises to Cathay and then to northern Russia. In 1551, a consortium of wealthy merchants, the Mystery and Company of Merchant Adventurers for the Discovery of Regions, Dominions, Islands, and Places Unknown was founded in London by Richard Chamberlain, Hugh Willoughby, and Sebastian Cabot.[41] Their goal was simple: a shipping route to China that would allow British trade interests to undercut Spain's monopoly on spice routes. As one of England's first joint-stock companies (others had ventured to Africa), the company presaged the modern corporation: it collected individual investors to underwrite nautical expeditions, distributing profit (and risk) among shareholders. Stock was held by more than two hundred and fifty individuals. In 1553, 10,000 English pounds were raised to fund the voyages of "three shippes" to Arctic Asia, led by Chamberlain and Willoughby.[42] But only a single vessel survived.[43] Two other craft were completely lost, their crews, we know, frozen to death while trying to overwinter. (We will hear more about this later.) Despite such a disaster, the company was pleased that "good" prospects existed for profit in Muscovy. Cabot, who had planned the doomed expedition, was made "governor for life" and received a bonus.[44] Trade in Russian pelts and lumber became brisk. But by 1568, the Muscovy Company, as it was then called, would be sued for "greedy covetousness" and "evil behavior" in its Arctic dealings.[45]

But in Holbein's painting, the globe aligns such entrepreneurship with a multisurfaced celebration of new technology — and with painting's ability to *frame* such innovation as possession. Next to the ambassadors' own orb lies a set of squares and dividers, an armillary sphere, an open, printed book, and a lute with a broken string. These things are all not just precious — they are new; during the commission, Holbein was working with Henry VIII's court astronomer and designer of instruments, Nicolas Kratzer.[46] Holbein had used the same crimson paint to mark the globe's longitudinal grids as he did for the book cover lying nearby, which is propped open with a T square. This book, visibly opened to show sums and addition tables, has been identified as *Kauffmanns Rechnung* (Merchant's arithmetic), a 1527 tract published in Ingolstadt by the same Petrus Apianus of the hand orb *Cosmographia*.[47] On Holbein's lower shelf, then, are linked computation and mapmaking as combined means to gauge Europe's new discoveries. Even the woolliest wilds of the unknown Northern Hemisphere, the picture suggests, may be quantified, overseen, and

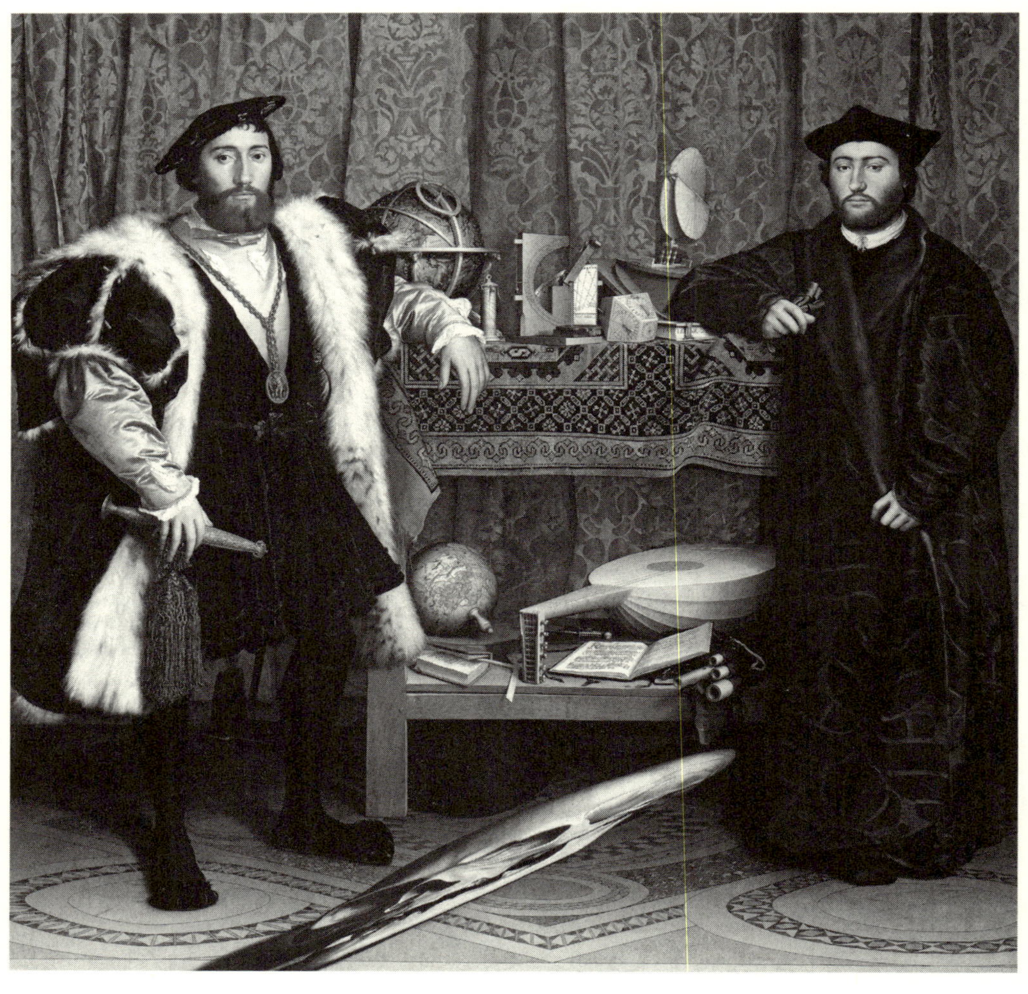

Figure 2.4. Hans Holbein the Younger, *Jean de Dinteville and Georges de Selve ("The Ambassadors")*, 1533, oil on oak, 207 x 209.5 cm, National Gallery, London, NG1314.

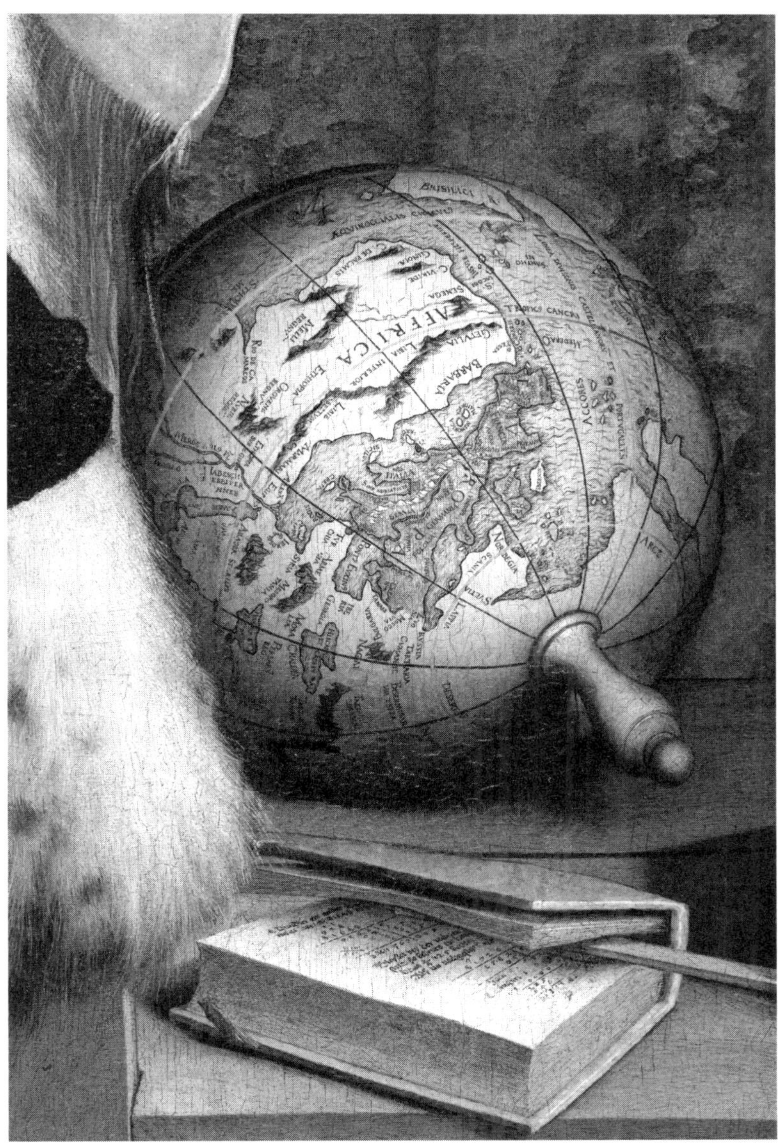

Figure 2.5. Hans Holbein the Younger, *Jean de Dinteville and Georges de Selve ("The Ambassadors")* (detail).

managed by a humanist intelligence.[48] In fact, an inscription on a later globe from 1596 — this one dedicated to Elizabeth I — presented the English contribution to world cartography as the specific mapping of the areas around the North Pole.[49]

A grayish smear famously tears through the Holbein painting's lower half. When viewed from an oblique angle, this floating patch, of course, resolves into a giant human skull in shadow. While anamorphic projection was not exactly new at the time, even in England,[50] the *vanitas* symbolism on such a scale was unprecedented. The death's head is actually one of two in the picture, the other in the form of a tiny hat pin atop de Dinteville's black cap at the upper left. A gold crucifix secreted in the extreme upper left of the picture, meanwhile, posits a visual rhyme with the slanting skull. Such facets traditionally alluded to the transience of human pursuits and voyages, the folly of human actions undertaken without faith. (We know that both de Selve and de Dinteville were liberal Catholics.)[51]

But as befits the occupation of Holbein's sitters — ambassadors — the unique construction of the skull renders the picture not just about vanity, but about movement. To view the full amassment of scalar things (rulers, lutes), one must physically dislocate one's actual body. One must, before the picture, travel. What is "revealed," then, is not just some hidden iconography, but the relational dependence of such emblems on a particular somatics of picture viewing, of world viewing, on the mobile body. Incredibly for a portrait (usually about stasis, about identity), the work thus becomes about kinesis and unfamiliarity — with the Arctic at its pivot. This is, on the one hand, a dim echo of the medieval idea of the Christian as a *homo viator* — a wayfarer between heaven and the afterlife.[52] But on a more immediate level, such thematization of travel refers, of course, to what exactly it is that ambassadors *do*. (We know that at the time of the commission, de Selve was journeying to England in secret, negotiating the divorce proceedings of Henry VIII.)[53] The painting thus connects discovery — as of the Far North — with bodily displacement, with experiential rupture. Meanwhile, the picture's visual proffering of epistemological mastery and possession *to* us is violently cancelled by an anamorphosis that *ungrounds* us, revealing, as Lacan once wrote of the *Ambassadors*, "the subject as annihilated."[54] Anamorphosis, like Arctic cartography, became a rip in the perspectival scheme of the world.[55] But in this, mortality is also an easily assimilable possession. In Holbein's picture, just as movement shows you death, so does it ingeniously *dramatize* a confrontation with unformed matter, presenting its resolution as a wholly individual act — one conditioned by operations of number. For Holbein's skull is not just distorted, it is enormous: utterly out of proportion with the bodies of de Dinteville and de Selve. Precisely as would Ellis's iceberg (see Figure 1.1), a "true form" emerges only to shift again as a viewer changes orientation in the face of disjunctive size.

Whisked Away

For many humanists, Northern climes were specifically associated with shape-shifting and sorcery. "The devil seemith to have in those Septentrionall Countries, greater dominion & more libertie than in other parts," wrote Antonio de Torquemada, "visions and Spirits... appearing to them in likens of some of theyr knowne friends, and suddainly vanishing away."[56] Pierre le Loyer's 1586 *Discours et histoires des spectres* was even more specific about why sorcery was most common in septentrional lands: "Demons tend to haunt the lands lying to the north, where Satan has established his throne...despite this, people do not leave [such lands] where God goes unrecognized and his religion is ignored, and where people, their eyes whisked away by fallacy [*les yeux fillez d'erreur*], rush after idolatry and venerate the new gods."[57]

It was Luther's ally Melanchthon who held that God occasionally intervenes in natural phenomena to transmit a "message."[58] Among the many portents that attracted the attention of Reformation evangelicals were aurorae borealis, the northern lights. Heinrich Bullinger owned a number of broadsheets addressing the vision.[59] During the later sixteenth century, aurorae appear to have been common as far south as Nuremberg; broadsheets report sightings in Bohemia, England, and Hungary. These were likened to fires in the sky and almost never were seen as harbingers of good news: "Take such terrible portents to heart and diligently pray to God, that we will soften his punishments and bring us back into his favour," read the text on one report from Kuttenberg by the printer Michael Manger.[60] To be sure, the origins of the phenomena at the poles were unknown. But the aurorae's mystery grew when actually viewed (and described) in Northern lands such as Scandinavia. The Bergen preacher Absolon Pederssøn Beyer (1528–1575) kept a diary where he described his experience of "flames, smoke, and light" in the sky on Christmas of 1563, and even made an anthropomorphizing drawing (Figure 2.6).[61] The Louvain natural philosopher Cornelis Gemma included one of the first printed illustrations of the northern lights in a 1575 treatise on natural wonders (Figure 2.7).[62] Bullinger spoke of such phenomena as "false appearances" from the North that deceive with "false similitude."[63]

That matter — and its anamorphic distortions — might affect any faithful understandings of the Far North had long been a concern for cartographers. A lost book known through Dutch glosses from the 1540s, the *Inventio fortunata*, told of a magnetic rock at the North Pole. The account circulated in manuscript, but was included in print on a conic map text from 1507 by the Cologne monk Johannes Ruysch (Figure 2.8):

> It is said in the book concerning the fortunate discovery that at the Arctic pole there is a high magnetic rock, thirty-three German miles in circumference. A surging sea surrounds this rock, as if the water were discharged downward from a vase through an opening. Around it are four islands, two of which are inhabited.... Here the ship's compass loses its property, and no vessel with iron on board is able to get away.[64]

Daunting as such a prospect may appear, this vision was attractive to early explorers for two reasons: first, it suggested the idea that Arctic regions could in fact support human life, and second, it seemed to posit the extreme north of the globe not as continent, but a sequence of navigable islands.

This was the basis for the world map published in 1569 by the cartographer Gerard Kremer, known as Mercator. Kremer took a particular

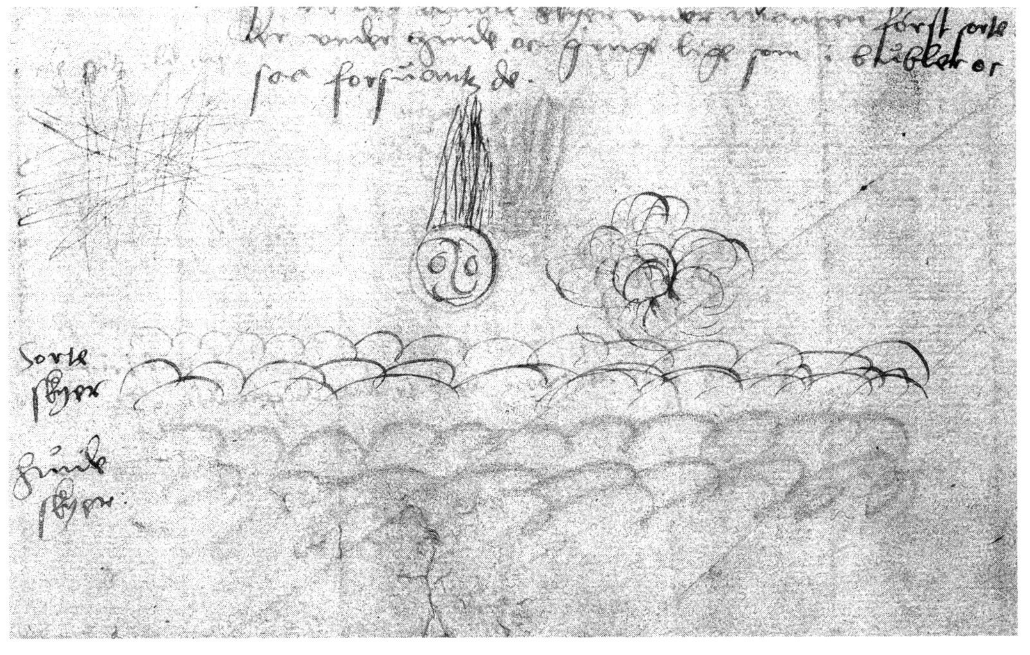

Figure 2.6. Absolon Pederssøn Beyer, "Northern lights," in Ragnvald Iversen, Edvard Edvardsen, Oluf Kolsrud, Kristen Valkner, and Halkild Nilsen (eds.), *Dagbok og Oration om Mester Geble* (Oslo: Universitetsforlaget, 1963), vol. 1, fol. 107r.

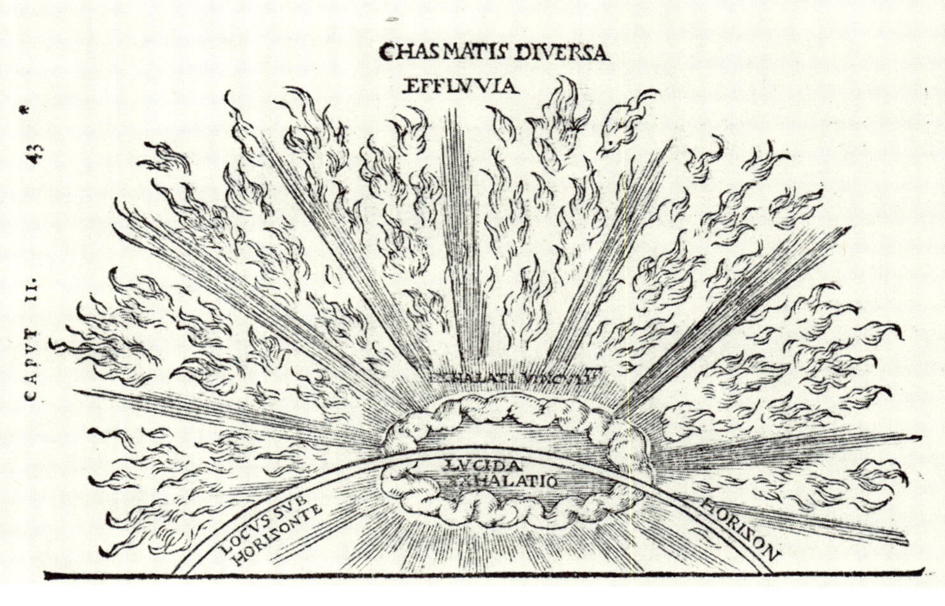

Figure 2.7. Cornelis Gemma, *De Naturae Divinis Characterismis Sev*, 2nd book (Antwerp: Plantin, 1575), p. 63, Houghton Library, Harvard University, Cambridge.

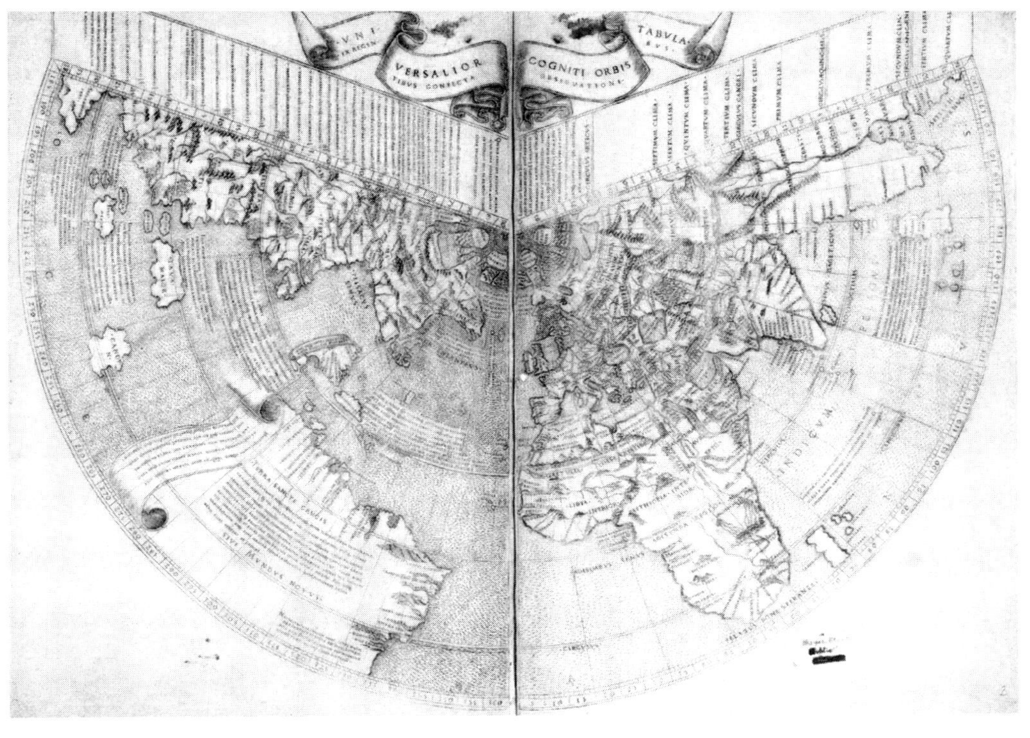

Figure 2.8. Johannes Ruysch, *Vniversailor cogniti orbis tabula ex recentibus confecta observationibus* (Rome: Ruysch, 1507), Beinecke Library, Yale University, New Haven.

interest in the Far North; it offered a means to introduce a new graphic system for representing the world, the projection of which still bears his name. Mercator, son of Huguenots, was actively engaged with the religious controversies of his day and wrote several religious essays in his youth attempting to reconcile biblical teachings with Aristotle.[65] Mercator's mapmaking overlapped with his faith: in February 1544, while at the University of Louvain, he had been imprisoned for having written "suspicious letters" in a Lutheran vein. His system — still in use today — basically reimagined the globe as an upright cylinder with curved poles, laced by absolutely straight north-south and east-west lines. The upshot for cartography, and for the image of the Arctic, was profound. On the one hand, navigators now had a means to chart point-to-point distances using a straight line; on the other, Mercator's grid accounted for the curvature of the earth only at the equator.[66] The earth, of course, is not a cylinder, so at the globe's extremities — say 88 or 89 degrees latitude, near the North Pole — precise linear scale becomes literally impossible. The farther north (or south) one moved from the equator, the greater visual distortion spread. (Google Maps runs on a Mercator projection. That is why Antarctica and Greenland appear enormous there.)[67] Mercator's scheme was what cartographers called "conformal" — it preserved angles throughout the globe, but at its extreme edges, left contours unbound. Its Arctic was, literally, anamorphic.

To account for the incongruity of the poles on his whole-world projection, Mercator devoted a map to the roof of the globe in 1595 (Figure 2.9). This posited four islands around the black magnetic rock suggested in the *Inventio fortunata*. This hulk was the anchor for the "indrawing sea." Mercator, echoing the medieval accounts, explained it thus:

> In the midst of the four countries is a Whirl-pool . . . into which there empty these four indrawing Seas which divide the North. And the water rushes round and descends into the earth just as if one were pouring it through a filter funnel. It is four degrees wide on every side of the Pole, that is to say eight degrees altogether. Except that right under the Pole there lies a bare rock in the midst of the Sea. Its circumference is almost 33 French miles, and it is all of magnetic stone.[68]

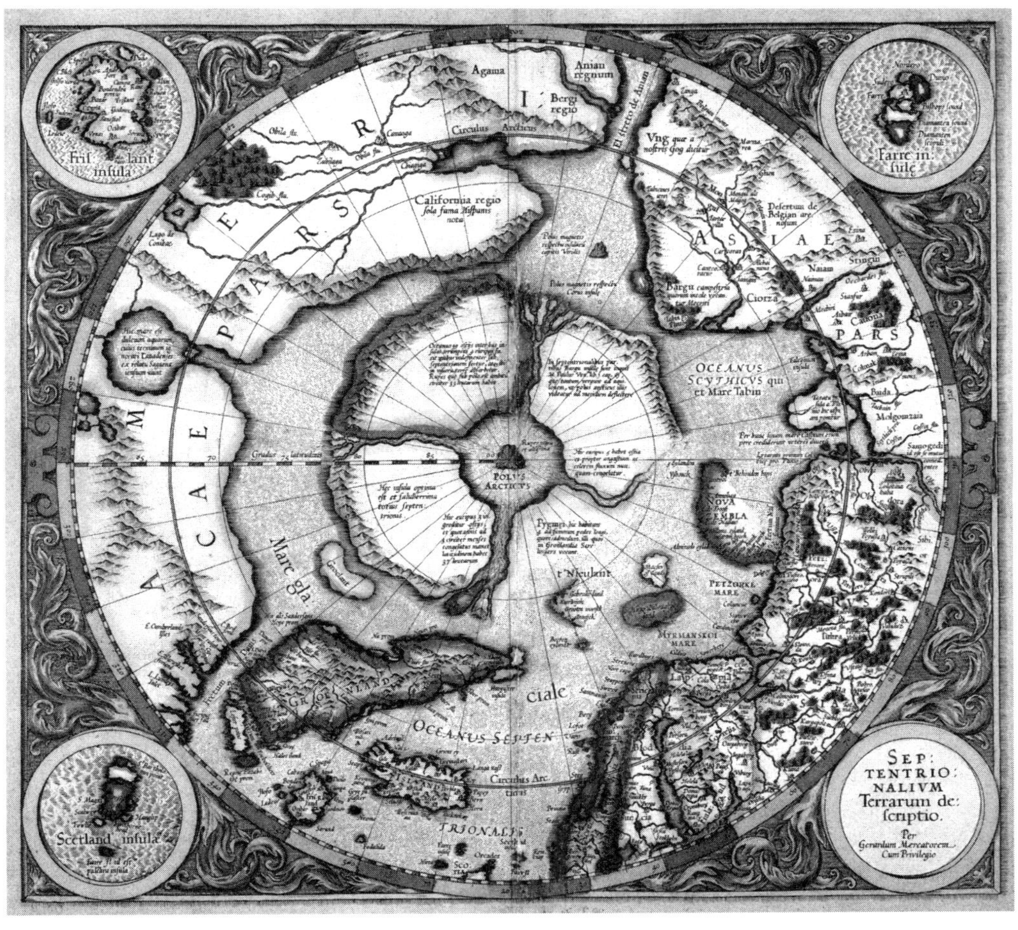

Figure 2.9. Gerardus Mercator, *Septentrionalium terrarum descriptio*, 1595, engraving, private collection.

This was the magnet that pulled mariners' compasses north (Arab cosmographers had suggested the same) and trapped sailors sailing too far north. Swapping German miles for French, Mercator explained that there seemed to be different locations for a magnetic meridian, depending on different observations. He thus labeled one point "the magnetic pole with respect to the Cape Verde Islands" and the other, with a tiny circle, "the magnetic pole in relation to the Island of Corvo." In the sixteenth century, both sites were believed to fall upon the magnetic meridian. Less than admitting the ambiguity of precise location determination, Mercator was laying out two different cosmological possibilities.[69] Even on a chart dedicated to the Northern realms, true north remains a plural, contingent concept and is literally captioned as such.[70] Like Holbein's skull, Mercator's Arctic mapmaking practice is disruptive. It, too, relies on distortion.

Like a giant eye, site, symbol, and system of islands, the chart aestheticizes the old Greek myths as points of uncertainty about the zones as a cartographic conceit, a shareholder's fantasy. Ruysch's 1507 map, too, associates the Far North with an archipelago. Between Iceland and Greenland, it revealed a tiny island, Huitsarc, which, as Ruysch notes, no longer exists: in 1456, claims the inscription, the island vanished — it became completely burned up (*fuit totaliter combusta*) — likely due to a volcano.[71] The Arctic, that is, entered the early modern imagination not as a place, but as a mode of disappearance. And reappearance.

CHAPTER THREE

"A Strange Quantity of Ice"

Arctic enterprises occurred at a moment when various Reformations were uprooting the authority of images. In England, the first onrushes of polar curiosity (and investment) coincided with soft bans on images, at the behest of Henry VIII. Henry's successor, Edward VI, urged full-on iconoclasm. By 1547, the archbishop of Canterbury had called for "idolatry destroyed, the tyranny of the Bishops in Rome banished from your subjects, and images removed."[1] As had occurred earlier in Switzerland and the German lands, English image breaking hinged on a fundamentalist reading of the Second Commandment, but also on a modern-seeming cleavage between structure and supplement. For as much as sixteenth-century Reformers trafficked in a language of negation, they were often entranced by rhetorics of comparison: churches true and false, acts versus words, seen and unseen gods, images shattered or revered. "Popish ornament," in the words of one English report from March 1566, was fine, as long as it was "defaced and broken in peces."[2]

Encounters with the Far North often shared in this hermeneutics of suspicion, this language of comparison. For the break or ban an image was not to discount the idol's power, as Joseph Koerner has noted, but to uphold it.[3] The iconoclast submerges, not destroys, figuration — hides it, puts it away. For many reformed polemicists, this was not an idealist question of essence versus appearance or even of sign and referent, but a theatricalizing of the *dimly* visible.

The same years that saw the Muscovy Company's forays into Siberia witnessed the spread of "blanchers" — church whitewashers, as one period preacher termed them — in England.[4] As the Arctic was being investigated, church spaces were becoming dramatically "naked, bare, and unclad" in the words of one source.[5] This cleansing took place at locales throughout the continent. One period visitor to Reformed Rotterdam conjoined chromatic whiteness and absence: "We went to the Great Church, where there is *nothing to consider*; it is big enough and completely whitewashed on the inside."[6]

And often it was the perspectival image, with its clean distinction between I and thou, that especially troubled, that cried out for cancellation: as the preacher Thomas Tenison put it, citing Maimonides, "the worse and more flat the work is, the less danger there is of its abuse."[7] Bespeaking this Reformation milieu, Thomas Ellis's iceberg woodcut (see Figure 1.1) presented a white picture made up of "broken peces." The berg itself — moving and melting — formed part of an equivocating material circumstance, a disturbingly plural "perplexitie." Printed, flattened, the icy form's lumpy unresolvedness stands empty on its own blank page — without backdrop, without scenery. Ellis is not just sequencing his ship's drift past a mountain of ice; he is attending to the multiplicity of "shapes" that appeared, or seemed to appear, somewhere in the North Atlantic in 1578. The "sight" that this iceberg offered Ellis — and Ellis offers us — is numbered and captioned, but willfully provisional.

The image revels in a strange optical experience, yet turns upon a distrust of the cleanly measurable. As we have just seen, a relative metric like cartographic scale had long been pressured by far Northern geography.[8] And in fact comparativisms of all kinds — of numbers, experience, and belief — were being challenged by the Reformation in similar ways. In fact on certain Arctic voyages, as in more recent art-world expeditions to the far North, the very idea of analogy collapsed, often when it seemed — for many travellers — that they, too, faced environments whitewashed or deserted, with "nothing to consider."

Coastlines

Frobisher sailed to Baffin Island in 1576, 1577, and 1578.[9] What seems to have happened was this: Around 1575, Elizabeth I's advisor John

Dee (an alchemist and also an owner of physical America *curosiae*),[10] had begun discussions with London Merchants about a potential Northwest expedition, since earlier North*east* ventures had proven so disastrous. These led to privately funded voyages commanded by Frobisher. The first trip, in 1576, had yielded a "peece of a blacke stone . . . which by the weighte seemed to be some kind of metal or Mynerall."[11] Initial assays seemed to suggest the presence of gold. Thus, a second voyage was organized, which enlisted fifteen ships and extracted around 150 tons of ore from ten sites on what is now Kodlunarn Island. For a third voyage — the iceberg voyage of 1578, Queen Elizabeth personally invested 1,000 pounds.

The 1578 expedition had several books written about it.[12] Abridged, these were collected in Richard Hakluyt's *Divers voyages touching the discoverie of America* (1582) and later incorporated into the same editor's sprawling, three-volume history of British exploration, *The principal navigations, voiages, traffiques and discoueries of the English nation* (1600). Both projects of nascent national propaganda far outpaced (and outlasted) their original sources in popularity. The narratives sprang from a contested web of third-party interventions by printers, bankers, editors, and sailors, all in published aggregates of verse, bookkeeping, and storytelling. Reportage was never the sole content. Ellis's own iceberg account of 1578 contained poems by multiple authors; Humphrey Gilbert's account of the second Frobisher voyage opened with a sonnet; Dionyse Settle's *A true reporte of the laste voyage into the west and northwest regions* (published in 1577) contained quatrains, and Best, who commanded the ship *Anne Frances* in 1577, included a tabulated list of the "instructions [that] may be reaped by diligent reading [of] this Discourse."[13] Frobisher himself wrote almost nothing.

Bewilderment recurs as a theme of the many Arctic narratives in Hakluyt. There is the ice, the constant ice, which occupies the sailors' attention and frustrates attempts at both navigation and quantification. Ellis, for one, goes on about the iceberg:

> We came near a marvellous huge mountaine of yce, which surpassed all
> the rest that ever we sawe: for we judged him to be neere a foure score

fadams above water, and we thought him to be a ground for any thing that we could perceive, being there nine score fadams deepe, and of compasse about halfe a mile, of which Island I have, as neere as I could, drawne and here set downe the true proportion, as he appeared in diverse shapes passing alongest by him.... These Foure being but one Island of Yce, and as we came neere unto it, and departed from it, in so many shapes it appeared.[14]

This geography is a plurality of forms, rather than a list of objects. Ellis acknowledges any single image's failure to match his own visual experience, to recoup its "many shapes," and captions his four views with numbers. A cognate account of the same voyage, by George Best, included a "general Mappe" that, too, scattered single outlines on a colossal page folding out of the text (Figure 3.1). Along with "Frobisshers Streights" and "Hattons Headland,"[15] the labels traffic in the provisional; to the west of Baffin Island is "The Way Trending to Catania" (the way that seems to go to the East), and even more forcefully, the "Supposed Fyrmeland of America." Best begs the reader's forgiveness for a map "roughly framed, without degrees of Latitude and Longitude,"[16] while the book's printer even admits, in a preface, the need to suppress certain information, it being "secretes, not fitte to be published or revealed to the world."[17] "The old knowne parts have their boundes traced and drawne with whole lines," Best went on, "and the newe discovered Countries have their boundes drawn with points or broken lines."[18] The sheet's points and lines, however, were not so distinct.

Best's Arctic chart, one of history's earliest, was different from other maps of early modern coastlines. One precedent for both Ellis and Best could have been the 1558 *Onderwijsinge vander zee* (Figure 3.2) by Cornelis Anthonisz., a Dutch painter with ties to the English court.[19] Such books' stacked views of coastal tracts between Flanders and Reval — also in woodcut — layered horizontal bands of shoreline with textual labelings of villages and islands along Netherlandish shipping lanes. The silhouettes provided a means for sailors to determine a vessel's location.[20] And Anthonisz.'s coastlines, like Ellis's

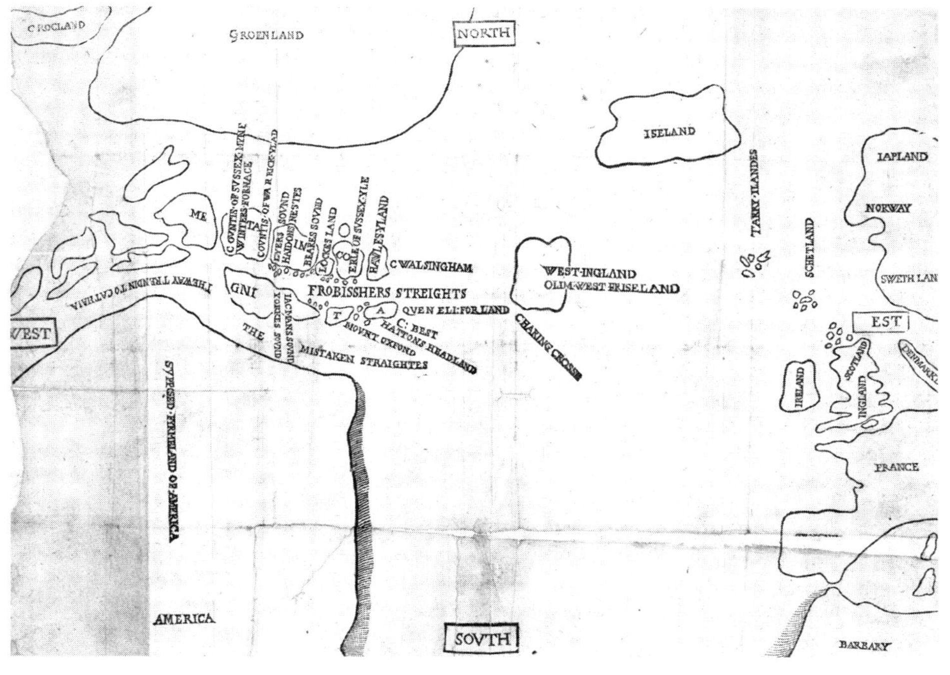

Figure 3.1. George Best, *A True Discourse of the late voyages of discoverie* (London: Henry Bynnyman, 1578), map plate.

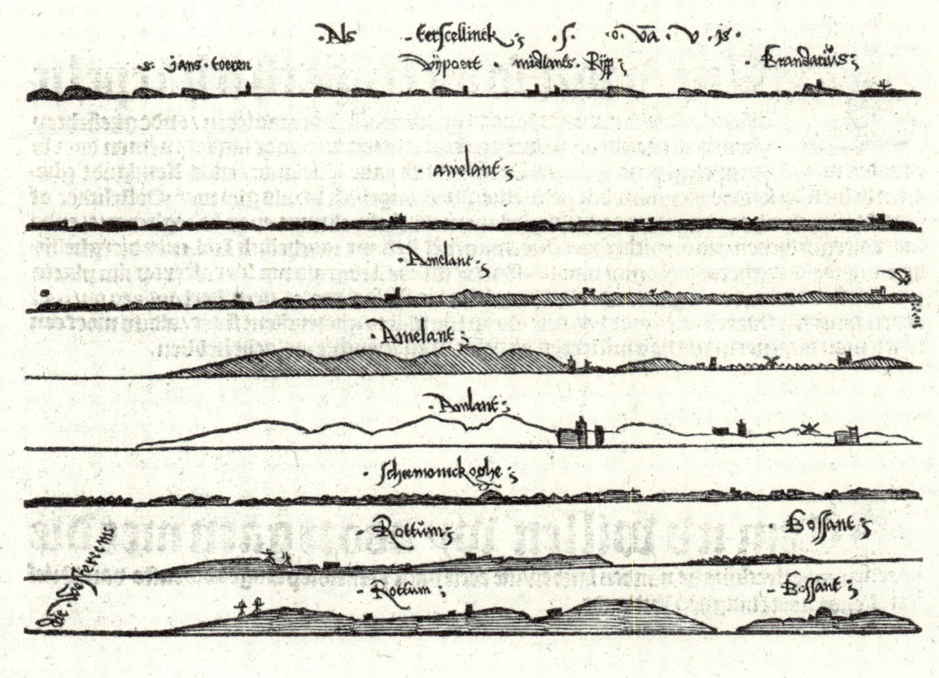

Figure 3.2. Cornelis Anthonisz., *Onderwijsinge vander Zee*, 3rd ed. (Amsterdam: Jan Ewoutz, 1558), fol. 6, 16 x 21 cm, Houghton Library, Harvard University, Cambridge.

iceberg views, were printed on pages that actually folded out of the book foliation itself. Anthonisz.'s book saw at least three German translations and two into Danish and English, and could have modeled the design strategy of Ellis.[21]

George Best, however, spoke precisely to the breakdown of such coastal wayfaring in the face of the unknown North. Describing the gloomy rocks off Newfoundland, he was dismayed at "the thicke fogge which along time hung upon the coast, and the newe falling snow which yeerly altereth the shape of the land and taketh away oftentimes the Mariners markes."[22] Consequently, "the Fleete lay thus doubtfull amongst great store of yce in a place they knew not without sight of Sunne, whereby to take the height, and so to know the true eleuation of the pole, and without any cleere of light to make perfite the coast."[23] Best went on to connect this difficulty to concrete measuring practices. Speaking of a navigation of (what is now) eastern Baffin Island, Best described the futility of sounding depth using weighted rope and plumb: "If you shall sounde upon the side or hollownesse of one hil or rocke under water, and have a hundredth, fiftie, or fourtieth fadome depth: and before the next cast, ere you shall be able to have your lead again [that is, pull up the rope fully], you shall be upon the toppe thereof, and come aground, to your utter confusion."[24] The language of Best is one of struggles to see and to gauge. In such a light, Ellis's woodcut (see Figure 1.1) thus emerges as an emblem for Frobisher's last expedition, in which one kind of rock was disastrously mistaken for another, when "assessment" itself was corrupted — a condensed allegory, perhaps, of the search for the Northwest Passage itself.[25]

But for a few visitors to the actual Arctic, a common point of comparison was the desert. It was a terrain "vast and void,"[26] as one explorer wrote, fraught with biblical overtones of barrenness, confusion, and itinerancy.[27] Certain pamphleteers, for their part, traded on Northern dullness; "there is nothing but stuck-fish, whetstones, and cods-heads,"[28] wrote one wit about Iceland; "it seemed to be the true pattern of desolation," complained another.[29] Or as Stephen Parmenius, a Hungarian poet who sailed to Newfoundland (and drowned there) in 1583, rhetorically posed in a letter, "What shall I say . . . when I see nothing but solitude?"[30] (Of course in the Spanish West, barrenness could also be a topography: "There are very few people, the land is sterile, and the roads are wretched," wrote a Spanish friar in New Mexico around 1517.)[31]

And yet, being *like* nothing else, the Arctic was particularly vexing. Figural description of the Arctic turned away from lists of things seen; recounting, indeed, the specifics of the Atlantic crossing itself or narrating, remarkably, voyagers' *internal* wrestling with the removal of normal means of recognition, of sight. One account of a 1580 English voyage through the Asian Arctic described one sailor's frustration at being unable to distinguish ocean from land.[32] Another sailor off Greenland related an episode wherein his crewmates mistook frozen water for earth. Thinking they had hit solid terrain, they "sent our pinnesse [a small boat] off to discover it . . . but we were informed that it was only ice."[33]

This sensory confusion affected communication: Edward Hayes, who narrated Humphrey Gilbert's voyage to Newfoundland in 1583, described how his crewmen "were incombred with much fogge and mists in manner palpable, in which we could not keepe so well together, but were disservered."[34] Then there is John Davis, sailor on one Frobisher voyage, daunted by "a strange quantity of ice, in one intyre masse, so bigge, as that we know not the limits thereof . . . incredible to be reported in truth as it was, and therefore I omit to speake any further of."[35]

Often, this was a confusion posed for rhetorical effect. And in the North, literary silence was often matched by the landscapes' endemic blanks. This bred responses that could turn quietly self-reflective. Best apologized that, in his account "of me there is nothing else to be lo[o]ked for."[36] More than a defense of plain style, such phrasing summoned, on the one hand, a set of anxieties about sensory experience and, on the other, an ambivalence about how visual information — vital for the description of New World phenomena — could be transmitted for terrain that largely disavowed an aesthetic of precision, or could be reconciled with a faith that often disavowed the reliability of optical sight alone.

Scaling

The Northern voyages occurred at a moment when the relational measuring processes we now term "scale" were being written about in England in very concrete ways, as we have begun to see.[37] Scale, in the early modern sense, subsisted in explanations — it was a crucial aspect of the way abstract information (data, measurements) was made legible. ("Scale" derives from the Latin *scala*, "staircase," signaling nuances of access, gradation, verticality, and dislocation.)[38] The Egyptians and the Greeks all had used scale compasses. Although the early modern Italians rarely isolated this mode as a discrete metric,[39] architects and surveyors, unsurprisingly, had much to say about the way scale could negotiate between a preparatory drawing and actual-sized buildings. Here, for example, is Filarete around 1460, describing how the mechanics of scale permitted a virtual inhabitation of a picture: "By pretending that man is small, all the measures drawn from him are small. . . . Even though this drawing seems small in appearance to us who are large, if men were as small as it is, it would seem as large to them as it will to us when it is all walled up and completed."[40] In fact, before Descartes, scale rarely appeared as a matter of numerical dimensions in the mind, and certainly not as some code of standardization. Rather, scale remained a very bodily metric (think of Apianus's hand), a comparative vehicle, and one reliant — like linear perspective — upon the human senses. In 1435, Alberti began his own treatise on painting (a vital source for Filarete) with such an assertion:

> Mathematicians measure with their minds alone the forms of things separated from all matter. Since we wish the object to be seen, we will use a more sensate wisdom. . . . if the sky, the stars, the sea, mountains and all bodies should become reduced by half, nothing would appear to be diminished in any part to us. All knowledge . . . and every similar attribute is obtained by comparison.[41]

Painting, implies Alberti, is at its core a scaling process. It rests upon the creative instating of comparisons between a depiction and its experience, comparisons comprehensible most vividly via the body. In fact, exactly contemporary with the Frobisher voyages was Edward Worsop's short treatise on *real* landscapes in surveying, *A discoverie of sundrie errours and faults daily committed by land-meaters.* Through an (unwitting) echo of Alberti, Worsop explained scale as a process of simulation: "A measure used in platting . . . upon paper, or any other superfice."[42] Worsop even cited Atlantic voyages as evidence of the need for better measurement.[43] To give something scale, both claimed, is to pull it into a *system.* But this is what Ellis was unable to do with his account of the Arctic iceberg and what his own era's mapmakers (again, as we have seen) found impossible when picturing the Arctic. Best, we recall, felt the need to apologize for his own map's abandonment of latitude and longitude. And some of the precise charts that we know were carried by Frobisher (for example, maps by Mercator) eschewed scale when picturing high latitudes.[44] Worsop's own scalar illustrations dispense with corpora altogether (Figure 3.3), leaving disembodied grids, like Best's "points and broken lines" to the shaky measure by which an empty terrain now accrues an image.

It was often problems of scale that contoured voyagers' thinking about the Arctic environment as a concept. The question was how to reconcile the vastness and the nothingness of the tundra with the apparent imperceptibility of its actual contents. Sailors were often conflicted, differently than elsewhere,[45] by the scalar disjunctive between what they saw and what their charts (say) told them to be true. Southern explorers had encountered the same concerns, of course. But they generally faced an entirely different problem: the issue of too *much,* rather than too *little* to comprehend. There is Cortés's blustering report to Emperor Charles V on a Mexico market (first published in 1522) where he saw avocados, obsidian knives, feathered masks, and more:

> There are found . . . articles of food, as well as jewels of gold and silver, lead,
> brass, copper, tin, precious stones, bones, shells, snails, and feathers . . . deer-
> skins dressed and undressed, dyed different colors; earthenware of a large

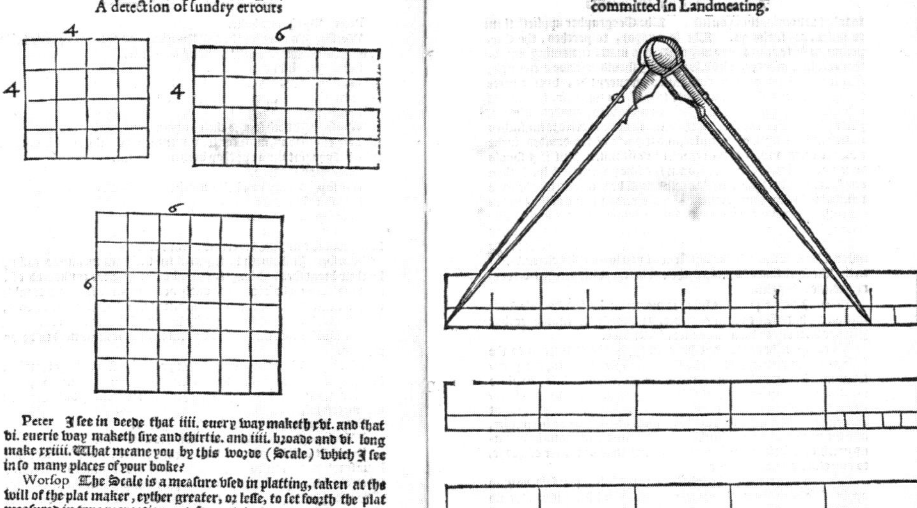

Peter   I see in deede that iiii. euery way maketh xbi. and that
bi. euerie way maketh sixe and thirtie. and iiii. broade and bi. long
make xxiiii. What meane you by this worde (Scale) which I see
in so many places of your booke?

Worsop   The Scale is a measure vsed in platting, taken at the
will of the plat maker, eyther greater, or lesse, to set foorth the plat
measured in true proportion, and Symetrie, vpon paper, or any o-
ther superfice.

Watkins   I vnderstand not this definition.

Worsop   Here (as ye see) are sundry scales, and euerie of them is
iust fiue inches long.

      The

The first, hath one inche diuided into iiii. partes, the second into fiue, the third into ten, ye may apply these inches and diuisions,

B 3   to

Figure 3.3. Edward Worsop, *A discoverie of sundrie errours and faults daily committed by landmeaters, ignorant of arithmetike and geometrie, to the damage, and preiudice of many her Maiesties subiects* (London: Henrie Middleton for Gregorie Seton, 1582), fols. B2v–B3r, Huntington Library, San Marino.

size and excellent quality; large and small jars, jugs, pots, bricks, and an end-
less variety of vessels, all made of fine clay, and all or most of them glazed and
painted.... They sell in the market everything else to be found in this land,
but they are so many and so varied that because of their great number and
because I cannot remember many of them nor do I know what they are called
I shall not mention them.[46]

On the one hand, what we see at work here is the aesthetic of the
inventory as an exploration model — new worlds subsisting in vast
quantities of stuff.[47] On the other, there is the trope of linguistic
inadequacy, the desperation to scale New World phenomena within
a European epistemological syntax. Cortés was not alone. "I am
obliged to admit, if asked how I have treated it, that I do not know,
especially when it is a question of information that reached me from
different sources," wrote Peter Martyr in his gloss of one account of
Guyana, and later, of local flora: "For my own part, I do not know
what Latin name to give to these trees and vegetables."[48]

And yet even when they failed, such accounts trafficked in languages of disparate, yet present *things*. This was, again, utterly the
opposite of the Arctic — "nothing but solitude." The Atlantic South,
for one, seemed alluringly scandalous because of its sheer abundance
of referents. At the markets, Cortés reported, "They sell everything
by the piece or the measure of size."[49] Comparatively, the North's
dominant experience was of monotony and dearth, which was *itself*
difficult to convey. It emptied description, just as the terrain seemed
exotically barren.[50] A sailor to Greenland in 1612 wrote of a "waste
wilderness, where there are huge mountains without wood, valleys
without corn or grass, and the sea with small store of fish."[51] "The
Countrie is barren and unfertile," as Dionyse Settle put it. "There are
no rivers, or running springes," natives "of no capacity to culture."[52]
"I finde in all the Countrie nothing that maye be to delite in, either
of pleasure or of accompte," Best elsewhere wrote.[53] With virtually
no exotic foods, glittering native handicrafts, or enchanting civilizations to plunder, exploit, or enslave, with perennially blurred,
void topographies mingling land, sea, and air, the North seemed a

region refusing stable for / against, inside / outside, and self / other dichotomies that many sailors had expected. As one disappointed crewman on Frobisher's second voyage claimed: "In place of odiferous and fragrant smels of sweet gums & pleasant notes of musciall birdes, which other Contreys in more temperate Zones do yield, wee tasted the most boisterous Boreal blasts mixt with snow and haile."[54] For fellow writers and cartographers, the most urgent questions, then, became not the "what" or the "how" of some cultural encounter, but an uncertainty as to whether anything had, in fact, been encountered at all.[55]

And while the geographic South — home to advanced Aztec civilization — seemed to invite analogic judgments, the Far North repelled them. We can imagine how Northern sailors, like the conquistadors they knew from accounts, expected to assess treasures freely and vibrantly. But the Far North could seem imprisoning. "We were," recalled Edward Fenton, second lieutenant on Frobisher's third voyage, "by the great abundance of ize constrayned."[56] For while everything from Virginia south appeared to teem with new bodies and things, with conditions mystifying, but at once insistently *visible*, the dominant aesthetic of the Arctic was aridity, or even more unsettingly, absence. The resonances with Reformation church spaces was not lost on certain sailors. For even at their most bizarre, new human or natural curiosities (described in books, for example) were at least mappable onto contemporary notions of object-subject relationships: land as a stage, curiosa as props and cast, site as ground, exotic things as figure — the model of linear perspective (actually a relatively late arrival in sixteenth-century English painting, poetry, and theatre design).[57] But without much to see, dark and intractable, the Arctic seemed to resist both projection *and* difference.

Place as Process

One of the strangest episodes from Frobisher's last *Meta Incognita* landing in 1578 involved the construction, on Baffin Island, of a house "of lyme and stone" that sailors filled with trifles and then abandoned: "We left therein dyvers of oure countrie toyes, as belles, and knives. . . . Also pictures of men & women in lead, men on horse-backe, lookinglasses, whistles, and pipes."[58] It seemed a little Arctic *Wunderkammer*, proffering items to be taken away. The crew even left bread baking in the oven.[59] Why? To some extent the house continued the trend of bartering with locals that the sailors had maintained over three voyages. As a triumphant proclamation of European technological superiority, the selection of the objects most astonishing might be the prints, drawings, or badges ("pictures . . . in lead") and the "look-inglasses." As Sophie Lemercier-Goddard has argued, the latter were likely convex glass mirrors, cheaply imported to England as early as the fourteenth century.[60] These shifted both shape and, importantly, size, depending upon beholder's place before them, precisely like Holbein's skull (see Figure 2.4). Leaving such a mirror behind, along with replicated images fashioned by "European" artisanship, amounted to a kind of secular offering to the New World. As much as a colonialist overture, the little house — the first semipermanent architecture the English ever built in North America — was meant to seed a colony that never happened, at least not on Baffin Island.[61] The abandoned mirror, instrument of empire and trade, instead was left to reflect and, more accurately, *refract* the ever-shifting nothingness around it.

This installation would be succeeded in later centuries. In September 1969, the American critic Lucy Lippard flew to the Canadian settlement of Inuvik (68.3° N).[62] Here, accompanied by six artists and curators, she documented two days of ephemeral artworks, most of which would later appear in an exhibition at the Edmonton Art Gallery entitled *Place and Process*. Most of the pieces involved the movement of earth, stones, or waterways. In three different iterations of *a natural water course diverted reduced or displaced*, for example, Lawrence Weiner constructed a dam out of found rocks. In other pieces, tree branches and gravel were piled across streams and, in a separate action, *The Arctic Circle Shattered*, Weiner fired bullets across the tundra with a borrowed .22-caliber rifle, creasing rocks in a gravel pit (Figure 3.4). Other *Place and Process* artworks, meanwhile, turned to the local. In *Circular Walk inside the Arctic Circle around Inuvik, NWT* and *Sixteen Compass Points inside the Arctic Circle*, for example, Iain and

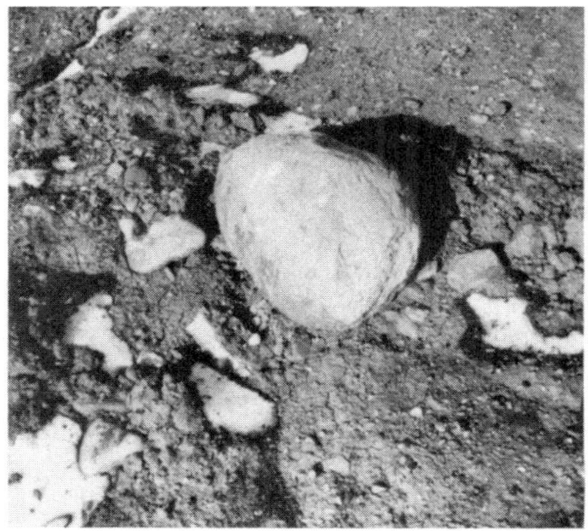

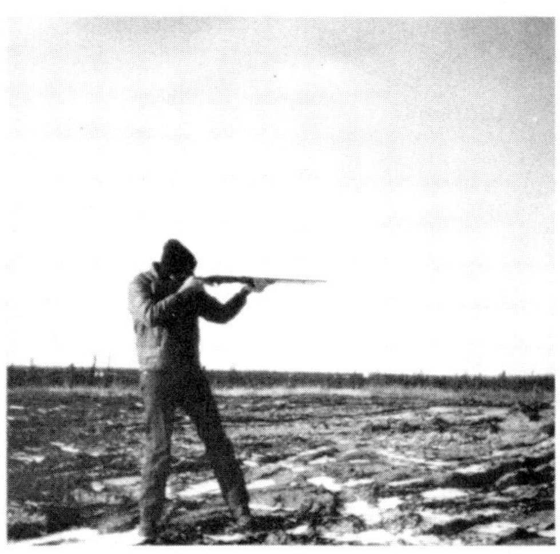

Figure 3.4. Lawrence Weiner, *The Arctic Circle Shattered*, 1969 in Lucy R. Lippard, "Art within the Arctic Circle," *Hudson Review* 22.4 (Winter 1969-1970), full plate after p. 672.

Ingrid Baxter, operating as the pseudocorporate "N.E. Thing Co.," made C-print photographs at stages along a 3.5-mile hike, a total of 10,314 steps. For the Edmonton show, these images were mounted on gridded paper alongside maps or framed as snapshots from a mobile viewpoint.

In these, the landscape was gritty and unscenic. Kodachrome shots of garbage bins, marshy roadways, muddy tundra, and telephone poles were mounted onto preprinted NETCo placards and hung in random sequence. In another piece, known only through Lippard's account, Baxter spray painted a white east-west paint line directly in the brushy taiga. And in still another NETCo work, *Territorial Claim*, photos were made of a small patch of ice that had been urinated on by Baxter. Invoking the processes of mapping and measuring, but also the animalian gesture of territory marking, the pieces parodied more Southern (read: American) mythologies of the Arctic as a space of majesty resistant to human presence. Instead, the piece impassively sequenced mud-spattered trucks in fields and bulldozer tracks on puddled ground.

Lippard photographed many of the pieces and published a diaristic article about the junket in the *Hudson Review* the same year. Although not explicitly political, Lippard's piece alluded to the bizarre culture of resource exploration coeval with the art actions (Inuvik had been founded ex nihilo in 1958 to support petrochemical exploration nearby; it was, to some extent, a modernist experiment itself).[63] Lippard's greatest interest, however, remained the relation between these human environmental conditions and the "barren" Arctic topography, an interest redolent of Frobisher, as rooted in a cancelled comparativism:

> Northern spaces are grand, bleak, infinite, and reject autonomous man-made objects almost by definition.... Under such conditions, imposed somewhat differently by a rolling tundra and a flat snow landscape, a work of art has no scale, or rather no relative scale, and does not compete with nature, partly because few people will see it, partly because it need be compared to no other art, partly because it is impermanent anyway.[64]

In Lippard's reading, the Arctic actions (specifically those of Weiner) sought to demotivate pictorial monumentality: made with the most mundane of gestures, wielding detritus from the vast Arctic wasteland, the pieces denied the idea of the artwork as something heroically, systematically fabricated, something that has conquered its spatial surroundings. Within Weiner's pieces and Lippard's writing about them, the indeterminacy of the Arctic topography hosted a tension between natural vastness and what one critic later called "abstract discursive denominations":[65] cartographic phenomena such as an "Arctic circle," which, as we have seen, even the Greeks had found problematic. For Lippard, Weiner's travestying of body-object relations was aimed at the disavowal of sculptural bigness or smallness altogether. (The same interest colored Lippard's review of the Corcoran's *Scale as Content* exhibition of 1968, consisting of works by Ronald Bladen, Barnett Newman, and Tony Smith from exactly a year before the Arctic trip.)[66] Laid bare across the Inuvik pieces (and across Lippard's writing about them) was both a very historical interest in the Arctic's storied aesthetic of visual indeterminacy and an interest in the role journalistic reportage plays in the transmission and fashioning of that aesthetic.

For Lippard, the trek to the site, the scale of distance between home and away, was as much a part of the pieces as any arrangement of sticks, dirt, and film. "Spent night in Edmonton and set out on the 1200mile flight to Inuvik," she recounted. "The distances involved are impressive. Edmonton is about 2400 miles from New York, near the 55th parallel."[67] Indeed, scale figures in the *Hudson Review* essay as a metric of global travel as much as a visual experience, a journey that had itself become "dematerialized" by jet travel. Lippard's tales of mundanity also recall travel accounts from centuries past. She writes of Inuvik as "uninteresting to describe . . . the infinite sameness of the terrain" and "is not so exotic as I had expected."[68]

Yet as elsewhere, the narrative of the journey *to* the art site created its own literary environment; the article relays anecdotes about truck drivers, drunken locals, and oil wells. At the same time,

Lippard's photodocumentation establishes (as in so many records of land art) a sense of moving around the pieces, of the phenomenological relation between the artworks and a particular (image-making) body. Lippard's essay even quotes the nineteenth-century Norwegian explorer of the Arctic Vilhjálmur Stefánson, who wrote: "One sees things under circumstances that give one no idea of the distance, and consequently one has no scale for comparison" because, "under certain conditions of Arctic light, [there is] nothing to give you a measure of the distance, nothing to furnish a scale to determine size by comparison." This is an antiproperty aesthetic, Lippard contends, akin to "the Eskimo language," which "contains no words for measurement of space or time."[69] Emergent here, of course, was the utopian (some would say naïve) faith in the critical potential of an objectless art, somehow resistant to commodification — at precisely the moment in United States history, the late 1960s, when a goods-based economy was giving way to a finance culture of vast abstraction and an economy of futures, derivatives, and swaps. Such economic invisibilities were, of course, inventions of Frobisher's age.

Weiner, for his part, disavowed any rhetoric of evanescence, as would Lippard herself later. Arctic or not, "no one dematerializes objects, that doesn't mean anything," he claimed. "As soon as you know something, it's an object."[70] For their part, Weiner's Arctic works were perhaps most profound less for their *countering* of the object (and accordingly for some supposed disavowal of a conventional gallery system) than for their privileging of the *material* over the *optical* properties of the Northern landscape — for exploring the Arctic as stuff, rather than scenery. It was the relation *between* objects and humans — the basis for scale — that structured Weiner's understanding of sculpture: "Art is and must be an empirical reality concerned with the relationships of human beings to objects and objects in relation to human beings."[71] Like the early voyages, of course, many later land art projects framed themselves as "expeditions . . . into uninhabited regions," as one gallerist put it.[72] And like the North of Frobisher, such undertakings became known only via their scattering amid large-scale networks of medial environments, sites, and displays.[73]

The *Place as Process* artists, with their banal defilement of the Inuvik landscape (rifle shots, spray paint, and urination, interventions by transient artists), amplified as well as critiqued the Arctic landscape's debasement and pseudopossession by visiting forces, both material and academic. Frobisher is not far away. Vancouver critic Charity Mewburn argued that the actions manifested a parodic "colonialism," a statement against a Greenbergian, flatness-based high-art discourse. And at the same time, the Inuvik works, fasioned by cool kids from New York, represented "highly ironic symbol *itself* of neo-colonialism."[74] In 1963, in fact, Greenberg had expressed great interest in Canadian painting, actually betting (without having visited) that Saskatchewan might be "New York's only competitor"[75] for an art scene of his liking. In fact, in 1962, Greenberg had actually hosted a writers' workshop at Emma Lake in Saskatchewan.[76] Greenberg would go on to write a (highly critical) piece for the journal *Canadian Art* in which he posed local painting's landscape mode as one logical future for advanced art, now that its New York profile was dead. Greenberg despised the Canadian painting he actually saw, however.

Idols?

Lippard's account brings full circle the Arctic's earliest clash with certain early modern ideas of environment and media — nature understood as a social, as much as an ecological concept, something almost simulative.[77] Of course, it was not just Northern climactic conditions that frustrated relational situations of measurement and analogy, but, as back in Europe, theological ones. The difficulty often lay in distinguishing between the two. Arctic exploration, as we have begun to see, took place in cultures particularly anxious not only about pictures, but about pictorialism.[78] Speech supplied a surrogate fascination. On the 1576 trip, for example, one of Frobisher's men, Christopher Hall, transcribed a list of seventeen Inukitut words (Figure 3.5).[79]

Frobisher's crew — again looking to Spanish and Portuguese accounts — assumed the locals "to be Idolaters and worship the Sun." We will turn to this more fully in the next chapter, but for the Englishmen, most puzzling was how the Inuit seemed to intermingle

The language of the people of *Meta incognita.*

- Argotteyt, a hand.
- Cangnawe, a nose.
- Arered, an eye.
- Keiotot, a tooth.
- Mutchatet, the head.
- Chewat, an eare.
- Comagaye, a legge.
- Atoniagay, a foote.
- Callagay, a paire of breeches.
- Attegay, a coate.
- Polleuetagay, a knife.
- Accaskay, a shippe.
- Coblone, a thumbe.
- Teckkere, the foremost finger.
- Ketteckle, the middle finger.
- Mekellacane, the fourth finger.
- Yackettrone, the little finger.

Figure 3.5. Christopher Hall, "The first voyage of Mr Martin Frobisher to the Northwest for the search of a passage to China; anno 1576," in Richard Hakluyt, *The principal navigations voiages, traffiques and discoueries of the English nation, made by sea or ouer-land, to the remote and farthest distant quarters of the eEarth* (London: George Bishop, Ralph Newberie and Robert Barker, 1600), p. 622, Library of Congress, Rare Books & Special Collections Division, The Kraus Collection of Sir Francis Drake, G240.H142.

physically with their gods: "Many little images cut in wood"[80] discovered in tents, on kayaks, even on clothing; Davis described "carved wooden idols . . . carried on their person." The Inuit "have images great store,"[81] he concluded. Whether or not these were amulets or small carved driftwood figures (Figure 3.6), they struck Best as strange for being scattered throughout the camp, as if blurred into the landscape. Later seeking to trade with the locals, Frobisher's crew had feigned idolatry themselves:

> At length one of the locals, pointing up to the sun with his hand, would presently strike his breast so hard that we might bear the blow. This he did many times before he would in any way trust us. Then John Davis . . . was appointed to use his best polity to gain their friendship who struck his breast, and pointed to the sun after their order. Which then he had divers times done, they began to trust him.[82]

The sailor John Davis later chuckled about the natives' gullibility, deeming them "a very tractable people." Of course, not far from the site of the sun worship, Frobisher's crew would soon load their ships with Arctic stone that, from a European financier's point of view, was just as laughable. Wooden idols, black ore; intersubjective judgment mattered here, too.

Why was this intermingling of images and trade — even at a humble scale — strange to the English? Around 1600, the van Doetecum publishing firm set a curious triad of figures in a map of Northern Scandinavia (Figure 3.7). Three Sami hunters are posed on a barren landscape, a herder sleds with reindeer, and profile views of seven "Sami idols" (Figure 3.8) stand, frontal and erect, pressed to the surface.[83] The map accompanied an account of Jan Huygen van Linschoten's 1594–95 voyage to Lapland. In nearby text, van Linschoten described his crew's encounter with the haunting *Afgoden*:

> At the first spit of land, near the south side of the island, there stood something like three or four hundred wooden idols, large and small, carved from wood so crudely and clumsily that one can barely tell if they were to be human figures or not; they were each raised against a support, all facing to the east, and around them were scattered a lot of reindeer antlers, which appeared

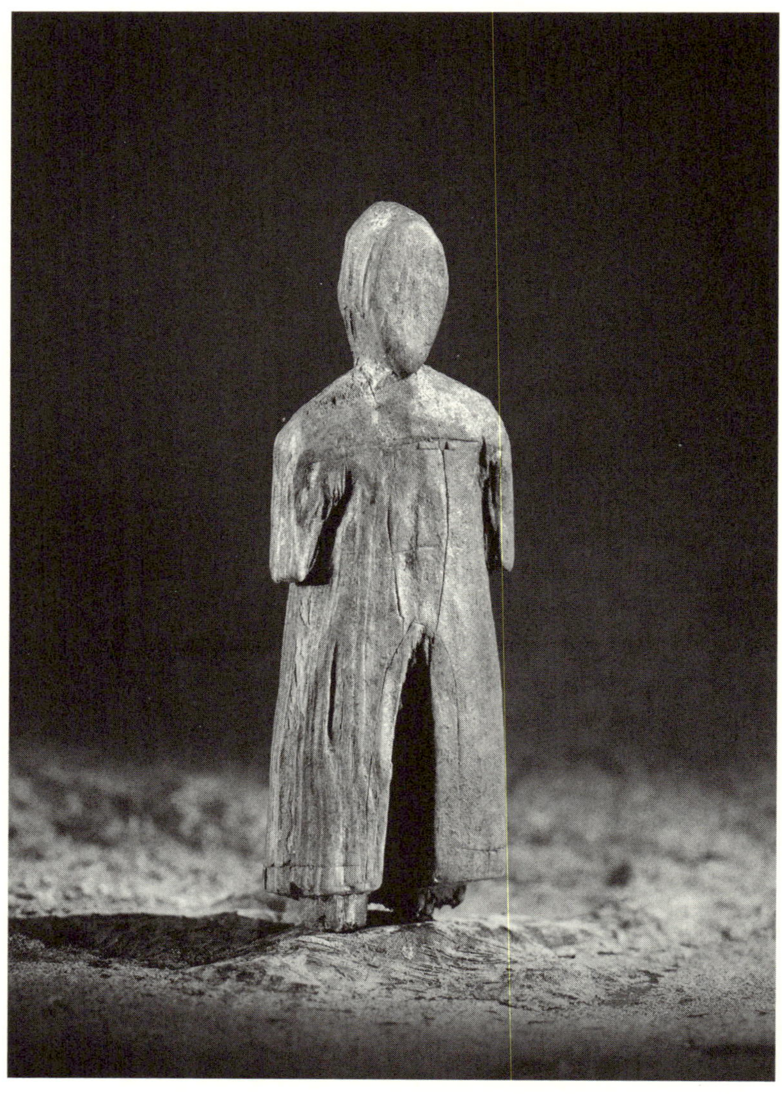

Figure 3.6. Inuit, *Human figure*, c. 1250-1700, driftwood, h. 53.8 mm, Ottawa, Canadian Museum of History, KeDq-7:325.

brought almost as offerings (as if the horns and idols were crosses). . . . I cannot guess how it is that such a large gathering of sculptures came to be. I was led to the idea that, perhaps after one dies, a sculpture is brought here in the place of the dead. For it appeared that some sculptures were roughened by age, while others seemed entirely new, made quite recently. Also: some were men, some women, some were children, some men and woman together in one piece — in some places four, five, six, seven, eight and more together, as if a whole household. Or it must be that they come on a pilgrimage there in some part of the year, and that they bring each a likeness and image [*ghelijckenisse ende Beeldt*] and leave it there. We also saw there a litter of stakes with similarly carved faces, instruments that they, presumably, used to carry the idols in a procession. At first, we assumed that the place must be something like a cemetery, but we could find no sign of graves or bones, other than the reindeer antlers that I mentioned before and of which there were a lot. . . . Although we walked around the point over and over again, we could find no traces of houses or men so far. But it was clear from the sculptures and the idols that humans live here. Yet we have yet to discover exactly where.[84]

These sculptures were likely wooden stave fetishes amidst sacrificial bone piles, or *sieidi*, erected by local Nenets.[85] The island of Vaygach, where van Linschoten arrived, was a holy place; Nenets mythology maintained it was where the world began.[86] Reindeer antlers were customary offerings. As fulcrums for animism, the *sieidi* consecrated not just dead locals, but land that was *not* human — a dematerialized divinity. For van Linschoten, however, this was why the staves seemed perplexing. He believed that "neither the Lapps nor the Finns — the inhabitants of the land are pagans." In fact, the Sami and Nenets adopted monotheism only syncretically, erecting small Christian churches, but continuing to plant such staves for centuries.[87]

In the van Doetecums's detail, the seven anthropomorphic sculptures are frontally posed, framed alongside renderings of actual Nenets hunters and a herdsman, all of which overlay the larger map itself. A related figure, from "Muscovy," was likely in the collection of natural historian Berent ten Broeke (1550–1633) and was illustrated in a seventeenth-century *Wunderkammer* guide alongside other kinds of divine

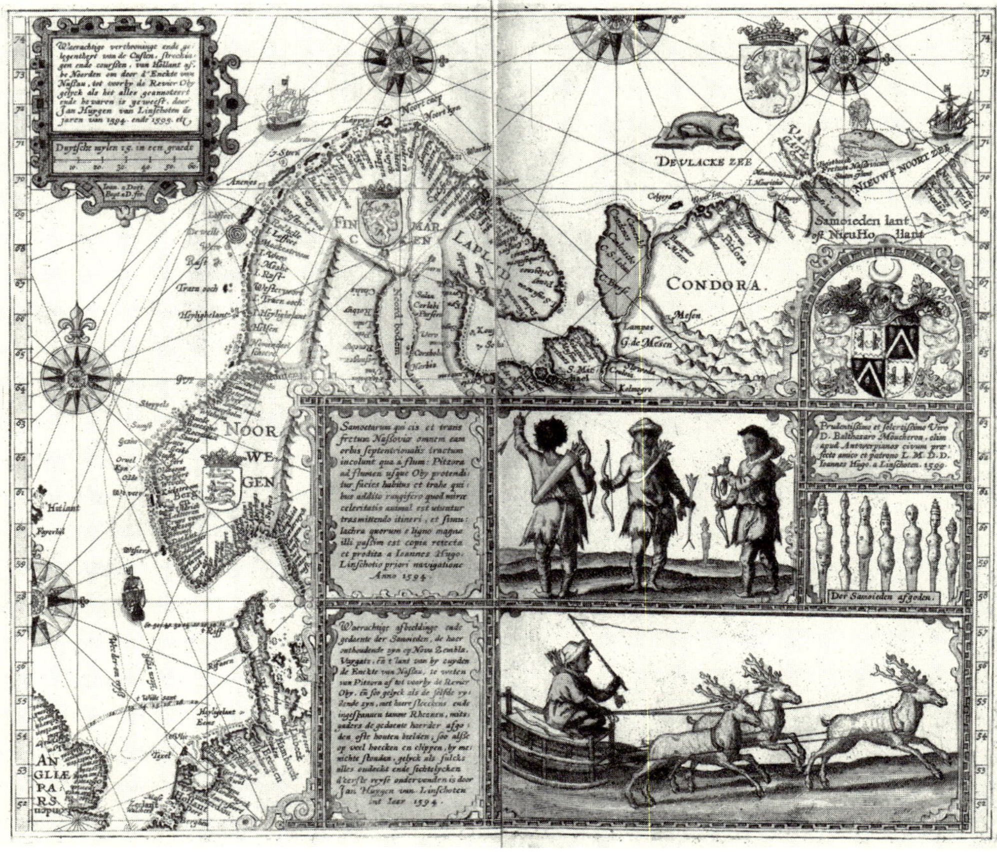

Figure 3.7. Jan Huygen van Linschoten, *Voyagie, ofte schip-vaert, Jan Huygen van Linschoten, van by Noorden om langes Noorvvegen de Noortcaep, Laplant, Vinlant, Ruslandt, de VVitte Zee, de custen van candenoes, Svvetenoes, Pitzora*... (Franeker: Gerard Ketel, 1601), map after fol. 23r, John Carter Brown Library, Brown University, Providence.

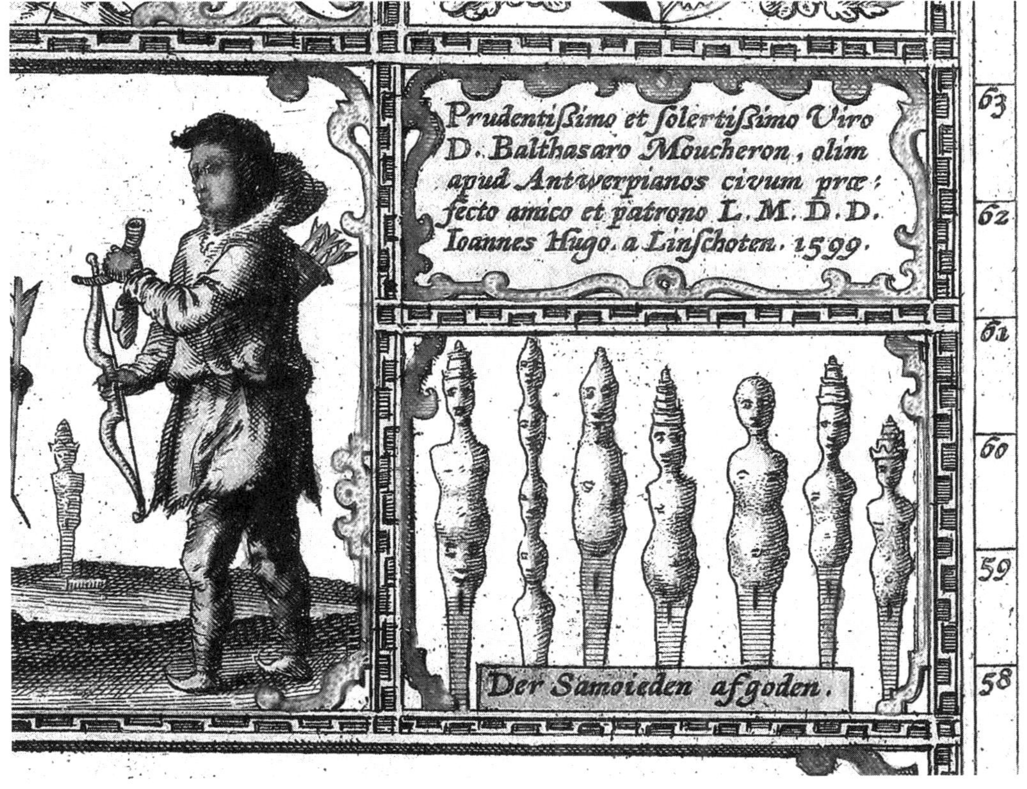

Figure 3.8. Jan Huygen van Linschoten, *Voyagie, ofte schip-vaert, Jan Huygen van Linschoten, van by Noorden om langes Noorvvegen de Noortcaep, Laplant, Vinlant, Ruslandt, de VVitte Zee, de custen van candenoes, Svvetenoes, Pitzora...* (detail).

effigies (Figure 3.9), images allegedly from India and Egypt: this Arctic idol was "dressed with rough sheep skin, feathers of birds, and small teeth of fish." In the engraving, the "Arctic" idol ("5") stands in a lineup near an icon of St. Nicolai (numbered "6"), which is itself presented by the author as ridiculous, something "before which one must utter a prayer of praise every time one enters the interior of a house [where it is hung], as one would a God."[88] The author, Adam Ölschläger, librarian to the court of Frederick III of Schleswig-Holstein, offers all of the figures as desacralized possessions that submit to comparative scrutiny. But van Doetecum's own juxtaposition of god and person, idol and man (Figure 3.7), invites a different kind of analogy. Diagonally across from the sculptures on the square map's upper corner lies a ruler inside a cartouche, a secular foil to the Nenets works and their makers, who are banished from its grid, *outside* of any cartographic assessment.

For van Linschoten, the Arctic "idols" retained a particular air of menace precisely for their refusal to stay cleanly "apart" from the spit of land, to mark themselves loudly *as* effigies. In 1556, the English navigator Stephen Borough had seen the staves too. He reacted more ardently, appalled by:

> a heap of Samoyed idols, which were in number above 300, the worst and the most unartificial work that I ever saw. The eyes and mouths of sundry of them were bloody, they had the shape of men, women, and children, very grossly wrought, and that which they had made for other parts was also sprinkled with blood. Some of their idols were an old stick with two or three notches, made with a knife, in it. There was one of their sleds broken, and lay by the heap of idols … before certain of their idols blocks were made as high as their mouths, being all bloody.[89]

Lying in a "heap," the carvings defy Borough's expectations of how an idolator's locus was supposed to exist. The Arctic, here, contrasted violently with other regions new to the European West. Conquistadors at Tenochtitlan had marveled at the "great and highe aulter buylded foure square of marble compacte together," an account that Borough and van Linschoten could have known.[90] And yet the Nenets *sieidi* — "grossly wrought" — were not set up on altars;

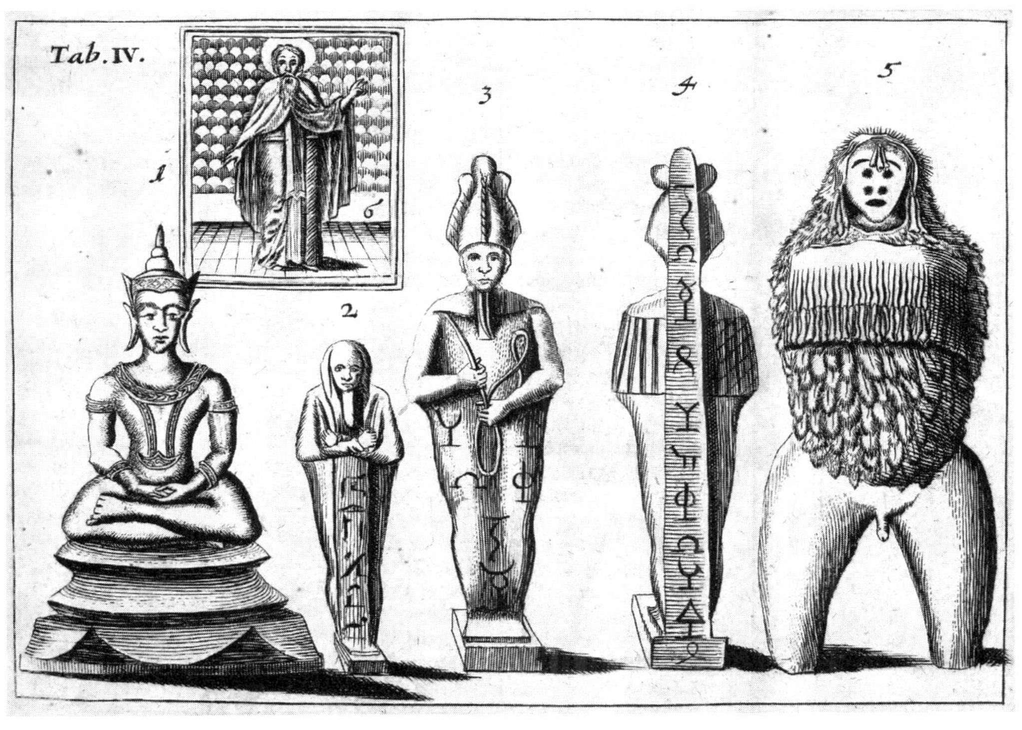

Figure 3.9. Adam Ölschläger, *Gottorffische Kunst-Kammer: worinnen allerhand ungemeine Sachen, so theils die Natur, theils künstliche Hände hervor gebracht und bereitet* (Schleswig: Gottfried Schultzens Kosten, 1674), 2nd ed., plate 4, Getty Research Institute, AM401.G68.

they dotted the island landscape and could not even be distinguished *as* gods: "One could not tell if they were to be human figures or not." The specifics of the carving did not help: "Roughened by age," their appearance blurred any distinction between figure and substrate, even between natural or human-crafted thing. Only in the space of the chart can the sculptures be isolated and set off as clearly man-made items — human manufacture, since Augustine, remaining the defining trait of the idol. But these were at once both highly personal effigies and universalized gods. Van Linschoten's, in fact, was not dissimilar to other Netherlandish reactions to non-European fetishes around the same year (say, in West Africa), objects that also per-plexed by defying exchange value.[91] But the Arctic *Afgoden* were more quietly strange. They, like Lucy Lippard's Inuvik, were haunting, precisely because they were "not so exotic . . . as expected."

Reformation polemicists and Catholic counterattacks traded on charges of idolatry. For Martin Luther, idolatry was a vanity, a fruit-less devotion not to material things, but to material things falsely instantiating the divine. Arctic consternation about pretend-gods and nothingness were enwrapped with Reformation critiques of material-ism closer to home. There, labeling practices as "pagan" hinged upon rhetorics of analogy. "Thus are the believers differentiated from the unbelievers," wrote Zwingli, "in that the believers, or those who are trusting, go to God alone; but the unbelievers go to the created."[92] Iconomachy, which we will turn to in the next chapter, was the most lurid outcome of this binarism. For Protestants, idolatry was false because it wielded crude matter to render the ethereal. It involved an all-or-none proposition of either image or "dumb wood" — precisely a dichotomy that the rough Sami idols elided.[93] To state the obvious: this mandated not just a distinction, but a comparison, the same made by iconodules and iconoclasts alike, between true and false deities. Thus could the Arctic's *lack* of comparanda be transformed along famil-iarly Christian lines into a potentially desirable spiritual condition.

As Robert Heath put it in the next century: "When the body is wholly depriv'd of sight, the eyes of the soul then see best."[94] Such terrain, encountered during a moment of transatlantic financial and theological shift, insisted on modes of description (of weather, of people) that disallowed a clean, dichotomous relativism. And this shaped how the Arctic was represented in word and image. To put it another way: in the sixteenth century, the Far Northern landscape itself was not yet a "place," in the sense of a governed, chartable finitude. It was a worryingly borderless concern on maps, an incomplete geography (Figure 3.10), a terrain ripe for cultural conditioning by newly global instruments of religious zealotry as well as of capital.

In our own moment, Atlantic travel writing is often discussed in terms of "spaces," both physical and discursive. It often reads as a concrete topography peopled by exotic creatures and flora and as a European intellectual conceit.[95] To be sure, the early modern Arctic, like the rest of the New World, was often fashioned within the various arenas of Renaissance culture and finance: the stage, the pamphlet, the map, and the stock exchange.[96] In many published travel accounts, the story goes, points of contact with New World phenomena forced the issue of analogy. How to explain (say) pineapples and kayaks within old descriptive rubrics or via the authority of the ancients? Numerous scholars have pointed out how this incompatibility — or "wonder" — arose as a rhetorical contention in and of itself, nourishing creativity and humanist soul-searching back in Europe, but also serving as a justification for material exploitation. But as a new kind of theology, wonder always presumed a subject and an object. Within such a comparativism, the New World's vast numbers of bodies and things could be tucked within the epistemological systems of the old: time and space, as in a map, become compressed.[97]

And yet in the Arctic, figural description often turned away from lists of treasures *seen*, tabulating instead what the new land did *not* have, and what signs it might hold (see Figure 3.5). The Far North was, in some sense, an iconoclastic landscape. That descriptions of this Arctic ("I find in all the countrie nothing") recall those of whitewashed churches ("there is nothing to consider") is coincidental, but

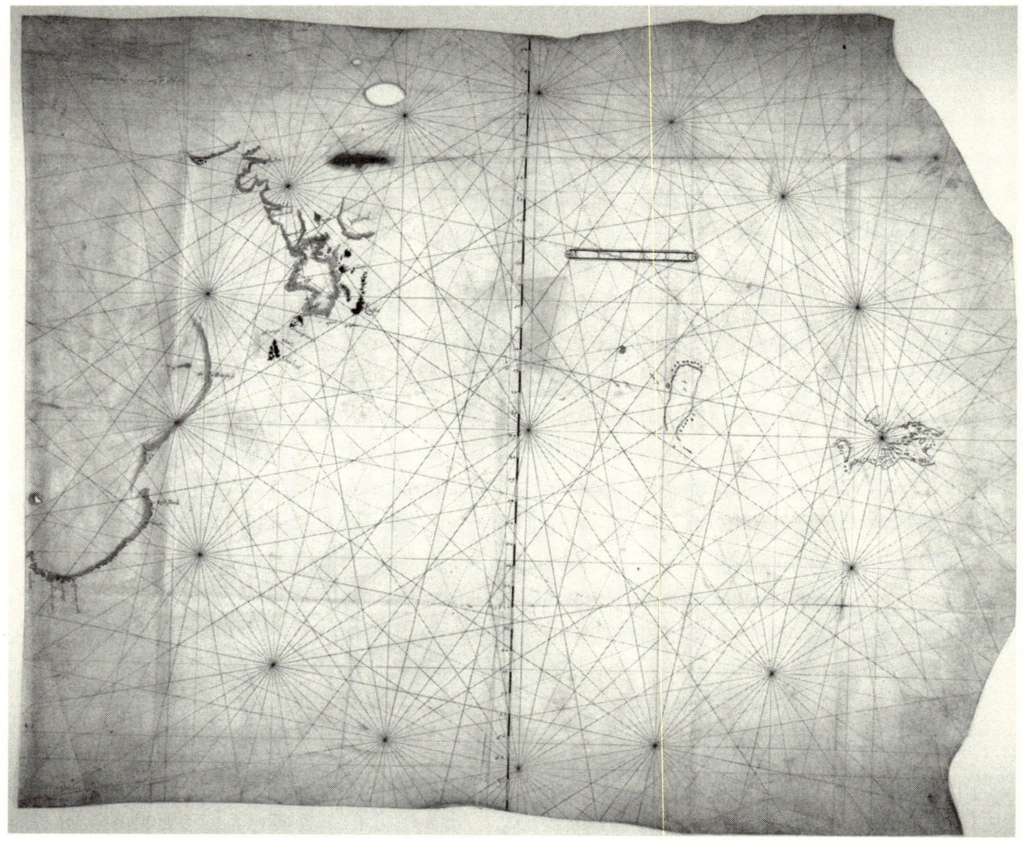

Figure 3.10. Navigational chart of the North Atlantic drawn by William Borough, ca. 1576. Hatfield House, Hertfordshire, UKCPM1/69.

illuminative in its language of dearth. Read today, the rhetorics of blindness and disorientation — Protestant or not — clash with a certain portrait of early modern exploration as a "seeing into," discovery as an unproblematic eye gazing upon verdant *thou*.[98] Not so for the Arctic: "The air is so darkened with continuall mistes and foges so neere the Pole, that no man can well see, either to guide his ship, or to direct his course," wrote a sailor.[99] Of course, to conceptualize (say) a permanently habitable Arctic, one had to disbelieve everything the body says and willfully suspend the idea of vision as a means to progress, even in terrifying circumstances. This was a peculiarity that contemporaries noted, often with astonishment. Consider the words of a Spanish spy on the Frobisher voyages, in 1578, disbelieving the persistence of the English: "It is incomprehensible that a land so cold as this can produce anything."[100] The straining accounts of ice, snow, and fog are, by turns, pathetic and heroic in their own exhaustiveness, tending to collage description to make up for what often turned out to be directionless projects. Many of the reports emerging from the Arctic failures, perhaps, do not just illustrate disaster, but present the act of image making *itself* as a disaster.[101] Here things rightly have no place.

Is it only coincidental that modernity's grandest statement about spatial transparency in art, about the stable "seeing into" that is Renaissance perspective, Erwin Panofsky's 1924 "Symbolic Form" lecture, was delivered in a major port on the North Sea during the wintertime?[102] Panofsky offered the talk at the Bibliothek Warburg, posing an Italianate visual-order system as a salvific metaphor for historical distance. Perhaps the idea of a warm Renaissance rooted in linear perspective, modeled upon *measurement*, arose in art history to palliate anxieties over aleatory, dank Northern cold.[103]

Epistemically, Panofsky's perspective maintained that humans fit comfortably within the world, something his own catastrophic decades had thrown into question. Early Arctic actors, many born into their own intellectually ravaged landscape, were different. When confronted with phenomena such as hull-crushing storms and bloody staves, many chroniclers reverted to language of the mystical or the incommensurate. But an equally common response was silence.

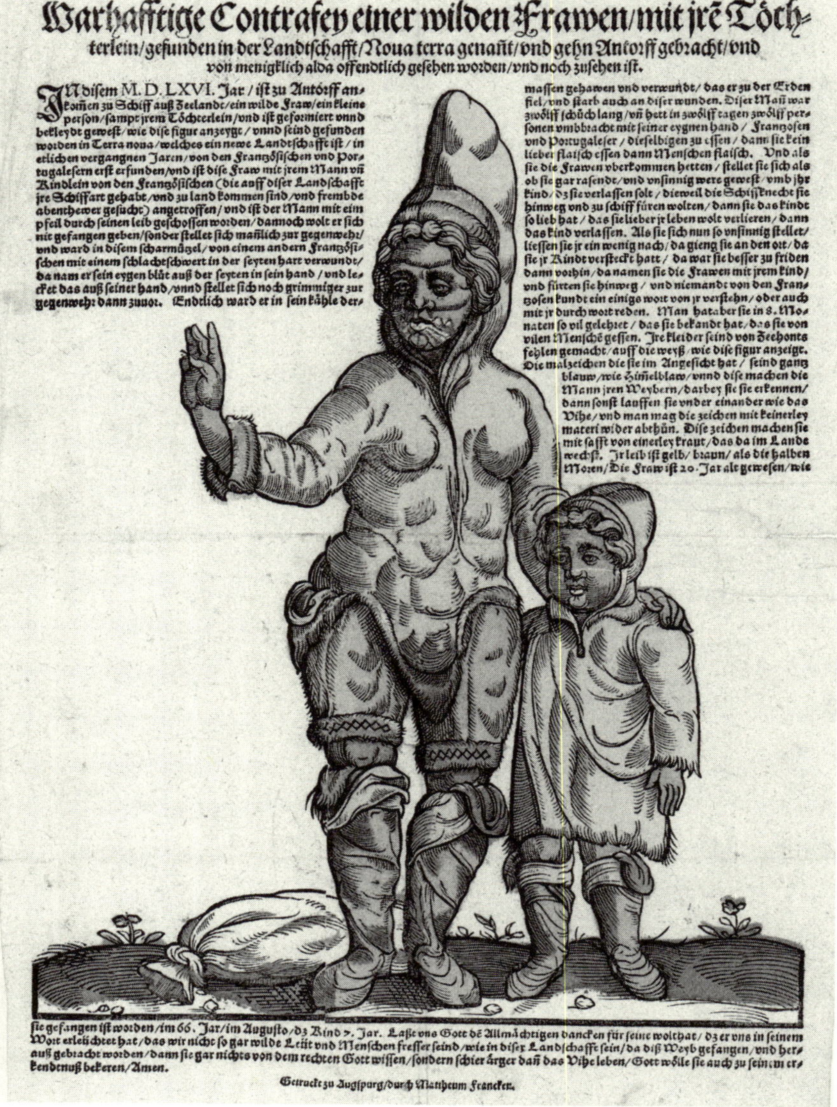

Warhafftige Contrafey einer wilden Frawen/ mit irē Töch-
terlein/gefunden in der Landtschafft/Noua terra genaͩt/vnd gehn Antorff gebracht/vnd
von menigklich alda offendtlich gesehen worden/vnd noch zusehen ist.

IN disem M.D.LXVI. Jar / ist zu Antorff ankommen zu Schiff auß Zeelandt/ein wilde Fraw/ein kleine person/sampt jrem Töchterlein/vnd ist geformiert vnnd bekleydt geweßt/wie dise figur anzeyge/vnnd seind gefunden worden in Terra nova/welches ein newe Landtschafft ist/in etlichen vergangnen Jaren/von den Frantzösischen vnd Portugalesern erst erfunden/vnd ist dise Fraw mit jrem Mann vñ Kindlein von den Frantzösischen (die auff diser Landschaffe jre Schiffart gehabt/vnd zu land kommen sind/vnd frembde abenthewer gesucht) angetroffen/vnd ist der Mann mit ein pfeil durch seinen leib geschossen worden/dannoch wolt er sich nit gefangen geben/sonder stellet sich mässlich zur gegenwehr/vnd ward in disem scharmützel/von einem andern Frantzösischen mit einem schlachtschwert in der seyten hart verwundt/da nam er sein eygen blüt auß der seyten in sein hand/vnd lecket das auß seiner hand/vnnd stellet sich noch grimmiger zur gegenwehr: dann zuuor. Endtlich ward er in sein kähle der-

massen gehawen vnd verwundt/das er zu der Erden fiel/vnd starb auch an diser wunden. Diser Mann war zwölff schüch lang/vñ hett in zwölff tagen zwölff personen vmbbracht mit seiner eygnen hand/Frantzosen vnd Portugaleser/dieselbigen zu essen/dann sie kein lieber flaisch essen dann Menschen flaisch. Vnd als sie die Frawen vberkommen hetten/stellet sie sich als ob sie gar rasende/vnd vnsinnig were geweßt/vmb jr kind/dz sie verlassen solt/dieweil die Schiffknecht sie hinweg vnd zu schiff füren wolten/dann sie das kind so lieb hat/das sie lieber jr leben wolt verlieren/dann das kind verlassen. Als sie sich nun so vnsinnig stellet/liessen sie jr ein wenig nach/da gieng sie an den ort/da sie jr kindt versteckt hatt/da war sie besser zu friden dann vorhin/da namen sie die Frawen mit jrem kind/vnd fürten sie hinweg/vnd niemandt von den Frantzosen kundt ein einigs wort von jr verstehn/oder auch mit jr durch wort reden. Man hat aber sie in 8. Monaten so vil gelehret/das sie bekandt hat/das sie von vilen Menschē gessen. Jre kleider seind von Seehontsfehlen gemacht/auff die weyß/wie dise figur anzeige. Die malzeichen die sie im Angesicht hat/seind gantz blauw/wie Himmelblaw/vnnd dise machen die Mann jren Weybern/darbey sie sie erkennen/dann sonst lauffen sie vnder einander wie das Vihe/vnd man mag die zeichen mit keinerley materi wider abthün. Dise zeichen machen sie mit safft von einerley kraut/das da im Lande wechst. Jr leib ist gelb/braun/als die halben Moren/Die Fraw ist 20. Jar alt gewesen/wie

sie gefangen ist worden/im 66. Jar/im Augusto/dz Kind 7. Jar. Laße vns Gott dē Allmächtigen dancken für seine wolthat/dz er vns in seinem Wort erleüchtet hat/das wir nicht so gar wilde Leüt vnd Menschenfresser seind/wie in diser Landschafft sein/da diß Weyb gefangen/vnd herauß gebracht worden/dann sie gar nichts von dem rechten Gott wissen/sondern schier ärger dañ das Vihe leben/Gott wölle sie auch zu seinem erkendtnuß bekeren/Amen.

Getruckt zu Augspurg/durch Mattheum Francken.

Figure 4.1. *Warhafftige Contrafey einer wilden Frawen/ mit ire Töchterlein* (Augsburg: durch Mattheum Francken, [1567]), woodcut, former collection of Johann Jakob Wick, Zentralbibliothek Zürich (Ms. F 18.74a).

CHAPTER FOUR

The Savage Episteme

Sometime in the summer of 1566, a broadsheet appeared in Augsburg announcing the public display of two Arctic abductees (Figure 4.1).[1] Issued by Matthäus Franck, the page, large at 40 by 36 centimeters, presented "a wild woman, with her little daughter, found in the district called Nova Terra." The unfortunates, the text tells us, were taken from the waters off Greenland by fishermen (Basque sailors had plied the area for a century) and then brought to Zeeland. They visited various cities, and then went to the Hague, where they were viewable, "for a fee."[2]

The two wear parkas and stand upon a small mound of earth, flanked by three sprouting green plants and a mysterious sack. The adult's right hand is outstretched, posed as if in a gesture of blessing, and waves of hair crest her forehead, with facial tattoos — a mark of maturity for Inuit women of Eastern Labrador — painted in blue.[3] Both mother and child are dressed in animal skins "with the fur side turned in." Tufts of hair can be seen emerging from the adult's folded right cuff. Her oblong sealskin hood forms part of a parka for carrying infants, an *amautik*.[4] The letterpress text, which encloses but never touches the two bodies, explains how the twenty-year-old "confessed that she had eaten many men," while her adult mate, abandoned back in Newfoundland, was dead from "an arrow through his body."

The broadsheet, it would seem, presents a tale of capture and display, *itself* put on display. It offered not just a curiosity, but also an event: the pair was actually shown in Antwerp, "publicly seen by everyone . . . and still to be seen."[5] And all of this was taking place around the precise moment that the Netherlands was experiencing the most violent iconoclastic riots in its history. In fact, the last line of the sheet collapses these two rips in the quotidian: the woman's savage habits and appearance are detailed, which the text then compares to the "completely wild people" (*gar wilde Leüt*) — that is, the image breakers — here at home.[6]

The first inscription presents the sheet as an *imago contrafactum* — an early modern species of image, a picture that was veridical for being made close to a prototype. Not a falsity, the *contrafactum* is an image that "stands in" for a thing it describes. It is a report authoritative and reliable for having been made proximate to its subject — an inchoately objective, protoscientific image, synonymous with mimetic *information*.[7] The *contrafactum* idea was specifically associated with print in early modern North Europe; it was a common label for broadsheets picturing natural wonders local and far off — often aberrant and portentous bodies, such as monstrous births and bizarre trees. (The same year the Inuit sheet appeared, the publisher Franck also issued a print describing the capture of a giant squid.)[8]

But to act as *contrafactum*, *contrafacta*, or *contrafeyt*, an image (Arctic or not) must, in a sense, *work* insofar as making content known. It must be, in some sense, alive. As a mode, that is to say, the *contrafactum* is demonstrative: it defines itself not through style or subject, but through function, through its capacity to communicate something.[9] But as what kind of *imago contrafactum* would this glimpse have acted in 1566 Antwerp? During a moment of iconoclasm and inchoate and incipient Netherlandish nationalism? At a moment when the ideas of "native" and, indeed, of "image" were hardly stable categories? By 1566, the New World was not always conceptualized as separate (or even distant) in a monolithic way.[10] And in certain cases we have begun to see, differences existed in the European understanding of the Far North, but not always along an axial episteme of self-other. And in certain cases of *Arctic* bodies, the neat binary inherent in the *imago contrafactum* seemed further to crack.

Stealing People and Things

The sheet documents another fable of domination: phenomena posited as ulterior in order to be owned. The forcible taking of New World individuals not just as slaves, but as specimens or proof was commonplace in the fifteenth and sixteenth centuries. Along with parrots and Taino jewelry, Columbus actually seized about twenty-five people from what is now Haiti on his first voyage. Eight survived the trip back to Spain, only to be sold at auction in Seville.[11] And Vespucci, returning from his first voyage in 1499, was allegedly accompanied by more than two hundred natives. In 1502, Sebastian Cabot presented three men from Newfoundland to Henry VII, men who were "clothed in beastes skinnes, and eate raw flesh but spake such a language as no man could understand them."[12] When Richard Hakluyt gave instructions to sailors to Siberia hoping to find a strait between North Europe and China in 1580, he asked them to bring back native foodstuffs, flora, and, if possible, "one or other young man."[13] If this occurred, an Englishman was to be left in his place, ordered Hakluyt.

This collectionist impulse extended a longstanding interest in specifically Northern animals and things. The chronicler Adam of Bremen, writing around 1075, tells of a polar bear from Greenland gifted to the Holy Roman Emperor Heinrich III.[14] In George Best's otherwise scantily illustrated account of the second Frobisher voyage, a woodcut of a narwhal was included by his London printer (Figure 4.2). The grinning cetacean formed the only noncartographic figure in the account and was picked up by continental translators.[15] Snowshoes sat alongside the Mexican featherwork and Brazilian axes in the Hapsburg collections in the Tyrol before 1585.[16] Inuit Kayaks seem to have been particularly prized. Exemplars were in German and Dutch collections by the seventeenth century;[17] and the famous engraving of Ole Worm's Copenhagen cabinet displays a kayak prominently, alongside parkas and sealskin coats (Figure 4.3).[18] An Inuit boat, now lost, was gifted to a Bavarian duke sometime between 1588 and 1597.[19] In 1521 Albrecht Dürer, in Antwerp, reported being given "a small Calicut round shield made of fish skin and two gloves

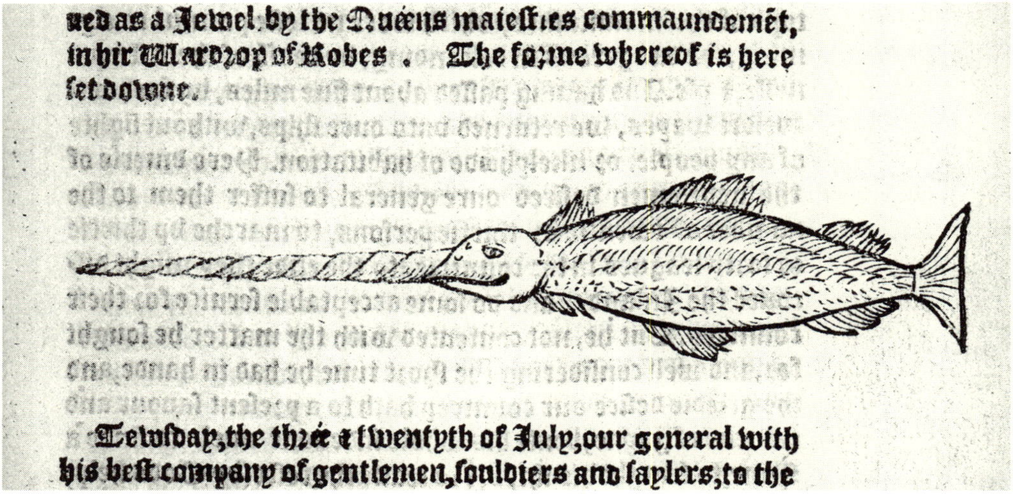

ued as a Iewel, by the Quæns maiesties commaundemét,
in hir Warorop of Robes .   The forme whereof is here
set downe.

Tewsday, the thre & twentyth of July, our general with
his best company of gentlemen, souldiers and saylers, to the

Figure 4.2. George Best, *A Trve Discovrse of the Late Voyages of Discouerie, for the Finding of a Passage to Cathaya, by the Northvveast, Vnder the Conduct of Martin Frobisher Generall* (London: Henry Bynnyman, 1578), p. 15.

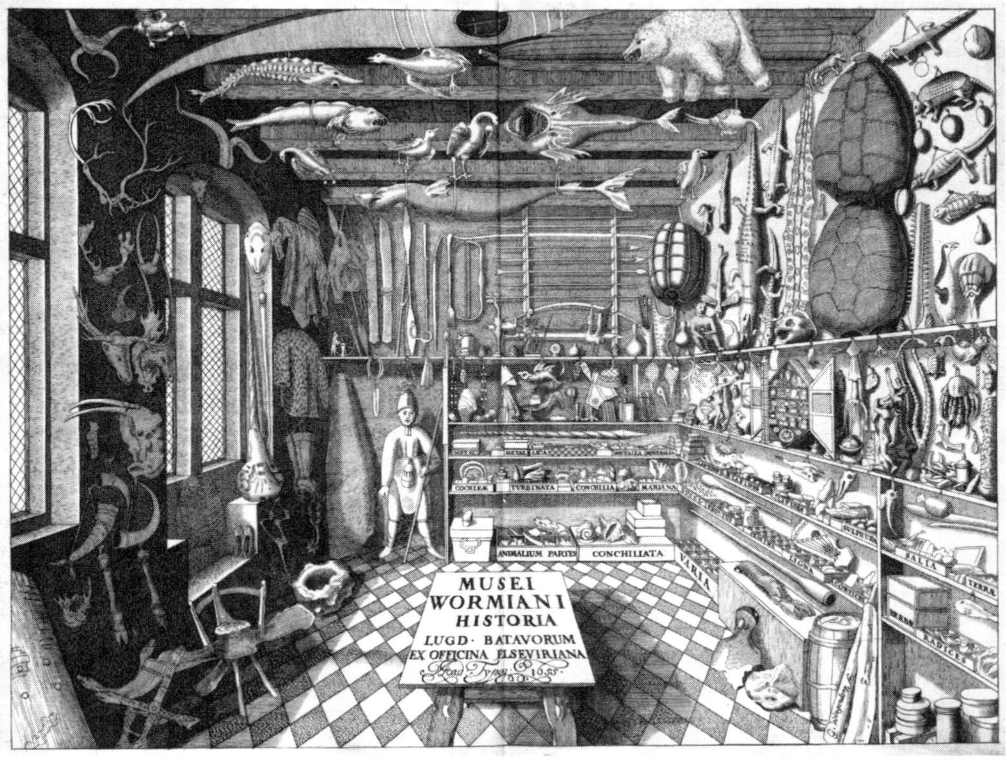

Figure 4.3. Frontispiece to Ole Worm, *Museum Wormianum, seu, Historia rerum rariorum : tam naturalium, quam artificialium, tam domesticarum, quam exoticarum, quae Hafniae Danorum in aedibus authoris servantur* (Amsterdam: Ludovic and Daniel Elzevir, 1655), Special Collections, Getty Research Institute, Los Angeles.

with which the natives there fight," possibly mittens and, it has been argued, a drum of Eastern Inuit manufacture.[20]

By the time Franck's Inuit prints appeared, specifically "American" bodily types had featured in book illustrations for decades. Columbus's letter about Hispaniola, first published in Basel in 1493, illustrated a cartoonish naked Taino population on shore. Anthropophagic Tupinamba were profiled in a lurid woodcut of 1505 by Christoph Froschauer, also made in Augsburg, to accompany Vespucci's published account of his third voyage (Figure 4.4) — itself the first printed representation of South American natives.[21] A stock iconography of grotesque "wildness" lingered as a common, even hackneyed visual idiom for many of these New World representations. (America and Asia were indistinct conceptually as well as cartographically at this moment for many audiences.)[22] While bespeaking recycled iconographies of cannibalism and paganism, this wildness often subsisted in the subjects being hopefully, semiotically, indeterminate. In an alternate edition of the Inuit sheet published in Nuremberg by Hans Glaser, in fact, the Inuit woman and her daughter have even been encaged in a woodcut border (Figure 4.5) collaged with the text.[23] More local painting and drawing traditions had defined "wild people" via their surrounding terrain (Figure 4.6). In the printed broadsheets, however, the two marginals have been literally and figuratively extracted from any landscape. Here, that is, the *text* now becomes the topography that gives them sense.

Whereas the Augsburg broadsheet presented the two Arctic abductees as an exoticism, the Nuremberg sheet pictured the reality of such exoticism *displaced*. Its cut-and-paste aesthetic literalized the two souls' removal and deployment somewhere else from the Arctic. What we might see in this juxtaposition is the place*ful*ness of the geographic Arctic — a specific, barren realm of strangeness — set into conflict with a certain kind of place*less*ness of what we might call an Arctic poetics, an unsettled, even indifferent way of relating to the early modern exotic.

When it came to natives, this tension between placefulness and placelessness played out in other ways. For Europeans, indigenes were often enfolded into more local modes of social difference: in words

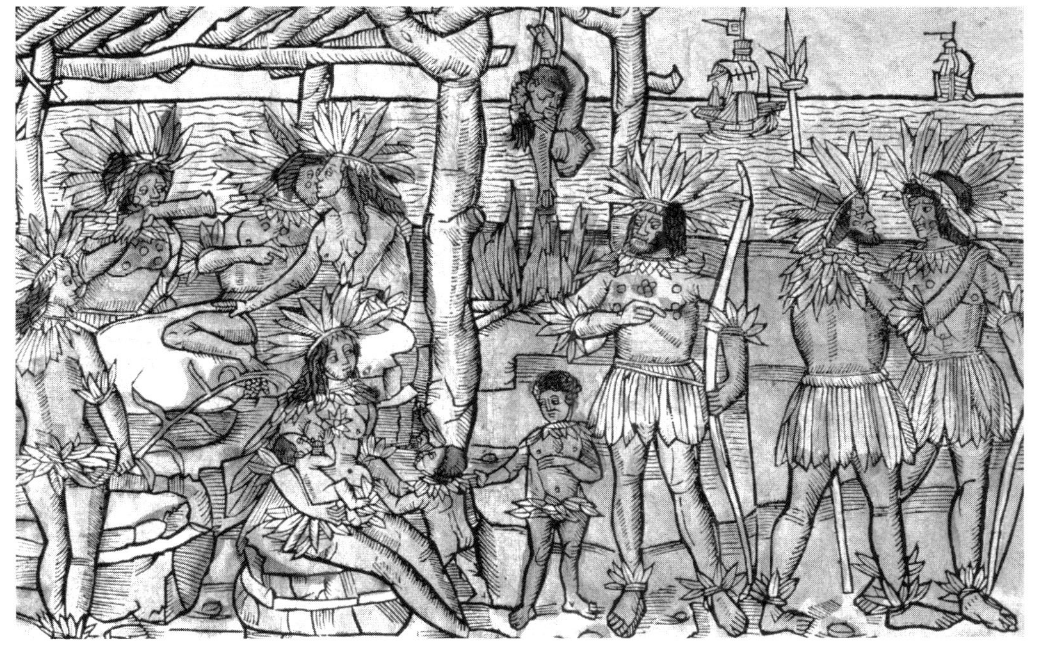

Figure 4.4. *Dise figur anzaigt uns das Folck und Insel die gefunden ist durch den christen-lichen Kunig zu Portigal oder con seinen Underthonen* (Augsburg: Froschauer, 1505), hand-colored woodcut, New York Public Library, Spencer Collection.

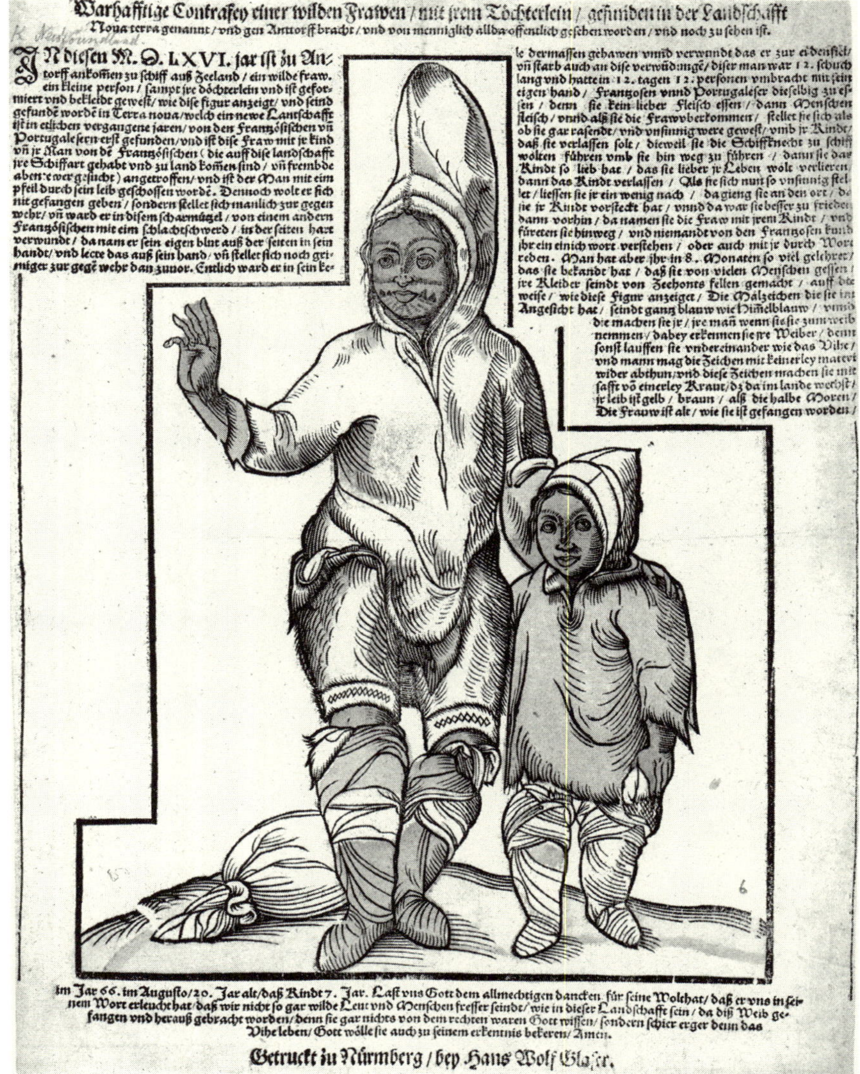

Figure 4.5. *Warhafftige Contrafey Einer Wilden Frawen, Mit Irem Töchterlein, Gefunden in Der Landschafft Nova Terra Genannt, Und Gen Anttorff Bracht* (Nuremberg: Hans Glaser, 1567).

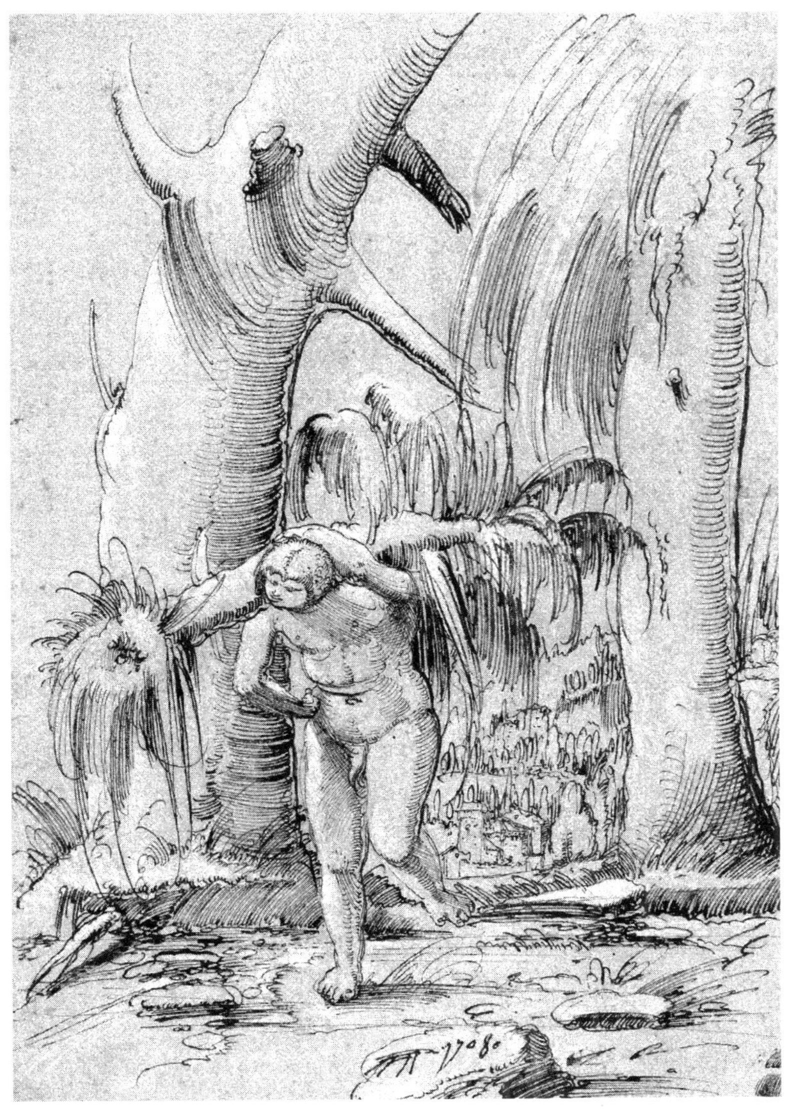

Figure 4.6. Albrecht Altdorfer, *Wild Man*, 1508, pen and black ink, heightened with white on red-brown prepared paper, 21.4 x 14.6 cm, British Museum, London, 1910.0611.1.

and image, the New World native could be blended with the wild man or the peasant into a kind of three-way natural other.[24] A key source here was, again, Tacitus's *Germania*. Rediscovered in Fulda in the 1420s and first published in German in Nuremberg in 1473, the tract established a contrast between rough but simple Northerners and civilized, vice-ridden Romans.[25] Augsburg, along with Netherlandish merchant cities such as Bruges, nurtured a local tradition of wild-man iconography on devices that, paradoxically, linked the city to a uniquely Roman past.[26] In Nuremberg, there was a fifteenth-century tradition of wild men running amok at the *Schembartlauf* festival, chasing participants and mixing with the crowd. In the 1520s and 1530s, such characters were increasingly confined to floats or, like the two Intuit in Antwerp, put on stages. By the Reformation the wild soul, that is, needed to be set safely apart, framed overtly as savage.[27]

From Tacitus derived the idea of a wild man both beastly and solitary; he was cannibalistic, brutely sensual, and particularly common in Northern European folklore: Celtic legends told of the *wodewose*, from the Old English *wōd*, Middle English *wode*, or Middle Dutch *woet*, meaning, literally, senseless or insane. In a 1492 address to students at the University of Ingolstadt, Conrad Celtis berated Germans for their warlike nature but claimed that Northern fervency, if tamed, could be an asset:

> The Scythian race is so fierce that, uncivilized and brutal as beasts of prey, they wander over wild, untrodden deserts like cattle, protecting themselves from the inclemency of the weather and the severity of their climate with the furs of animals . . . yet they were so inspired with eagerness for fame and glory that they thrice conquered and occupied the empire of Asia. . . . In the same way you who have taken over the empire of the Italians should cast off repulsive barbarism and seek to aquire Roman culure.[28]

This Northern man was a creature at once human and animal, or as Albertus Magnus put it, *similtudines hominis*.[29] He was a figure associated with the woods, both a hermit and, in a modern sense, an environmentalist; his iconography spread at the precise time that large-scale deforestation (for fuel and building materials) in central

Europe was taking place.[30] (That such eroding of the forest, in the name of trade-based expansion, was a real concern can be seen from the rise of civic injunctions against profligate logging, which existed as early as 1535 in Nuremberg.)[31]

In Elizabethan England, meanwhile, sponsor of so much Arctic exploration, the wild man became a stock feature of entertainments and pageants set in the countryside, where he often would often appear, armed and hairy, to welcome royals to ulterior realms.[32] Here he would invariably stand for barbarity. But real-world domestication went hand in hand with theatre: two of Cabot's Newfoundland prisoners of 1505, formerly eaters of "raw fleshe," were spied on at Westminster two years after, well-behaved and mannered, "clothed like Englishmen, and could not bee discerned from Englishmen."[33]

Within Tacitus also lies the recourse to geohumoralism, the idea that circumstantial factors such as climate explain behavior and appearance, that habitat shapes being.[34] Aristotle's linking of national character and temperature in the *Politics* centered Peloponnesian weather as an ideal. Nations "inhabiting the cold places," wrote Aristotle, "are full of spirit but somewhat deficient in intelligence and skill."[35] Jean Bodin, one of the first comparative ethnologists, made taxonomic human distinctions in terms of three Ptolemaic zones, much like Apianus: northern, temperate, southern.[36] Many early modern navigation accounts enthusiastically relayed these antique tropes. Richard Eden's translation of Peter Martyr's 1530 *De orbe novo decades* was explicit:

> There is another difference of regions caused of coulde and heate. For suche as are neare unto the poles, are vexed with too much coulde; And such as are under the line where the soone is of greateste force, are oppressed with heatte. . . . Under the pole, it is impossible that there shulde be populous cities bycause the lande is barren, and the carriage, or conveyaunce of fruites, vyttayles, and other necessaires, is incommodious. By reason whereof, it is necessarie that th[e] inhabitantes of suche regions lyue ever in continuall wanderynge from place to place.[37]

Paradoxically, central to this thinking was a Europe capable of "ethnographic" diversity precisely because it was only *loosely* connected to its geographical specifics. Europe, unlike (say) Africa or Asia, bore no rough nature of extreme cold or heat, and thus was free to insure that "civilization" was constructed through ideal climate (that of, say, the Mediterranean for the Greeks). Deviations not only of climate type (dry, wet, cold, hot), but of intensity existed at the margins of the world.[38] The satirist Joseph Hall (b. 1574), writing in the dystopian *Mundus alter et idem* (A world both different and same), could mock the essentialism of Aristotle with specific reference to the poles. Hall's fictional state of Moronia is in the Antarctic and accords with the land of the "Pygmies" situated under the Arctic Pole: "From the most truly intense cold of both regions," Hall wrote, "has been advanced both the stupidity of the Moronians and the puniness of the Pygmies."[39] Such effects are always pronounced "where the climate is more frigid" (*quo caelum frigidus*).[40] But refutation of the idea that Northerners were by nature "dolts and assheads" (as the Zeeland physician Levinius Lemnius would later put it) held an obvious attraction to British and Dutch natural philosophers.[41] Much of this rhetoric, that is, assumed that primitive cultures remained primitive because of their limited power to respond to the environment.[42]

But difference didn't always follow geography. New distinctions were not always sharp between indigenes from the North and the South once they arrived on European shores. But the Inuit often diverged quietly from expected types. They were not naked, for example. They had no adornment apart from facial tattoos, "marks that . . . are completely blue, like sky blue . . . the marks cannot be taken off again with any substance . . . indelible and made from the juice of a plant," as the Augsburg text reported. The tattoos, in fact, bred a fascination repeated by Becanus and by later English observers, who made the connection to Pictish tribes.[43] Further, the Inuit did not seem to farm or build houses, nor did they stay in one place year after year.[44] This nomadism suggested a more general, peasant-like austerity, which contrasted, again, with the Aztecs known to Spain. The Intuit's bulky clothing, for some, seemed to connect them to more domestic marginals.[45] Greenlanders taken by a Portuguese sailor in 1502 and displayed in Lisbon were notable for being "in all else the same form and image as ourselves."[46] In Northern Scandinavia, Jan Huygen van Linschoten described commonalities between the furry clothing of the Nenets, the Sami, and the Inuit.[47] And when a description of two Inuits exhibited in London in 1576 reached Muscovy, a representative of Tsar Ivan IV wrote to the English amabassador demanding the return of what — on the basis of their clothing — seemed to him Russian.[48] Hugo Grotius even claimed that Northern Americans were specifically descended from "Germans" who had crossed the Atlantic via Greenland and Iceland.[49]

Most jarring was the fact that the Inuit did not appear to *own* much at all. Cartier, in Labrador, complained that the natives he met in 1534 "had not anything above the value of five sous, their canoes and fishing nets excepted."[50] The French dramatist Antoine de Montchrestien (b. 1575), writing about North Atlantic natives, claimed, "they do not believe that land belongs to individuals, any more than does the light of the sun."[51] Even their art (see Figure 3.6), for some, seemed impoverished, worryingly redolent of old European sculpture: this "miserable Countrey" of the North, wrote George Best, had wrought an "ignorance" of art.[52]

In sum, the Arctic kidnappees seemed to signal a world that was, on the one hand, disappointingly empty in terms of resources, and on the other, worryingly *undifferent* from that of their Northern European captors. Where Spaniards had marveled at the splendid "orderliness and organization" of Tenochtitlan,[53] its plenteous resources and brilliant crafts, the Inuit, so it seemed, had nothing to offer. They suggested a mode of "wildness" that was, in its very austerity, disconcertingly familiar.

"She Had No Language"

The arrival of the Inuit pair took place at the exact time — August 1566 — when the Dutch revolt was in its most violent stage (Figure 4.7). Antwerp remained the wealthiest city in the Spanish Netherlands, an entrepôt for goods between the European hinterlands and the North Sea. In the spring of 1566, Hapsburg forces had begun suppressing Protestant dissent in the city's hinterlands with varying

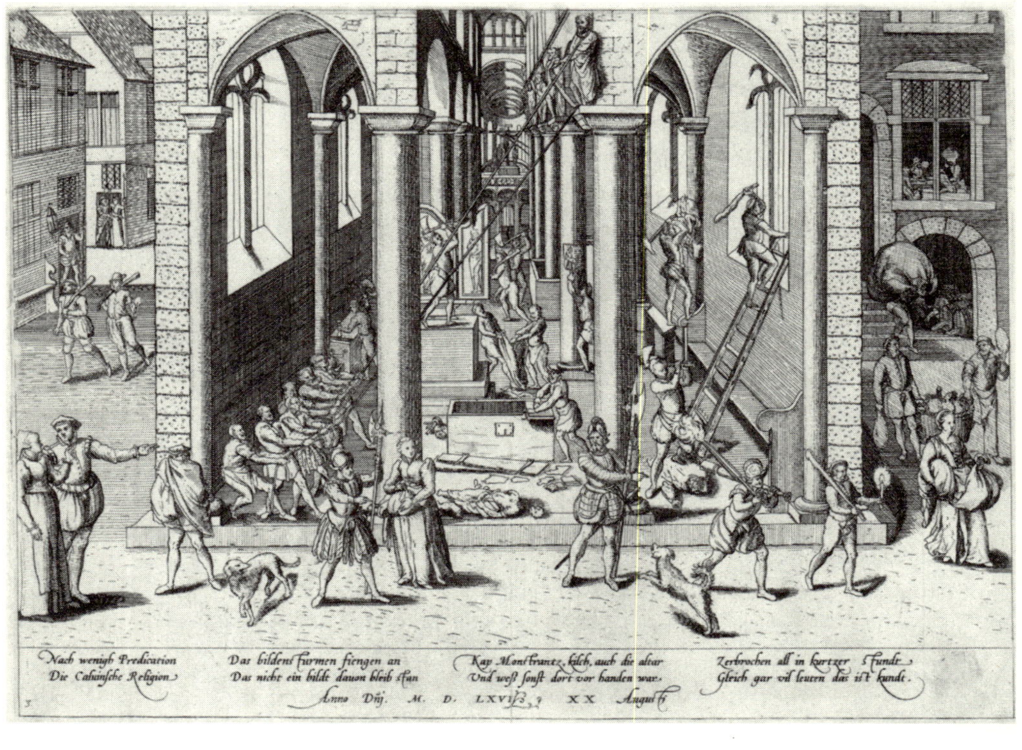

Figure 4.7. Frans Hogenberg, *Antwerp Iconoclasm, 1566*, 1566–1570, etching, 20.9 x 28.1 cm, Rijksmuseum, Amsterdam, RP-P-OB-77.720.

degrees of force. Groups of Calvinist nobles, who had long lamented the civil despotism and religious persecution of the Spanish, began to organize. April 5 of that year, a group of such nobles approached the regent, Margaret of Parma, with a list of grievances, which her councilor duly ignored as the gripes of "beggars" (*geuzen*). "Les Gueux" took on the name and solidified into an oppositional clan. Separatist rumblings soon fused with Reformation teachings against church profligacy.

Violence against images became enwrapped with political dissent. Drawing particular ire in Antwerp and Ghent were images associated with Marian cults (Figure 4.8). In August 1566, for example, the miracle-working statue of Onzelievevrouw op t'Stocken (the Beloved Lady of the Pole) was pelted with rocks while in procession.[54] When iconoclasts penetrated the Antwerp cathedral, they went first for the central Virgin statue, cutting off its head, hands, and arms, redirecting a punishment meted out on *real* bodies by the Spanish.[55] In Mechelen, one Gadifer vander Clyte decapitated a saint's statue and arranged it decoratively outside the church portal.[56] In s'Hertogenbosch, rioters emptied the St. Janskerk and made a bonfire of looted contents on the city square.[57] Such tumult became the background for a broader discussion of what today we might call Dutch identity formation. More than once, referring to the earlier protesters, iconoclasts paired their violence with cries of "Vivent le Gueux!" Image breakers often saw themselves as sharing bonds that previously did not exist. "Let our lord the king and his soldiers come to our land," cried one image-breaking rioter to his fellows, "for they will be defeated."[58] As Peter Arnade has revealed, in Flanders, iconoclasm became a rallying point to unite vastly different social contingents.[59]

The 1566 violence also provided the background for a rare first-hand description of the same Inuit pair illustrated in the broadsheet (see Figure 4.1). In the Hague, the ichthyologist Adriaen Coenen viewed the pair in front of a tavern owned by one Anna Pouwels, wife of a local sculptor.[60] Coenen recounted the experience:

> During the time of the image breaking . . . here in Holland, I, Adriaen Coenen-zoon, saw a wild woman with a child, and one could see them for money. This

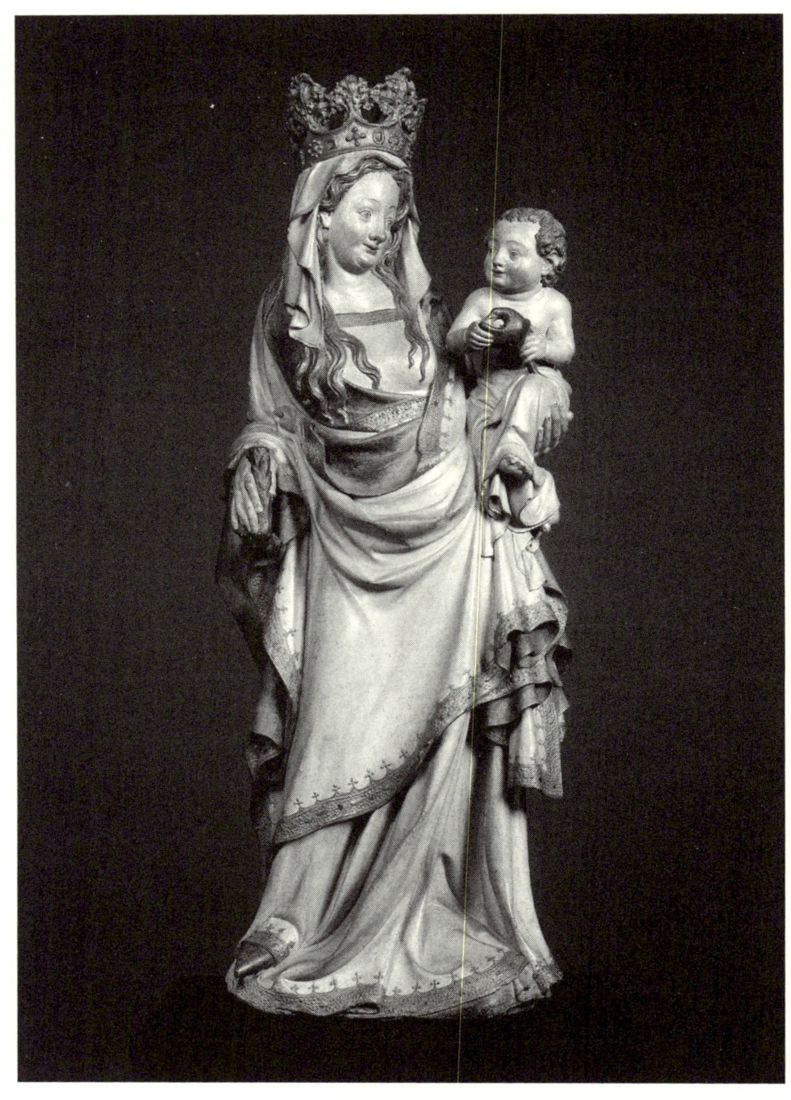

Figure 4.8. Flemish, *Madonna and Child*, 1390-1400, Bruges, limestone with original poly-chromy, h. 91 cm, Museum Mayer van den Bergh, Antwerp, Inv. nr. MMB.024.

woman was dressed . . . with seal skins with the hair on the outside and that child was dressed in the same way. She had no language or did not want to speak. I heard that the landlady [of the inn] called Anna Pouwels, said to that wild woman while showing her some statues, of which some were gilded and some were painted (because her husband was responsible for the St. Antonius altar, that is why those statues had escaped and were kept there). And Anna Pouwels pointed and said, "Look, put your hands together, this is your Lord, your God" and while she was pointing to the sculpture, the wild woman shook her head and raised her head up and put her hands together. From this it seemed that she had some knowledge of God in heaven. Thus it seemed to me in any case by watching her.[61]

There are several startling things in this passage. First, there is an imagined Christian conversion of a New World native "without language." Second, there is the imputed agency of a carved sculpture — rescued from iconoclastic destruction — in this conversion; the Inuit woman, in Coenen's account, is seen to dismiss the idol before her, pointing to the sky, in preference for a differently present God.[62] And third, there is the synchronicity of the exotic display and Netherlandish image breaking. In the Augsburg woodcut's own text, in fact, local iconomachy is mapped onto the supposed cannibalism of the Iunk captives to a salvific end; "Let us thank God the Almighty for his blessings," reads the text, "that he has enlightened us with his word, so that we are not such completely wild people and man eaters [*Menschen-fresser*] as are in this district."[63] For Coenen, the Inuit woman disbelieves the idol — shakes her head at it — not because it is Christian, but because it is a holy image and thus wrongly present in Christianity. In Coenen's creative reading, that is, the Inuit here opts for devotion to the unseen.

The proximity of the image controversy frames the descriptions of the pair for both texts. Coenen, adapting the shrugging exhaustion of other New World descriptive enterprises, concludes that there were "many other things" of interest about the natives, alas, "too many other things to tell about in detail."[64] Here, the mother and child stage a counterexample of the world, a miraculous and terrible apparition akin to other *Flugblatt* subjects, but now harbingers of a new kind of New World alterity — one parallel, in its barbarism, to the new confessional binaries at home. Theirs is the savage, idolatrous episteme now tamed — before eager onlookers — through a rejection of the image. Art is at the center of indigenous assimilation. The Coenen story assumes that there are two ways one can now act before images: wild or reverent.

But was sixteenth-century iconoclasm — like all iconoclasms, an othering of crafted bodies — a way of knowing? Iconomachy, modest as it was in the Netherlands in comparison with (say) Switzerland and France, resulted in an alternative visual reality introduced into the city. The same year as the Netherlandish destruction, 1566, Bullinger describes how:

> the object of delusion is of necessity something false, and it can never be called true because it pretends to be true by means of its external appearance and imitation. So if all imitation is not the thing itself but only play, then there is nothing of religion in images. Hence let us fashion a better, higher, and more spiritual notion of the Christ than when we look at him by means of paint and images, which differ from the truth as far as possible.[65]

Difference, for iconoclasts, was the goal. And in physical attacks, not only were figurative sculptures and paintings defaced, but rood screens, books, priestly vestments, even tombs — unfigured handiworks — hacked apart and assaulted. Sacramental wine would be drunk, effigies ceremonially hanged or split apart. Censure (as in the Hague) was not always violent (on occasion sculptures, say, would just be stowed out of sight). But its results defamiliarized long-known civic spaces in real terms. In the village of Lavantie in 1566, a day laborer actually recarved the face of a sculpted male saint in the "Turkish" style.[66] Iconoclasm, here, was less an absenting than an othering, a making exotic. It was not the objects themselves that were under attack, but a particular way of seeing.[67]

Image violence was ancient, of course, and religious chaos in the North summoned savage types and contemporary comparisons to the New World. Depending on whom you read, both iconodules and iconoclasts were barbarians — either because they were credulous or because they were base. Cornelis Gemma (of aurorae borealis fame from Chapter 3) detailed "Fauns, Satyrs, Androgynes, Ichthyophages . . . completely wild in appearance and way of life." And yet, claimed Gemma, "it is not necessary to go to the New World to find beings like this; most of them and others . . . can still be found here and there among us, now that the rules of justice are trampled underfoot, all humanity flouted, and all religion torn to bits."[68] Image worshippers, differently, could be framed as American primitives. The title page of a 1520 edition of Andreas Karlstadt's Lutheran tract *On the Removal of Images*, published in Wittenberg, was bordered with feathered natives connecting (imagined) American idolatry to more local European church ceremony.[69] The Mass was frequently mocked as a savage right. In 1522, Pamphilus Gengenbach, trained as a printer in Dürer's Nuremberg, published a dramatic satire comparing the clergy to cannibals (Figure 4.9).[70] His cover for *Devourers of the Dead* depicts priests, nuns, and demons gathered around a corpse, which the pope cuts open in preparation for a meal. Three scholars debate, heedless to the feast behind them, as a beggar goes unnoticed at the table's edge. All the while a demon, looking on, entertains on a fiddle. Both idols and idolaters figure as codes for profuse, blasphemous consumption. This cannibalism, like iconoclasm, could be about making normative bodies disappear in public ways — eaten, smashed, or defaced.

Michel de Montaigne saw the encounter with the savage as being about the encounter with the self. He posed anthrophagy as an early kind of cultural relativism, reconfiguring wildness as a means to query Europe: "We may therefore well call these people barbarians," he said of Brazilian natives, "in respect to the rules of reason, but not in respect to ourselves, who surpass them in all sort of barbarity."[71] During the Dutch revolt, in fact, the Spanish were accused of defiling and eating corpses at Naarden, and one Netherlandish rebel claimed to have eaten the heart of a captor.[72] The figures of cannibals often appeared in the margins of maps that, like the poles, were otherwise

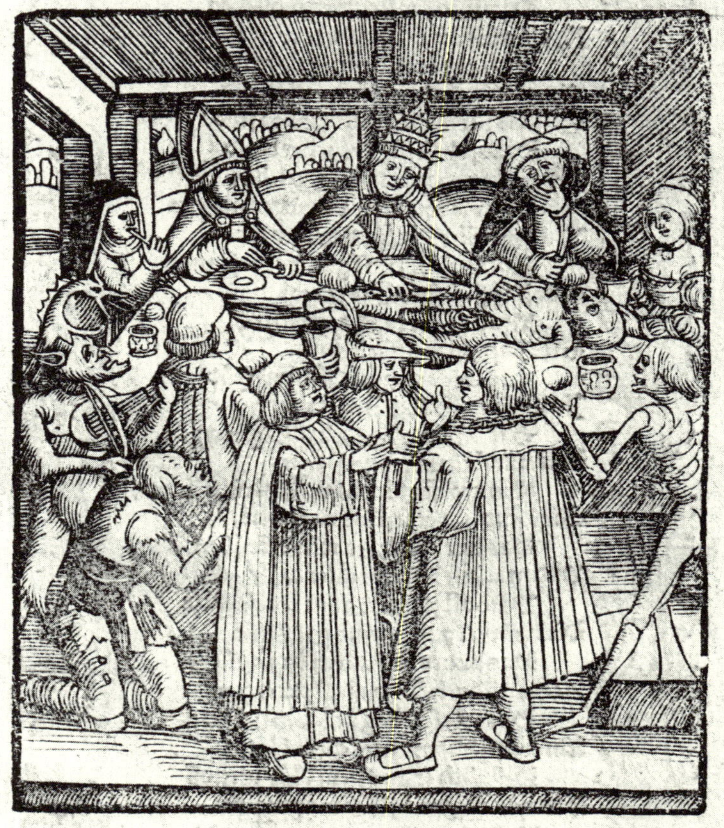

Figure 4.9. Pamphilus Gengenbach, *Diß ist ein jemerliche clag uber die Todtenfresser*, Augsburg [1522], title page.

empty — at the edges of the world, the same place one encountered grotesques and sea monsters. Usually the last thing to be noticed, such details bespoke both a far-off place and a low condition foreign to the civilized world.

And cannibalism — however unwitnessed — remained a way to map Northern natives onto more familiar descriptions from the South. This had roots in Herodotus, who used the term "Androphagi" to describe Hyperboreans.[73] Settle deemed the Inuit (without evidence) "Anthrophagi, or devourers of mans fleshe."[74] When the Brabantine physician and linguist Johannes Goropius Becanus (the same humanist who described Pytheas's *Thule*) viewed the Inuit pair in Antwerp in 1566, he referred to them as "Hyperborean" cannibals, assuming that they feared being eaten themselves.[75] Bodin even imagined a Northern cannibalism that was different from that in the South, one fueled by scarcity, a "bestial, hunger-driven rage." This was unlike man-eating in the tropics, Bodin wrote, which stemmed from a "melancholic, passionate fury."[76]

The figure of the cannibal embodied early modern sailors' fears about bodily vanishing.[77] And in practice, New World exoticism and Old World iconoclasm overlapped in several ways. Both trafficked in the idea of parallel realities adjacent to and apposite to immediately sensible states of existence. And all the while, accusations of idolatry in the sixteenth century bred, as Thomas Cummins has put it, "a symmetry of religious violence"[78] between Europe and the rest of the globe. Iconoclasm in the New World pitted Protestant forces against imagined idols of all kinds, with results that strangely paralleled acts at home. In March of 1599, for example, English pirates ransacked the cathedral at San Juan, Puerto Rico. The scene, as described by a Jeronymite monk is almost indistinguishable from European violence: "we came to the sancta sanctorum, which is the sacristy and the altar, and we found all the saints and figures of them cleaved and split into pieces and some had the noses cut off." And "in regard to Mary and the saints who were at Christ's side, their faces were erased [*borrados*] and the sculptures cut into pieces."[79] That the report recalls Netherlandish acts is hardly coincidental.

Atlantic sailors, in fact, seemed to relish image-breaking as an imaginative instrument of conquest. Francis Drake conducted Protestant services at sea and seemed to have kept John Foxe's rousing *Acts and Monuments* (1563) — lurid tales of Protestant suffering at the hands of Catholics — in his ship's library.[80] In 1576, his acolyte John Oxenham is recorded slashing and trampling "a veronica framed" on the island of Chapera (off present-day Panama) and later kicked an image of the Virgin into the sea.[81] And when joint colonial and British troops took over the French settlement of Point Royal (in what is now Nova Scotia) in 1690, a Catholic chapel was burned and, as a general proudly reported, its "Crosses & Images broken down."[82] Such destruction in the New World marked a redirection of fury against Old World images — themselves far off and inaccessible.[83]

While obviously a more complex gesture of othering, the portrayal of the Inuit pair in 1566, too, might have something to say about the figural "erasing" going on right at home. Coenen, for his sake, tasks the Inuit woman's reaction as example of a praiseworthy "natural" distrust of manufactured images, a refusal to engage in idolatry. With such a hoped-for validation of a different, new kind of devotion, the captive (in Coenen's eyes) almost refuses to submit to a clear category of alterity.

Captives and Ghosts

As stolen people, the Antwerp pair would not prove unique. In August of 1576, as we saw in the last chapter, Frobisher's crew encountered groups of Inuit on what is now Baffin Island. Communicating by signs, sailors lured a fisherman aboard ship with "trifles" and persuaded him to act as guide. When the local hunter led five men back to land in preparation, the whole party disappeared. Frobisher waited three days, and then, after a violent confrontation, captured a different (now injured) Inuit, with his kayak, to barter as a hostage. When the missing Englishmen did not reappear, Frobisher hauled anchor and sailed all the way back to England, where the native was put on display. "They have brought a man of the country with them and a bote; they toke him by force," wrote an English employee of the Muscovy Company, Thomas Wood.[84] The hunter arrived in London on October 9, 1576.

This Inuit's time in England was brief, but busy. Frobisher's financier, Michael Lok, described seeing a "strange man . . . which was such a wonder unto the whole City, & to the rest of the Realm that heard of yt, as seemed never to have happened the like great matter to any mans knowledge."[85] He sat for a wax cast. And he was actually painted eight times in London, clothed both in his native garb and "in Englishe apparell" by Gouda-born portraitist Cornelis Ketel. Records of Ketel's fees indicate that the artist was paid for portraits of the Inuit in full length, a Netherlandish format usually reserved, in midcentury Britain, for nobility.[86] A watercolor by Lucas de Heere (Figure 4.10) was likely based on one of these now-lost portraits.[87] De Heere, a Protestant tapestry designer and poet from Ghent, had fled to London during the 1566 iconoclastic riots. His watercolor appears in the last pages of a costume book that was begun in London in 1568. We see a figure in a sealskin *tuiliq* with an oar and bow and arrow, again demonstrably extracted from elsewhere. He has been reposed on a dusky shoreline and then doubled, in the background, paddling a small kayak. Essaying indigenous technology, de Heere's sheet places its sitter in a landscape few viewers would have ever seen. And instead of a captive dressed "in Englishe apparell," we are presented with a figure who reads as a European dressed as an Inuit.

The interest in portraiture continued. In July of 1577, Frobisher again landed in Baffin Island, again skirmished with locals, and actually inspected local dwellings that had been abandoned. Ever in search of fungibles, the crew then helped themselves to native objects, which Dionyse Settle dismissed as "trifles, more to be wondred at for their strangenesse, than for any other commoditie needfull for our use."[88] And the crew again took captives: a man, a woman, and a small child whose names were later transcribed as Kalicho, Arnaq, and Nutaaq. These have since been connected with the Nuguminut tribe.[89] The three were taken to England, landing in

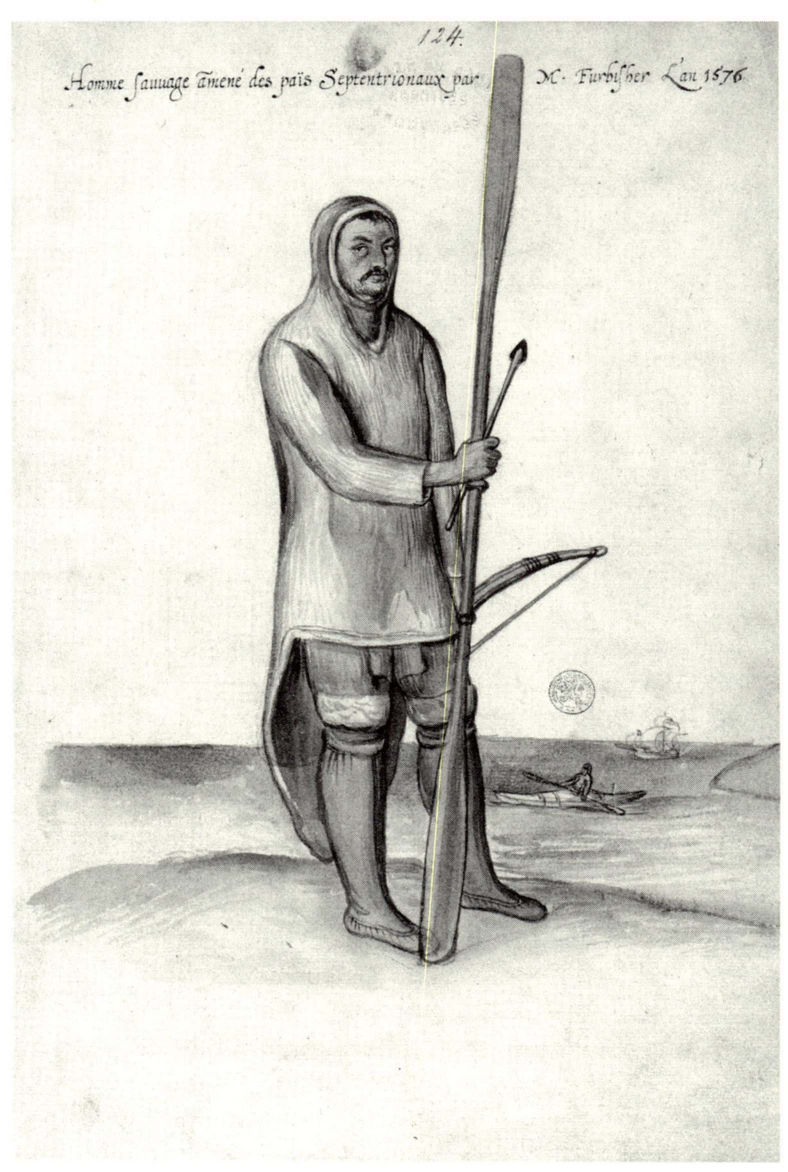

Figure 4.10. Lucas de Heere, *Portrait of an Inuit Man*, 1577, watercolor on paper, from Lucas de Heere, *Theatre de tous les peoples et nations de la terre*, Universiteitsbibliothek, Ghent.

early October 1577 in Bristol. They then made their way to London where they soon fell ill. Despite being cared for by an apothecary, the captives lived only fifteen days and even received autopsies.[90] But the short visit created a sensation. It was, in fact, Kalicho, possibly from the old Inuktitut *kaliksaq* — "to haul something" — who might have lent a name to Shakespeare's Caliban from the *Tempest*.[91]

Cornelis Ketel was again paid to make portraits in 1577. Two of them were commissioned by the Cathay Company — heirs to the Company of Merchant Adventurers — and one later was given to Elizabeth I.[92] A German visitor to Hampton Court in 1592 reported seeing "life-like portraits of the wild man and woman whom Martin Frobisser . . . brought live to England."[93] These paintings, too, have been lost, but the famous watercolors by John White give an indication of their appearance (Figure 4.11). In Bristol, Kalicho was put on display. He was made to hunt ducks with his "dart" on the Avon in his kayak, learned some phrases of English, and "beganne to growe more civill, familiar, pleasant, and docile amongst us in a verye short time."[94] The facial tattoos compelled again, recalling Pictish facial ornament. One William Camden described "the woman painted about the eyes and balls of the cheek with a blue color like the ancient Britons."[95]

But before his own visit to Europe, Kalicho was shown a painted portrait *in* the Arctic itself. One of the pictures of the previous year's captive by Ketel came over with Frobisher. (Archives note payment for a frame for "the strange mans picture to send over seas.")[96] Near Baffin Island, the English sailors staged a remarkable encounter of indigene and image. As George Best reports it:

> we shewed him the picture of his countryman, which the last year was brought into England (whose contrafet we had drawne, with boate and other furniture . . .). He was upon the sudden much amazed thereat, and beholding advisedly, the same with silence a good while, as though he would strain courtesy whether should begin the speech (for he thought him no doubt a lively creature) at length began to question with him, as with his companion and finding him dumme and mute, seemed to suspect him, as one disdainful, and would with a little help have grown into choler at the matter, until at last by

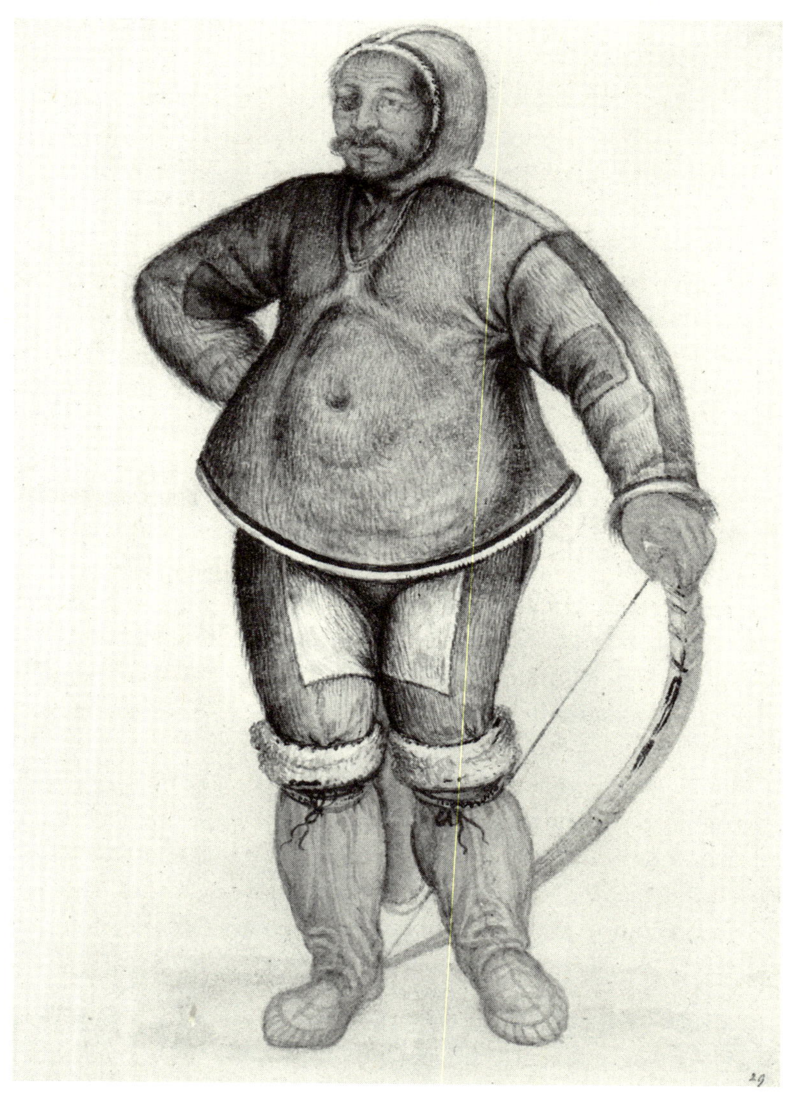

Figure 4.11. John White, "Kalicho," 1585-1593, pen and brown ink and watercolor over graphite, touched in white, 16.3 x 22.5 cm, British Museum, London, 1906.0509.1.29.

feeling and handling, he found him a deceiving picture. And then with great noise and cries, he ceased not wondering, thinking that we could make men live or die at our pleasure.[97]

Kalicho — at least in Best's eyes — here appears to be humbled by the subtlety of English representation *as* representation — the picture's capacity not just to duplicate, but to tack between mirror and symbol. Best here seems to be drawing, ironically, upon Spanish accounts of writing in the New World, wherein the Nahuatl were assumed to be mystified by the idea of communication that did not require face-to-face contact.[98] But Best imputes a credulity to Kalicho, assuming the latter's speech was unquestionably directed "to" the picture's absent subject, rather than "to" the actual object before him, painted by Ketel. Stephen Greenblatt has described the episode: Kalicho "thinks that the companion is alive, then he thinks that he has been turned into something 'dumme and mute' — that is, dead — then he concludes that the English have produced both of these experiences." To be sure, the encounter, whether or not it actually occurred, demonstrates the brandishing of colonial power through mimickry; the representable indeed becomes a piece with Shakespearean embrace of both paradox and paradox's unraveling.[99]

But there is also the question of Best's language. A pivotal term in the original English text is "contrafet," a version of the same word attached to the Augsburg and Nuremberg broadsheets.[100] The *imago contrafactum*, recall, was an image taken directly from a prototype, a particular kind of representation making claims to authority. As species of image, the *contrafactum* bore specific associations with identity; Dürer's friend Johannes Camerarius used *contrafacta* to refer specifically to faces.[101] A 1561 German-Latin lexicon published in Zürich even rendered the infinitive *abcontrafehen* as *effingere* — a species of imitation associated specifically with "portrayal."[102]

As elsewhere in the Arctic, with the Kalicho episode, pictures "shewed" are most powerful in their process of being revealed as unstable. What we find, that is, in Best, is the reverse of the other Inuit's experience in the Netherlands in 1566. Recall how the displayed native woman in the Hague was shown "gilded and painted statues," whereupon she took them as nothing *but* symbols. But what Kalicho, for his part, comes to grasp — against what Frobisher's crew triumphantly projects — is not just the bedazzlement of art followed by disillusionment, but the unreliability of sight alone at extricating truth from illusion where "pictures" are concerned. Only by gradual "feeling and handling" — by touch, not sight — does the native understand the displayed object to be "but a deceiving picture."

In 1578, in Strasbourg, a second woodcut of Frobisher's captives appeared, this time depicting three Inuit in situ (Figure 4.12).[103] The text of this broadsheet, authored by satirist Johann Fischart, freighted the natives' discovery with the portentous:

> The world demands wonders, and can hardly be satisfied with wondrous signs [*Wunderzeychen*]; now the Lord god accedes thereto, and every day shows people the most wonderful wonders [*wunderlichte Wunder*], and the best, most certain signs of his future coming. Which is namely, according to his own prophesizing word [*prophecienden sag*], that as a testimony to his kingdom, which the Christian belief, will extend over all peoples in the entire world from one sea to the other. Such he shows [*erzeygeter*] today, in that he has allowed the Christians out of Europe, and not the Turks out of Asia, to find, discover, edify, instruct, and discipline the most distant, most unknown, wildest ends of the world, where one would scarcely have looked for the habitations of animals, let alone humans.[104]

The sheet, with the text's astonishing distinction between signs and referents, is based upon a now-lost Dutch drawing taken from an English description of Frobisher's captives, apparently published by the printer John Aldee in 1578.[105] That publication is now entirely lost.[106] *That* English sheet likely was itself based on Inuit watercolors by John White and may have been attached to letters to the continent, themselves copied by German and Dutch printers.[107] Fischart's *contrafactum* brandishes this hectic chain of indexicalities. The Inuit now come to symbolize a wildness ripe for conversion. But this Arctic wildness is different from that of before: "I will be silent about the Spanish, Portuguese, and Floridian sea voyages which are now

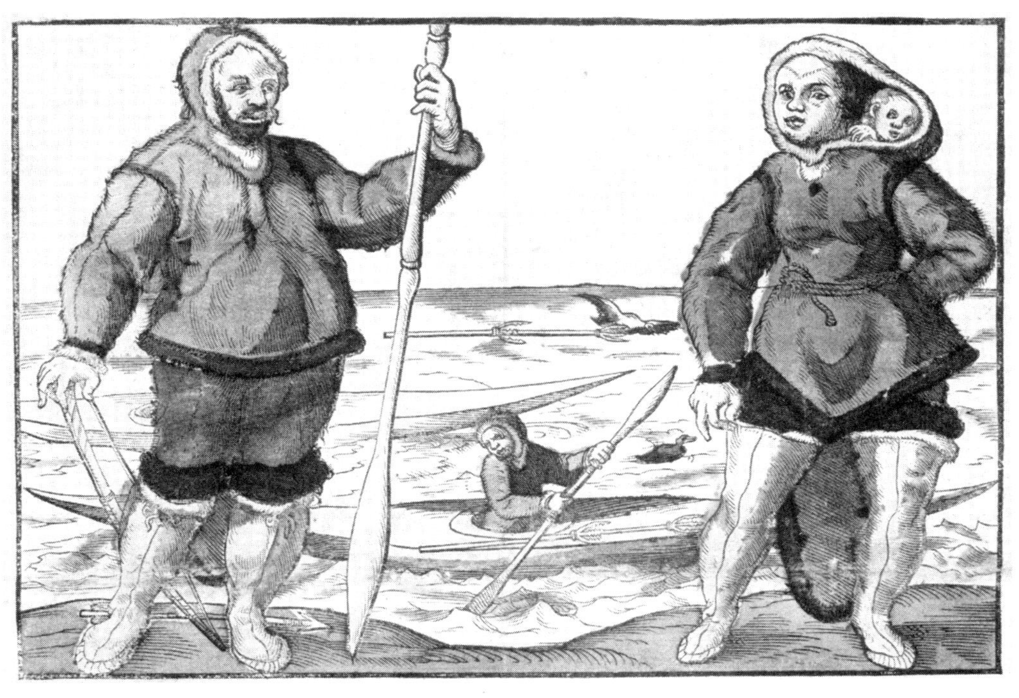

Figure 4.12. Johann Fischart (text), *Merckliche Beschreibung sampt eygenlicher Abbildung eynes frembden unbekanten Volcks*...(Strasbourg: Jobin [?], 1578), hand-colored woodcut and letterpress, 35.7 x 28.4 cm, Zentralbibliothek Zürich, PAS II 15/32.

sufficiently known and notorious," Fischart writes. "I will only remember the thoroughly newest, and still wholly unheard-of voyage of the English into strange islands . . . the strange men who were brought from the distant island to England . . . [and] are in appearance equal to ours." This wonder, that is, arises from uncanny *similarity*. It was the *context* of the broadsheet that framed the Inuit as wondrous, not some essence in the natives themselves.

Perhaps the idea across all the woodcuts, then, might be that wildness is place based and, at the same time, potentially inscribed within us all. This is — without being too confessionally determinist — the central Lutheran notion. But it flips during the early modern period, when the figure of the wild man, mapped on to exotic places newly available for viewing in prints and texts, is no longer "out there" beyond civilization, but, in a very real sense, here. The broadsheet form wields its medium's roughness as a means to index some primeval state, rendering savagery as local *news*. Franck's mother-and-child (see Figure 4.1) would also have recalled Marian sculptures that at the very same time were being attacked by iconoclasts (see Figure 4.8).[108] The printed pair forms a new graven image — they are presented as new idols. And this was the anxiety behind so many of the same worries about images among the natives, perhaps: the fact that the vanishings of bodies taking place amidst so-called "pagans" and amidst Europeans might not be very different after all. The Inuit pair's assumed wildness thus reads as both familiar and exotic, an indeterminacy shared, in iconoclastic Antwerp, by the idea of "image" itself.

The body features of certain Arctic captives that most entranced many North European viewers, as we have seen, were facial tattoos, what the Eastern Inuit call *tunniit*.[109] Tattoos were far from unknown in early modern Europe and could even carry a Christian charge. Reports exist of Italian pilgrims receiving cross tattoos when they visited Jerusalem.[110] But for Eastern Inuit mothers, these marks are apotropaic, a way to confuse evil spirits, to (say) ward off ghosts and disease in children.[111] They were ink lines deliberately meant to deflect attention away from the wearer, added less to harken than to disguise. And for (Protestant) Europeans, such marks were inscrutable: an inscription without language, they were signs that seemed to *foil* communication, disturb identity. And tattoos seemed further vexing for their unexchangeabilty: as Juliet Fleming points out, the tattoo is a property that (separate from its wearer) cannot be sold.[112]

The Antwerp broadsheet (see Figure 4.1) — itself an amassment of lines — similarly refuses to transcend, to transport the viewer, elsewhere to the New World. Rather it thrusts that New World's humanity into a Europe troubled by the possibility that images, and inscriptions of all kinds (facial or not), may not always "work" regarding information supposedly to be conveyed. In the Arctic, the *contrafactum* is no longer just pedagogue or double. It unevenly summons both friendship and enmity, vitality and death. Like the captives, it does not "want to speak." And like the traditional Inuit facial tattoo, the incised lines of the print enchant as they defamiliarize, asking us to, indeed, step up and stare at an unruly image culture.[113] To act like the savages we are. Or to look away.

Dispossessions

Eyewitnessing and testimonies of faith — crucial aspects of Protestant theology — helped to structure much New World reportage, wherein mystical and skeptical impulses easily cohabited.[114] One of the first and most eloquent Protestant writers to visit America was the Huguenot Jean de Léry, who sailed to Brazil in 1556. Léry's *Voyage* of 1578 (the same year of the last Frobisher expedition) took pains to render local indigenes as similar in comparison with Europeans; the bodies of the Tupi, Léry wrote, "are neither monstrous or prodigious with respect to ours." Such a defense was a piece with Léry's own take on images themselves; as a preacher in Geneva in 1562, writing the book, Léry is recorded as pleading unsuccessfully with iconoclasts to spare his church. Léry specifically wields the term "savage" throughout the book. It is a Renaissance word, a word used by Herodotus, Marco Polo, Columbus, and the American Declaration of Independence. But arguably the modern construction of the savage as supplement, subordinate, vitalistic, symbolically overdetermined (and the subsequent romanticization and demonization of the savage for precisely such values) is rooted in this sixteenth-century moment.[115]

Léry's writing was crucial for the work of Claude Lévi-Strauss, who claimed to adore its "surreality."[116] "Savage," for Lévi-Strauss, was not some debasing category of a human type or some presocial, primitivizing mode of existence. Rather, "savage," for Lévi-Strauss, was a particular intellectual relation of subjects to the world, a knowledge structure: savage was an episteme. It suggested an alternative to Enlightenment science, as it would for Foucault. For Lévi Strauss, the savage mind was "any mind in its untamed state" that constructs meaning via *bricolage*, working with what exists. This is distinct from the "scientific" mind, that of the engineer, where phenomena are cultivated or domesticated for the purpose of yielding a return.[117] Lévi-Strauss maintained that "savagery" is useful as a fiction against which to play mythologies of civilization. *Le pensée sauvage* is one that makes meaning and image out of things already in the world.

The appearance of the Inuit pair—as public spectacle—during a time of iconoclasm, however, may not be a "curious" disruption, but relies upon a potentially terrifying rhetoric of sameness and inclusion, the precise sameness that makes iconoclasm possible. Lévi-Strauss alluded to this via a quotation from Inuit specialist Franz Boas, who had worked with Arctic artifacts as early as the 1880s (Figure 4.13): "It would seem that mythological worlds have been built up, only to be shattered again, and that new worlds were built from the fragments"[118] using those "pieces" iconoclasm begets to know the other. For as we have seen, many initial reactions to the Arctic were often not wonder, not shock, not awe, not amazement, but rather frustration and fatigue, and a quietly failed incorporation of its scant phenomena into extant representational schemes. Print here was vital. Print intervened to make captives seem strange, but present, to make them "curious." Yet quiet doubts about the efficacy or the use of visual reportage meant that the Arctic bred more broken conceptions of fact. The English, for

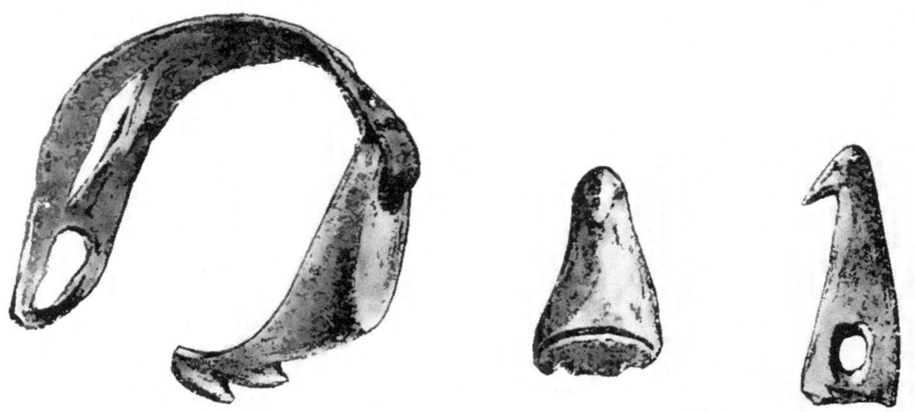

FIG. 394. Qilertuang or leather strap and clasps for holding coiled up harpoon lines. *a, c* (National Museum. Washington. *a*, 34128 ; *c*, 34132.) *b* (Museum für Völkerkunde, Berlin.) ⅓

Figure 4.13. Franz Boas, "The Central Eskimo," *Sixth Annual Report of the Bureau of American Ethnology to the Secretary of the Smithsonian Institution*, 1884-1885, p. 474.

their part, needed the Arctic to be somewhat undifferent from what was at home, if it was to be sold as a potential colony. Perhaps, then, what defined the specifically Arctic encounter was not an attempt at civilizing, but an awkward recognition that in the Far North, there might not be much to civilize. That is to say: difference existed in the European understanding of Arctic dwellers, but it was not difference along an axial episteme of opposing us and them.

Against Wonder

With the voyages of exploration, "wonders" physically moved home from these peripheries to the European center. To be wondrous, as with Old Work, was often to be collectable, if not necessarily explainable. Such was Dürer's famous image of Arctic fauna, itself documenting a media sensation. Sometime before 1521, Dürer drew the disembodied head of a walrus, a creature caught off Finnmark in the extreme north of Norway (Figure 4.14).[119] In the watercolor, Dürer's specimen confronts us with a tusky visage: at once terrifying and sympathetic, all rolling eyeballs, bristled mandible, mottled fur. The countenance, much like Franck's broadsheet, mingles wildness, menace, and pity.[120] Dürer inscribes it: "1521 this animal from those parts, whose head I *contrafeyted* here was caught in the Netherlandish sea."[121] The sheet would seem to align with Dürer's seemingly plotless watercolors of animals: the *Hare* watercolor, or the *Rhinoceros* woodcut, which Dürer claimed to have "*mit aller seiner gestalt Abcondertfet*" (to have shown in its entirety). The latter, too, proffered a specimen whose physiognomic "accuracy" mattered less than the evocation of an unknown geographic elsewhere.[122] We know, in fact, that the walrus head was a salted and preserved gift from Archbishop Erik Walkendorf of Trondheim, to Pope Leo X in Rome.[123] Dürer may have viewed the creature during its journey to the Vatican; it was actually displayed in Strasbourg in 1519, the same year Dürer himself visited Alsace.[124] Possible, too, is that Dürer may have seen an Italian woodcut of the walrus published by Conrad Gessner. The creature- would have been hunted by precisely the same groups of Basque fishermen who first captured the Antwerp woman and child in 1566.[125]

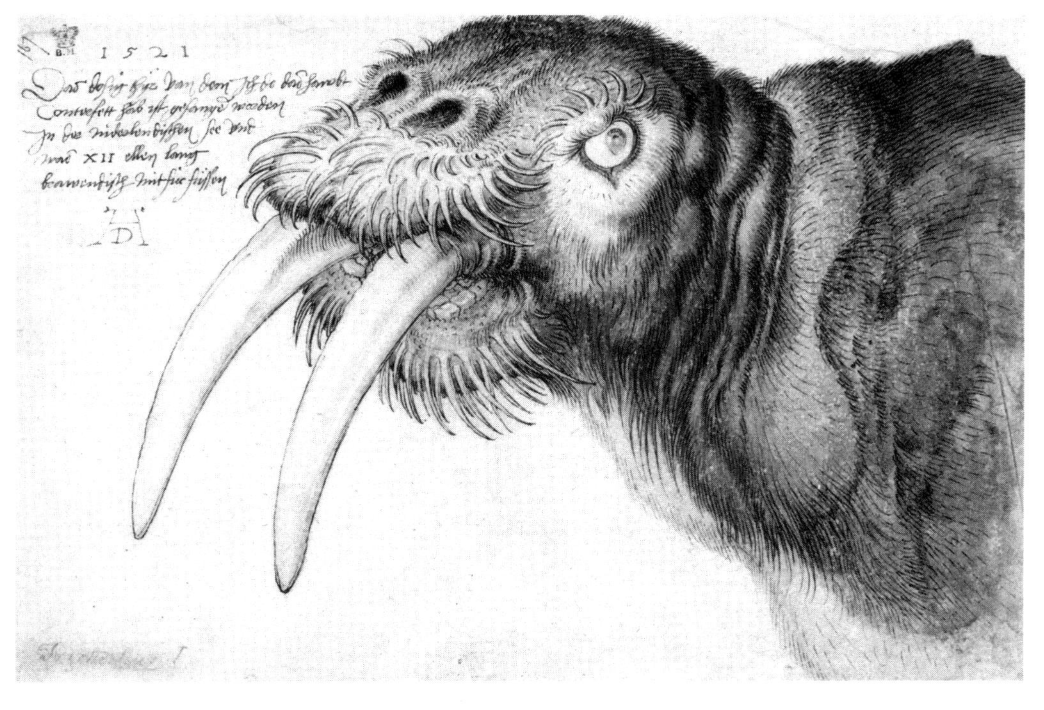

Figure 4.14. Albrecht Dürer, *Head of a Walrus*, watercolor, 1521, 21 x 31 cm, British Museum, London, SL.5261.167.

In the walrus sheet, Dürer reads as both "artist and scientist," as one scholar put it: "His studies from nature…belong to the incunabula of scientific illustration."[126] Yet in 1521, the pickled head was already in Rome.[127] The inscription on the sheet, that is, bears a different, impossible date, one placing the viewing during Dürer's sojourn in the Netherlands. This Arctic *contrafactum*, with its hairy referent, thus remains troubled with regard to any claims of "context," since Dürer (most likely ignorant of the Arctic provenance of the head) seems to have used the inscription to impart the work a date it likely could not have. But as *imago contrafactum*, it remains all the more truthful for depicting the specimen as dead.

And Dürer, as had generations of Anglo-Saxon carvers (Figure 4.15), repurposed this walrus body part to fashion something else.[128] Once back in Nuremberg in 1522, Dürer incorporated the creature into a drawing for *Madonna with Eight Saints*, an ink design for a *sacra conversazione* altarpiece (Figure 4.16).[129] There, the monstrous head — now hastily sketched in pen — lies at the feet of Saint Margaret among a riot of drapery, a decapitated dragon in profile. Like so many other altarpiece projects in Reformation Nuremberg, that commission disappeared.[130] And Dürer never referred to the walrus again. Yet the Northern subject provided the opportunity for him to dislocate natural "facts," setting Arctic observations into conversation (literally) with sacred belief.

Wonder, Caroline Bynum writes, "is deeply perspectival. It is a reaction of a particular 'us' to an 'other' that is 'other' only *relative to* the particular 'us.'"[131] Art's role in the exploration of marvelous phenomena such as Dürer's walrus — and, differently, New World novelties — is often presented as a relationship that is linear, map-like, legible, framed as near versus far, strange but *fixed*, with clear demarcations of inside and outside. Wonder is often portrayed as a matter of the relations between *selves* and *things*: "A sudden surprise of the soul which makes it tend to consider attentively those *objects* which seem to it rare and extraordinary," Descartes was to write.[132]

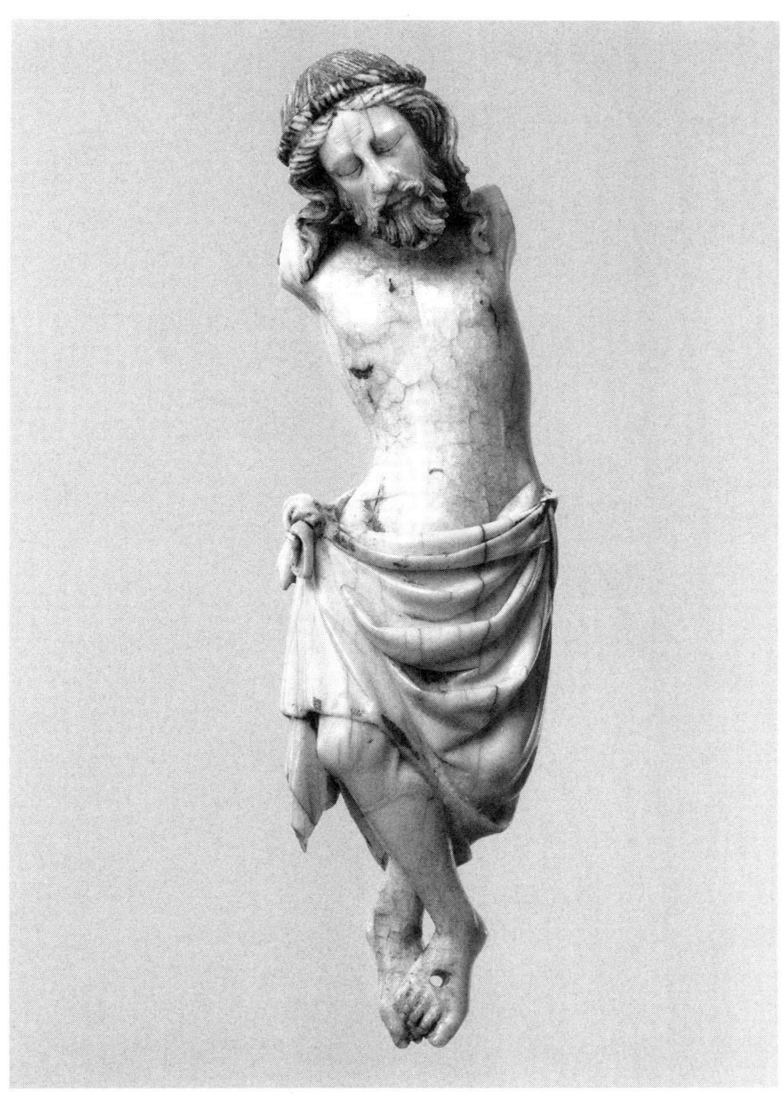

Figure 4.15. Northern European, *Crucified Christ*, ca. 1300, walrus ivory with traces of paint and gilding, 19.2 x 5.3 x 3.5 cm, Metropolitian Museum of Art, The Cloisters Collection, 2005, 2005.274.

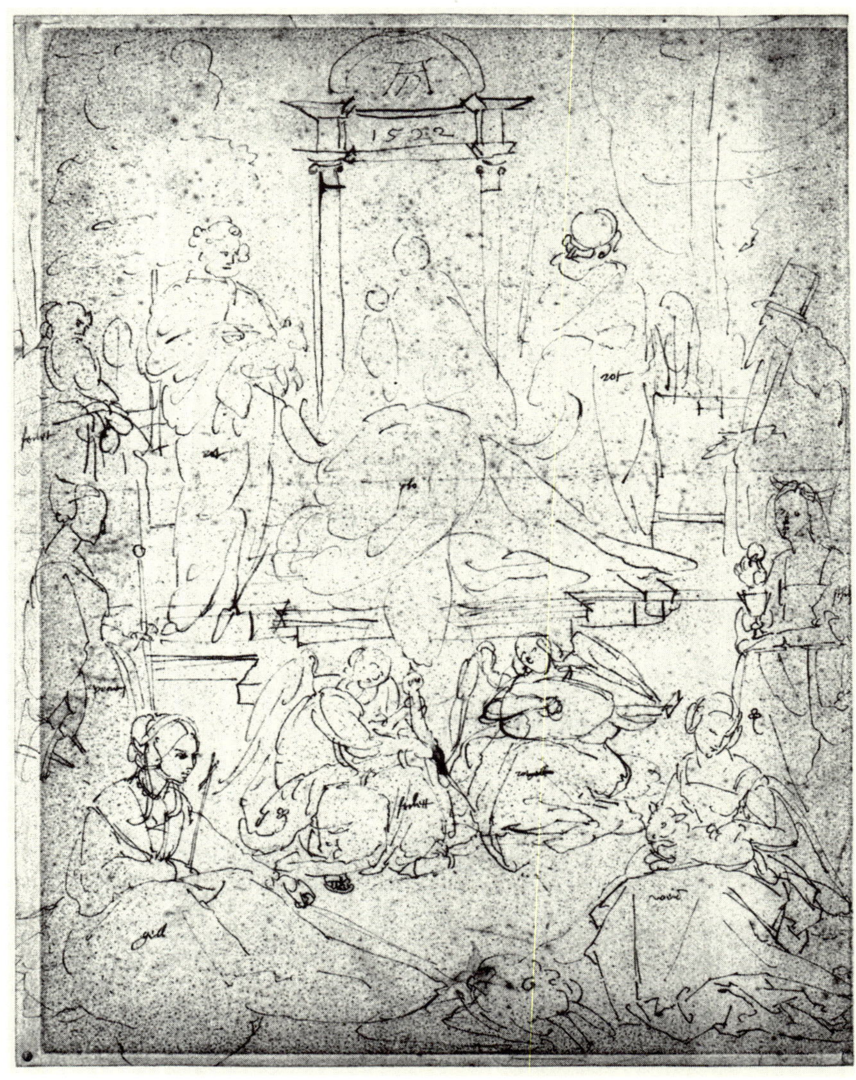

Figure 4.16. Albrecht Dürer, Madonna with Eight Saints, 1522, pen and ink drawing, 40.2 x 30.8 cm, Musée Bonnat-Helleu, Bayonne, Inv. NI1275; AI1504.

But what happens if one takes the epistemic image, the *imago con-trafactum*, as based not on prespectival access but on a certain opacity? An unlikely conceit at a time when certain images were being symbolically "killed"? An image based not upon "point of view" but on ungrounded notions of viewing itself? In the Arctic of the early moderns, difference did not yet lie in the hotly charged binary of other and self. It was like the cold Arctic terrain itself, broken and inconsistent. In the wildness that we have been examining — wild men and women, cannibals — there was a danger to the knowledge conditions now in operation. The "wild man," in this sense, serves not just as specimen from a far-off land, but as a conceptual tool to fashion — and blur — newly competing notions of the image at home. Cannibalism, particularly, "articulates the self (actively) assaulted but also the self (passively) disassembled and unbound," as Darcy Grigsby has put it.[133]

The Arctic experience was important, but the essaying of its conditions was equally critical, and not just for how it informed later narratives of can-do European identity, the myth of nation-hood planted atop the wilderness.[134] When Europeans began to travel more vigorously, identity came to be institutionalized as being about the relation between bodies and exterior places — places astrologi-cal, geographical, or economic. Atlantic whiteness — unmarkedness, in this sense — had forever been a dubious mode of race, based on assumptions of dark landscape illuminiated. But the idea of any New World as a *tabula rasa* demanded the constant visibility of nonwhite forces onto which Europeans could project "civilization." The con-querer, in this, demanded a stable "background" of rawness.[135] Per-haps this brings us back to Lévi-Strauss and to the famous opening sentence of *Tristes Tropiques*, his 1955 autobiography: "I hate travel-ling and explorers,"[136] he writes. The sentence is an ironic complaint *against* curiosity, *against* wonder, against the idea that to image is to master as to show is to access.

We know nothing of the ultimate fate of the captured mother and child in the 1566 Augsburg woodcut. Their sheet (see Figure 4.1), with its humble green mound of earth, is ultimately a landscape.

But we still grasp the pair as *images* unmoored. And to be sure, the spectacle world of Netherlandish capitalism — and iconoclasm — they now inhabited was a realm hostile to the very idea of place.[137] And rather than referring "simply or singly . . . to a 'person,' or to a dialectical power struggle between self and Other," as Homi Bhabha has noted, colonial control, for its sake, usually depends upon a "splitting . . . where the trace of what is disavowed is not repressed but repeated as something *different* — a mutation, a hybrid."[138] The earliest dreams of an uninhabited Arctic could enable mythologies of "figuring" and marking — and successfully knowing — a blank new world. But in their dependence upon a rhetoric of certainty, such myths were always haunted by very *local* anxieties about placelessness and desire.

CHAPTER FIVE

A Roman Interruption:

Olaus Magnus, 1555

In the 1550s, exiled and friendless in Rome, the Swedish bishop Olaus Magnus (1490–1557) began to write a colossal book about the Far North. His *Historia de gentibus septentrionalibus* (literally, Account of the people who live under the seven stars) (Figure 5.1) devoted 815 pages to obelisks, narwhals, comets, lawyers, dried fish, skis, avalanches, weddings, reindeer, yeast, giants, suicide, and, in one startling chapter, snowflakes:

> What a multiplicity of wonderful shapes and figures of snow can be found and examined everywhere, principally in the lands of the North . . . the farther one goes toward the Arctic Pole [*Polum Arcticum*], the more the falling snows seem to vary. It seems more a matter for amazement rather than inquiry [*ut potius stupenda, quam inquirenda ratio fit*] why and how so many shapes and forms, which elude the skill of any artist you choose to name, are so suddenly stamped [*imprimuntur*] upon such soft, tiny objects.[1]

Arctic snowflakes, that is, defy scrutiny precisely because they are diverse. A woodcut, possibly designed by Olaus's Roman publisher Giovanni Viotto, accompanied the section "On the Different Shapes of Snow" (Figure 5.2).[2] Three different views of snow crystals against a window are here collaged into a rectangle. At lower left, flurries are shown from afar, blowing downward in curled gusts. Ice crystals are pressed against a latticed pane with anthropomorphic and creatural mullions. And in a bay at far right, individual flakes are isolated

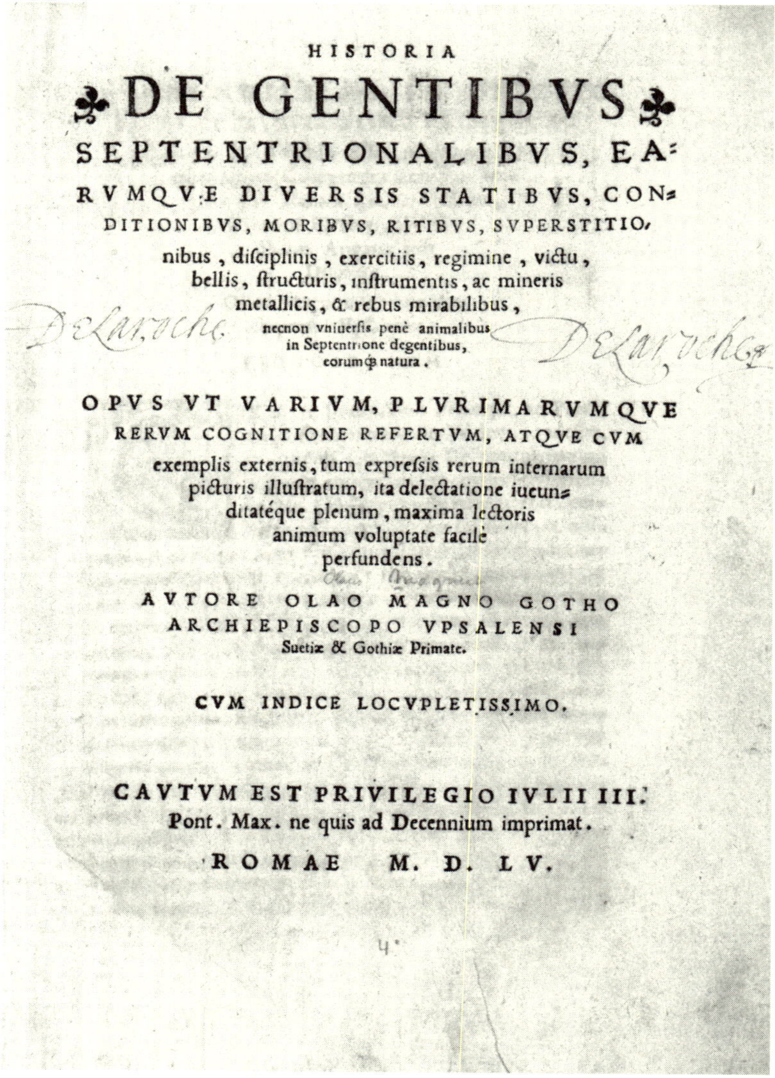

HISTORIA
❧ DE GENTIBVS ❧
SEPTENTRIONALIBVS, EA-
RVMQVÆ DIVERSIS STATIBVS, CON-
DITIONIBVS, MORIBVS, RITIBVS, SVPERSTITIO-
nibus , difciplinis , exercitiis , regimine , victu ,
bellis , ftructuris , inftrumentis , ac mineris
metallicis, & rebus mirabilibus ,
necnon vniuerfis penè animalibus
in Septentrione degentibus,
eorumq̃ natura .

OPVS VT VARIVM, PLVRIMARVMQVE
RERVM COGNITIONE REFERTVM, ATQVE CVM
exemplis externis, tum exprefsis rerum internarum
picturis illuftratum, ita delectatione iucun-
ditatéque plenum , maxima lectoris
animum voluptate facilè
perfundens .

AVTORE OLAO MAGNO GOTHO
ARCHIEPISCOPO VPSALENSI
Suetiæ & Gothiæ Primate.

CVM INDICE LOCVPLETISSIMO.

CAVTVM EST PRIVILEGIO IVLII III.
Pont. Max. ne quis ad Decennium imprimat.
ROMAE M. D. LV.

Figure 5.1. Olaus Magnus, *Historia De Gentibus Septentrionalibus, Earumque Diversis Statibus, Conditionibus, Moribus, Ritibus…Necnon Universis Pene Animalibus In Septentrione Degentibus, Eorumque Natura* (Rome: M. Viotto, 1555), title page, Nasjonalbiblioteket, Oslo.

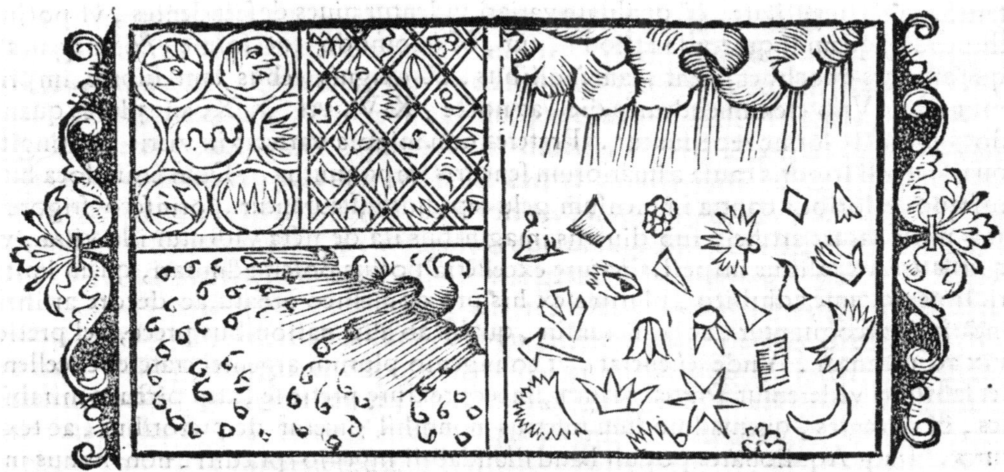

Figure 5.2. Olaus Magnus, *Historia De Gentibus Septentrionalibus, Earumque Diversis Statibus, Conditionibus, Moribus, Ritibus . . . Necnon Universis Pene Animalibus In Septentrione Degentibus, Eorumque Natura* (Rome: M. Viotto, 1555), p. 37, Nasjonalbiblioteket, Oslo.

to approximate moons, stars, or disembodied eyes. Olaus enfolds such precipitation into a statement about natural creation: "The cold outside and the wonderful handiwork of Nature are seen to have so embroidered those panes with such different patterns than any artist you like, when he looked at them, would be far more capable of marveling at her genius than copying it."[3] Flattened to crowd out the window's transparency, Olaus's snow (hardly endemic to Scandinavia, of course) offers a meditation on the idea of nature as artist—a discourse older than antiquity, but novel in a sub-Arctic context. This is a Northern nature of material patterns, a frozen window that, as Olaus puts it, actually disallows inquiry [*inquirere* - *in* "into" + *quaero* "seek"].

What was such a disquisition for? Olaus composed the strange tract while in exile at the Church of Santa Brigida off the Campo de' Fiori in Rome. His *Historia* remains one of the most famous books of the sixteenth century, translated into Dutch, French, Italian, and English before 1658. With its 728 chapters and 480 woodcuts, it is encyclopedic in scale, a work of profusion, modeled on Pliny. And yet it remains an unapologetically fragmented project. Anthropologists, folklorists, and historians of science have mined it for years.[4] But as much as it was a cultural history of the Far North, the *Historia*—particularly its strange first book—had something to say about images.

We know relatively little about Olaus Magnus as a person.[5] Born in Linköping in 1490, he seems to have studied at Rostock until 1517. Between 1519 and 1521, he wandered throughout Norway with his older brother, Johannes, as a sort of papal representative. In 1521, Johannes was made archbishop of Uppsala, but held his seat for a mere two years. When Lutheran-friendly forces under Gustav Vasa conquered Stockholm in 1523, Olaus made his way to Rome. For the next fifteen years, the brothers shuttled between Denmark and Sweden, landing in Gdańsk and, at one point, visiting Venice. The pair eventually settled in Rome in 1541, having been summoned by Pope Paul III. Johannes died in 1544. Olaus was promptly named archbishop in his brother's place, but never returned to Sweden.

Olaus attended the first Council of Trent between 1545 and 1549.[6] His stay there was a troubled one. Records indicate that he was one of two recipients of a charitable subsidy while in residence between December 1546 and March 1547, demonstrating that he had arrived impoverished.[7] But it was in Trent that Olaus conceived of a project intended to describe "the Far North, numbed by the constant merciless cold."[8] Such a book would depict a North not just of barbarians and darkness, but of ingenuity and resources, a North worthy of pilgrimage — and ideally, worthy of reconquest by papal forces. Such a text, Olaus wrote, was rendered all the more urgent "after the new disturbances and dangers broke out in Germany."[9] And the Reformation was of course the main topic of Trent. The council sessions that Olaus attended surveyed a number of reform questions, including the legitimacy of the Latin vulgate and the worrying pungency of Luther's teachings.[10] Olaus conceived of the book as an introduction for Catholic readers to a Northern New World. There, Olaus argued, the "harshness of the elements and the cruelty of the climate" were assets, rather than hindrances.[11]

Upon his return to Rome in 1547, Olaus installed two separate printing presses in his rooms and employed an émigré from Parma to work them.[12] The resulting *Historia*, as we know it today, is a sprawling jumble of storytelling, legend, and natural history (Jorge Luis Borges loved the book[13]) generously illustrated with woodcuts. Olaus begins with a pithy defense of images, glossing Franciscus Patricius:

> An illustration not only gives satisfaction and a singular delight, but also preserves a record of the past and constantly brings glimpses of history before our eyes. Indeed, when we look at paintings where spectacular feats are represented, we feel a need to strive for fame, and embark upon greater tasks . . . so we read how Plato, Cicero, and many others were enthusiasts of this art, which they conceived as a kind of silent poetry, since it combines in harmony lines, colors, proportions, and an extremely accurate copy of the real world, and is considered, as it were, an eloquent teacher in the school of life, an advantage for which it is highly esteemed.[14]

This is more than a kind of chilly take on *ut pictura poesis*. In the chapters of the first books, Olaus points to his own woodcuts' ekphrastic workings: "This image shows how, in an admirable way, different observations are made" (book 13, chapter 1). Or, elsewhere: "This picture explains itself" (book 1, chapter 24). He goes on to state that the dearth of (say) art collections in Scandinavia is perversely an advantage of creativity; it prompts craftsmen to emulate nature, rather than the works of other men. And in lieu of a homegrown antiquity, he writes, Northerners look to rocks, trees, and snow to produce a cold art that is difficult for the rest of the world to understand because of its detachment from the human.

In the chapters that follow, Olaus wanders between fine-grained description of fauna (bees, mice), to the retelling of mythical histories (Icelandic kings), to prosaic how-to advice (how best to cut down trees, the proper means of ice-skating, poisonous fish to avoid). Throughout all of this, Olaus—again, in unwilling exile—is constantly attacking Lutherans. They are "spreaders of every kind of crime and impurity." Olaus particularly seems to despise "Protestant" mythological pictures, alarmed at their secularism: "The Lutheran heretics, vilest of all mankind, have prescribed, and brought in naked, shameless effigies, to which higher authority turns a blind eye, alleging the merit of the paintings and admiration for the art. Although these portrayals have confused many virtuous individuals, they have never been able to quench the natural modesty of people trained in chaste habits."[15] Image theft and destruction, meanwhile, are even worse, a piece with attacks on actual ecclesiastics: "In case anyone deny the accursed impiety of these horrific crimes, sacrilege, heresy, and schism, we much judge that they are committed . . . wherever injury is inflicted on holy persons or places." Thus, the same "penalty is stipulated for those who violently attack priests or clergy, and another for those who seize holy virgins and objects dedicated to God in the churches."[16]

But Olaus remains most eager, above all else, to legitimize his Northern project and demonstrate his scholarly credentials; he cites Albertus Magnus, Aristotle, Strabo, and Herodotus and at one point overtly plagiarizes Thomas More's *Utopia* (1519).[17] He picks rhetorical fights and prods adversaries; the Augsburg reformer Jakob Ziegler, who had published his own history of the Far North in 1532 (Figure 5.3), is rebuked for his contention that the survival of paganism among the Sami signaled church corruption in the Far North.[18] Olaus admits that witchcraft remains pernicious in his homeland, but calls upon antique sources to frame them as curiosities, as much as real threats: "Among the Bothnian people of the North, wizards and magicians are found everywhere, as if it was their particular home," and "in the regions under the Seven Stars, in other words, the North (where in a quite literal sense the abode of Satan lies), demons, with unspeakable derision and in extreme shapes, express their encouragement to people who live in those parts."[19] Lapland magicians and Biarmian warlocks are presented as shape-shifting menaces nourished by frost.

But such visions of sorcery and hermeticism were aspects of a Gothic otherness that Olaus, writing for a Roman audience, is eager to suppress. The *Historia* correspondingly demonstrates a particular concern with communication, with a bridging of distance.[20] Olaus includes a curious chapter on runes (Figure 5.4), inscriptions that for many scholarly readers would already have held associations with ancient Scandinavia: "The kingdoms of the North had a script of their own. Evidence of this is furnished by stones of extraordinary size attached to the tombs and caverns of the ancients." Just "as letters written on paper are now sent from one person to another, so once the natives of the North directed to each other letters incised on wood They communicate [*communicant*] this secret to none except members of their own household."[21] Viotto's woodcut shows a runic alphabet put in Roman sequence.[22] The characters are not phonemes, Olaus implies, but figures, "shapes of different objects," almost like snowflakes.[23] He even claims to be able to decipher the inscriptions: "When the stones are marked with letters and put in a long straight line they mark the contests of champions, square stones show the fights of cavalry squadrons, rounded ones indicate the burials of near kinsmen."[24] Runes reappear on gravestones (Figure 5.5), where "lofty markings in Gothic letters give instruction."[25] The ancient Swedes "thought that by carving some brief inscription of famous deeds

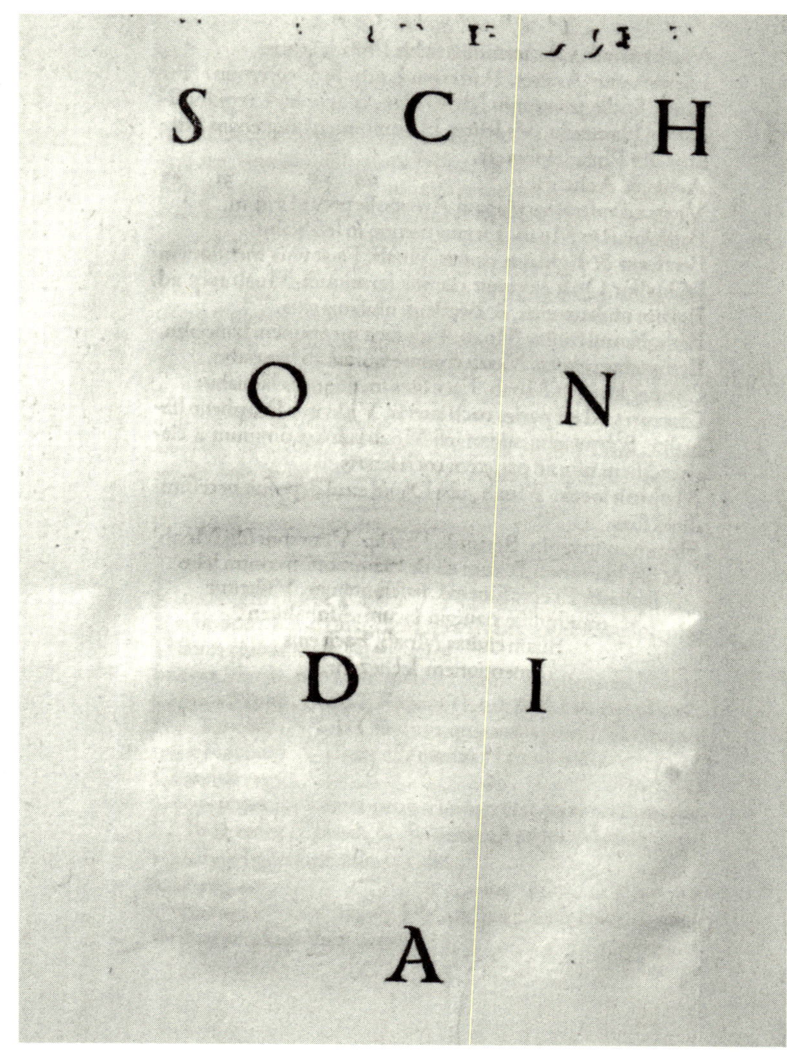

Figure 5.3. Jakob Ziegler, *Quae intus continentur: Syria, ad Ptolomaici operis rationem. Praeterea Strabone, Plinio & Antonio auctoribus locupletata. Palestina...Praeterea historia sacra...Arabia Petraea, sive itinera filiorum Israel per desertum...Aegyptus...Schondia... Holmiae...historia...*(Augsburg: Opilionis, 1532), n.p., Biblioteca Universitaria Alessandrina, Rome.

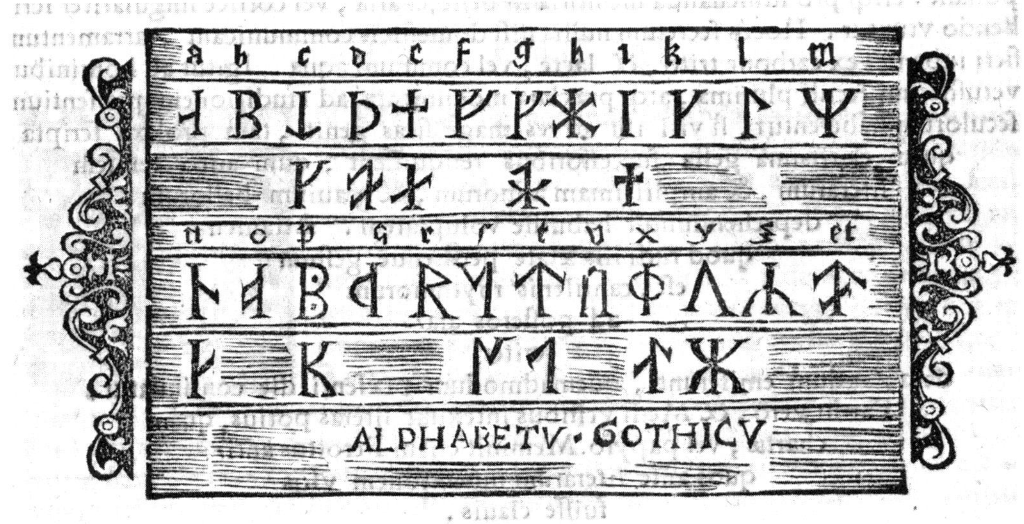

Figure 5.4. Olaus Magnus, *Historia De Gentibus Septentrionalibus, Earumque Diversis Statibus, Conditionibus, Moribus, Ritibus... Necnon Universis Pene Animalibus In Septentrione Degentibus, Eorumque Natura* (Rome: M. Viotto, 1555), p. 57, Nasjonalbiblioteket, Oslo.

on the stones they were perpetuating the memory of these men's names and exploits; similarly, by the customs of those times songs composed in rhythmic stanzas and handed down uninterruptedly through the centuries to the present day have transmitted an account of those feats to posterity."[26]

From where did Olaus derive this interest? An "Alphabetum Nortmannorum" had in fact appeared in the Sponheim lexographer Johannes Trithemius's 1518 history of polygraphic writing systems (Figure 5.6),[27] where it was summoned to argue that Northerners had been literate from ancient times. And runic script appears throughout the *Historia*.[28] The runes almost model Olaus's broader obsession with detail,[29] its cutting up of particulars to make nature speak.[30]

But the one topic that seeps into nearly every page of Olaus's early section is an invisibility: *cold*, a condition that marked the largest contrast with his adopted Southern home. "The huge power which the frost, or cold, possesses in the North, as if this were its own native region, can be demonstrated in many ways," wrote Olaus, "through the sense of feeling rather than by authorities." The bodily is awakened by such extreme conditions, which are ticked off in a list of effects:

> Cold burns the eyes of animals and stiffens their hairs
> Cold allows the pelts of all animals to be thicker and handsomer
> Cold allows fish to be kept fresh for five or six months without salt
> Cold causes copper, glass, and earthenware to break
> Cold allows games and delightful shows to be held on the ice[31]

Again, Olaus entreats upon the sensory, offering climate as a unifying factor between animals and humans. He even presents Scandinavian cold as a mode of seeing, a wayfinder that "opens up pathless territories to travelers and hunters."[32] And testimony about cold becomes quickly personal: "Since I was born and lived subject to this cold, even at a latitude of about 86 degrees," Olaus writes, "I think that I am capable of proving this."[33]

And yet, even when descibed, this Northern cold, this nature, this environment, ultimately splays and scatters itself to elude focused

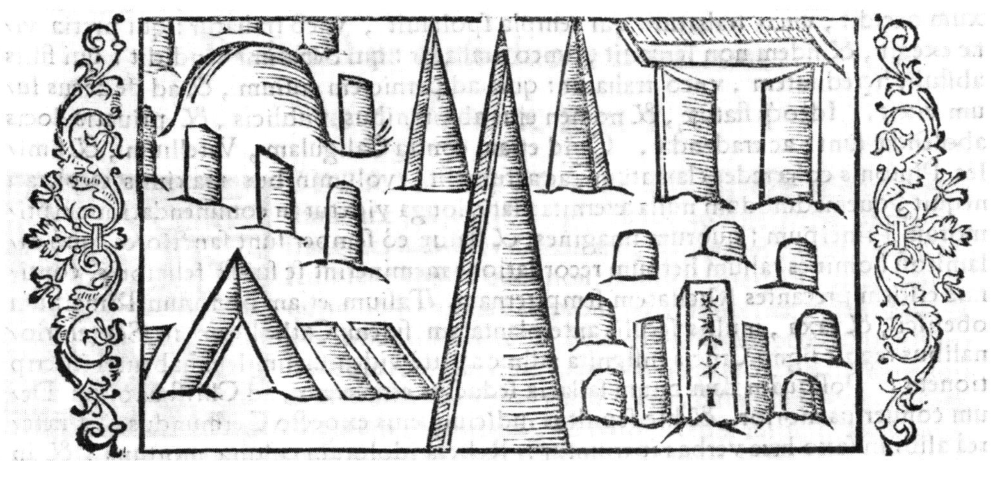

Figure 5.5. Olaus Magnus, *Historia De Gentibus Septentrionalibus, Earumque Diversis Statibus, Conditionibus, Moribus, Ritibus ... Necnon Universis Pene Animalibus In Septentrione Degentibus, Eorumque Natura* (Rome: M. Viotto, 1555), p. 49, Nasjonalbiblioteket, Oslo.

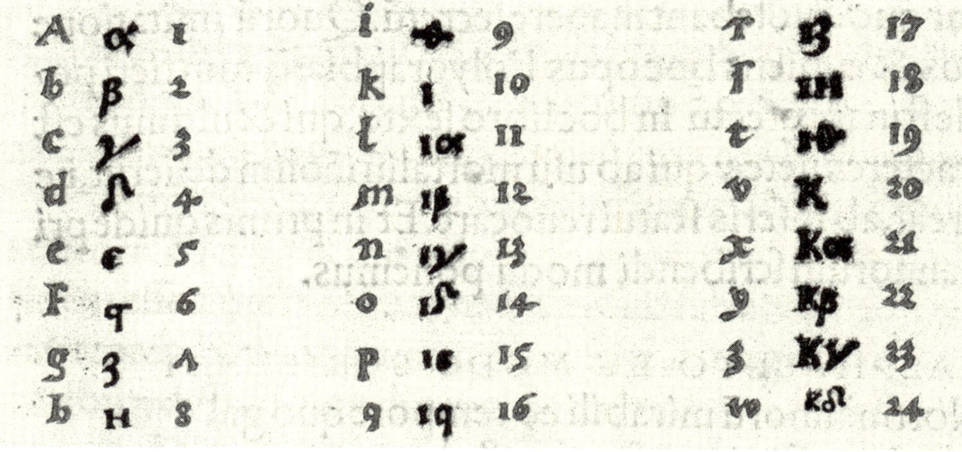

Figure 5.6. Johannes Trithemius, *Clavis polygraphiae libri sex Ioannis Trithemii* (Basel: Petri, 1518), fol. P7v, Houghton Library, Harvard University, Cambridge.

scrutiny. Like Viotto's blown snowflakes on a pane, Olaus's Arctic details almost seem to whip past the pictorial "wholeness" of a warm Roman South, and the remainder of the giant book largely abandons the theme.

Even so, the *Historia* proved influential, and the idea of cold as a welcome countervisual phenomenon would ingratiate Olaus to vastly different readers: Cotton Mather's *Winter Meditations*, published in Boston in 1693, cited Olaus as evidence that bitter weather — such as that in New England — breeds meditative properties.[34] Robert Burton's *Anatomy of Melancholy* (1621) quoted Olaus specifically as a source of information on "subterranean devils."[35] But Olaus never returned to Scandinavia. He died in 1557 in Rome. Arguing against the idea of the Arctic as one thing — a zone, perhaps a wasteland — what emerged was the hopeful idea that at least one section of the Far North was more like a vast archive, an active sender of messages, a place perversely *undifferent* from Italy itself.

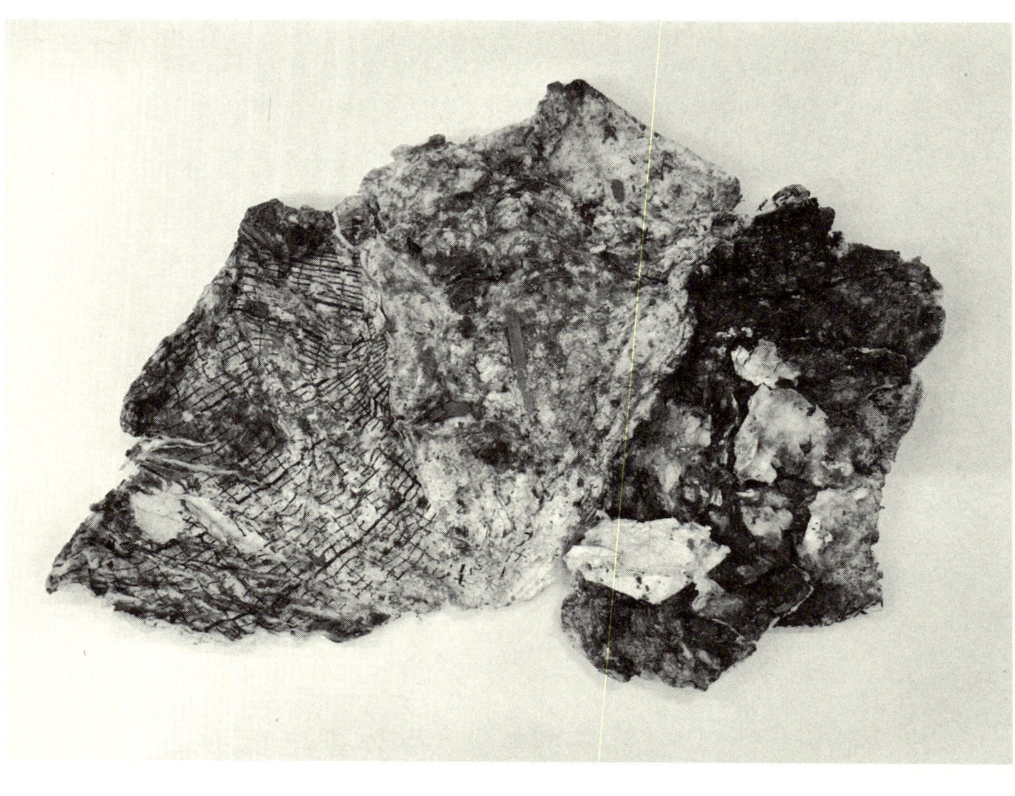

Figure 6.1. Fragment of compressed engravings, dimensions variable, Rijksmuseum, Amsterdam, NG-NM-7744-8.

Arctic Ink

In June of 1871, Norwegian hunters unearthed a mysterious chunk of pulp in the Russian Far North.[1] The find site, a deserted beach on the remote island of Nova Zembla, lay more than a thousand miles away from any permanent habitation. The mass (Figure 6.1), caked with gravel, ice, and moss, turned out to be a part of something astonishing: a cache of Netherlandish engravings — more than four hundred of them — works after Hendrick Goltzius, Karel van Mander, Bartholomeus Spranger, and others (Figure 6.2).[2]

Fused into blocks, the engravings had landed in North Siberia via shipwreck — one of the most spectacular marine fiascos in history: the disastrous 1596–97 expedition of Wilhelm Barents, on his way to a Northeast Passage to Asia.[3] But as physical allegories of Arctic survival, the engravings relate to more than naval history. They might raise questions regarding the ways we think about early modern print in general, a medium long associated with travel. The unexpected *informel*, three-dimensional concreteness foisted upon the mass by three centuries of interment has been largely unstudied by art history. In what literature exists on the Arctic sheets, the matter of the prints; remarkable cultural displacement has often been cleaved from the "matter" of their identification and restoration as objects — their history pitted against their thingness, as it were, the familiar analytic lament. There exist few models for making sense of the astonishing geographical framing, the unwanted Arctic stoppage of these highly wrought artworks. This chapter considers whether the icy provenance for the Dutch prints (now all in

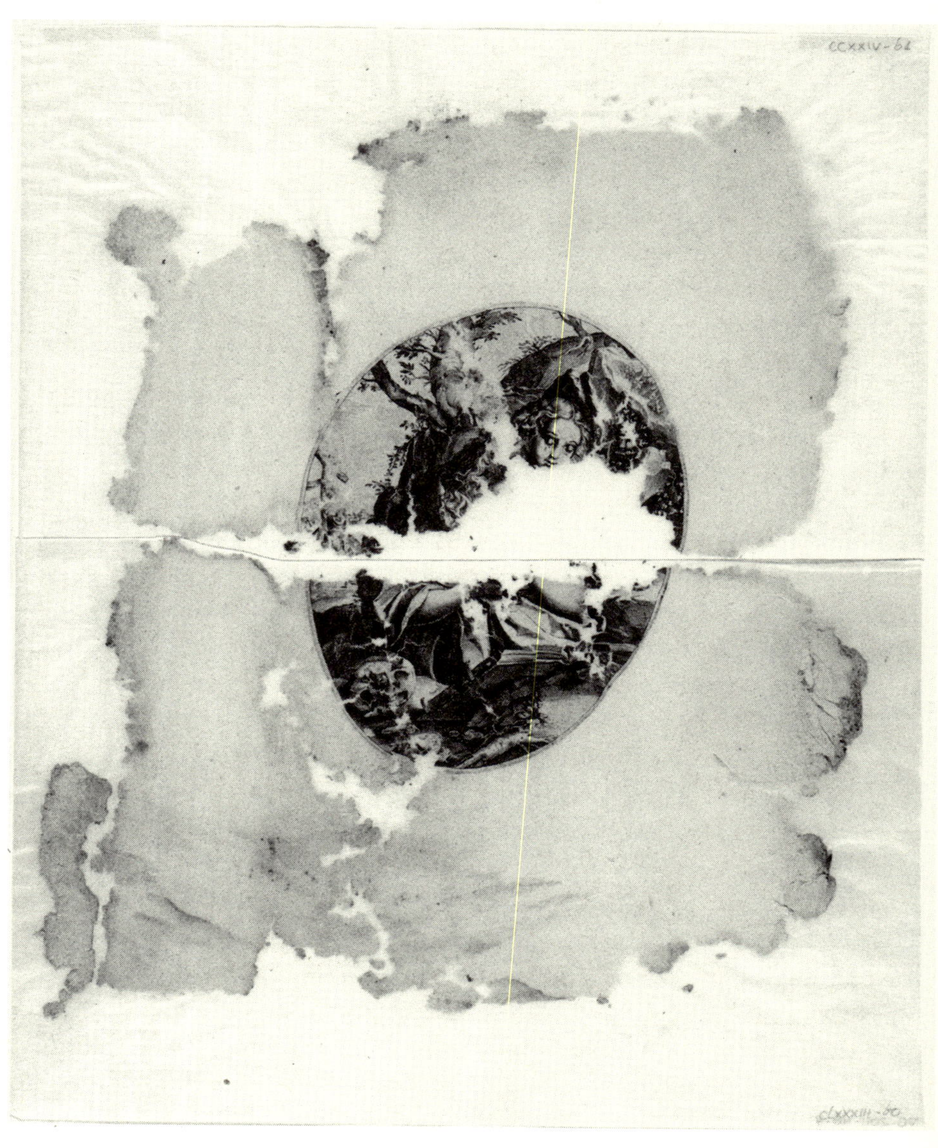

Figure 6.2. Hendrick Goltzius (copy after), *Maria Magdalena*, 1582–1590, engraving, 36.9 x 32.3 cm, Rijksmuseum, Amsterdam, NG-2011-48-7.

the Rijksprentenkabinet) remains just one more interesting bit of *Nachleben*, or something else.

Paper Voyages

On May 18, 1596, a seventeen-man crew led by Wilhelm Barents set out from Vlieland, in the West Frisian Islands, seeking passage to Cathay. The crew mistimed the winter ice, froze in it, and became marooned in Northern Siberia for more than nine months. To survive, the seventeen men constructed a shelter out of ship fragments. They endured darkness, polar bear attacks, scurvy, frostbite, insanity, and hunger. Astonishingly, most of them eventually escaped in a boat: first to the Russian mainland and eventually back to Holland, arriving in November 1597. On Nova Zembla, they left behind two dead crewmen, a ruined wood dwelling, a littering of luxury goods, and half-used navigation grids (Figure 6.3). One sailor on the voyage, a twenty-one year old officer named Gerrit de Veer, kept a diary and in 1598 published an illustrated account of the travails. The *Waerachtighe beschryvinghe*, which appeared in Dutch, Latin, and German, sold out of its initial run of more than fifteen hundred copies.[4] The text became a European sensation, a literary event in which, as one later author put it, "awareness of the Arctic burst upon European consciousness."[5] Shakespeare likely knew the de Veer book: in *Twelfth Night*, Fabian speaks of "an icicle on a Dutchman's beard," and, in *Measure for Measure*, Claudio invokes the "thrilling region of thick-ribbed ice," a world of "cold obstruction."[6] Shakespeare's London publisher, Thomas Pavier, was actually the first to print the English translation of de Veer in 1609.[7]

The abandoned Netherlandish engravings — which de Veer does not mention — were intended as merchandise. Some were on uncut sheets, others tied into bundles. All date from the early 1590s and come from a single Amsterdam print shop owned by Cornelis Claesz.[8] Of the more than four hundred impressions (all engravings and etchings), one hundred and fifty different designs were found, including, for example, twenty-seven exemplars of a single design after Jacques de Gheyn. Little topical consistency exists across the sheets. Many seem to be pirated copies of Haarlem School compositions — in effect,

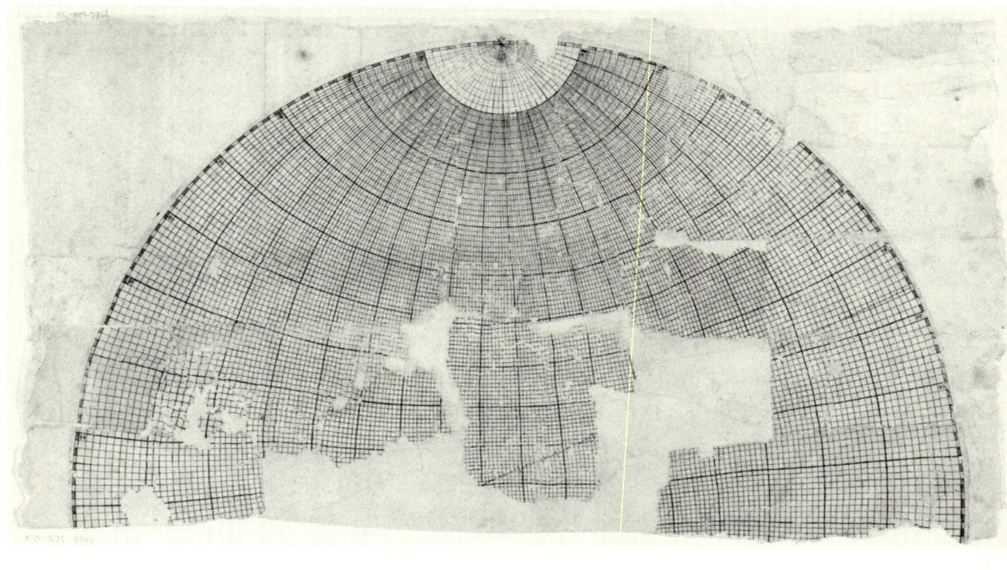

Figure 6.3. Anonymous, *Navigational Grid of Northern Hemisphere*, in or before 1596, engraving, 31.5 cm x 57.2 cm, Rijksmuseum, Amsterdam, NG-NM-7744.

second-rate artworks. (The specific impressions tally closely with those in another recorded shipment of prints made to the East in 1602, suggesting these engravings could have been made, legally or illegally, for export.)[9] They vary in subject matter: mythical and biblical scenes, costume prints, a series of Roman heroes, Karel van Mander's *History of Tobit*, and Collaert landscape designs after Hans Bol. After being dug up, the prints were acquired by the young Rijksmuseum in the 1880s, where they sat in storage, untouched, for nearly a century, often as mere scatterings of torn paper (Figure 6.4). No manifest survives for what else exactly was in Barents's hold, but other goods were recovered: medallions, etched silverware, astrolabes, compasses, a flute, and a Dutch clock that, we know from de Veer's account, actually stopped on November 1, 1596 because of the cold (Figure 6.5).[10]

The Dutch began exploring the Arctic coast of Asia at the precise moment that England directed military attention toward Spain.[11] With Spanish forces preoccupied, Netherlandish merchants could attempt a northerly route to China, which, as one sailor wrote in 1585, would "prevent our competitors from gaining an advantage over us."[12] All the while, state-licensed privateering flourished; piracy developed into a key source of income in the young republic between 1584 and 1586.[13] As earlier in England, financial backers promoted the Northeast Passage as a potential means to outflank Iberian forces along spice routes. And thanks to the calamity-ridden voyages of Frobisher, detailed in publications by Best and others, the Dutch had learned what the North*west* Passage held. But they, too, sought to make contact with traders in Asia — Barents's stopped clock, in fact, was to have been a gift of European technology to the emperor of China, and among the few books to have survived the overwintering were Flemish-language accounts of the Far East.[14]

The idea that an ice-free sea existed on the Far Northern Russian coast was proselytized by an influential Flemish cartographer named Peter Platevoet (1552–1622). Platevoet, Latinized to Petrus Plancius, helped raise money for the Barents voyage, maintaining to backers that no sea could freeze entirely, due to its motion and depth. Barents, and possibly de Veer, seem to have studied navigation with him.

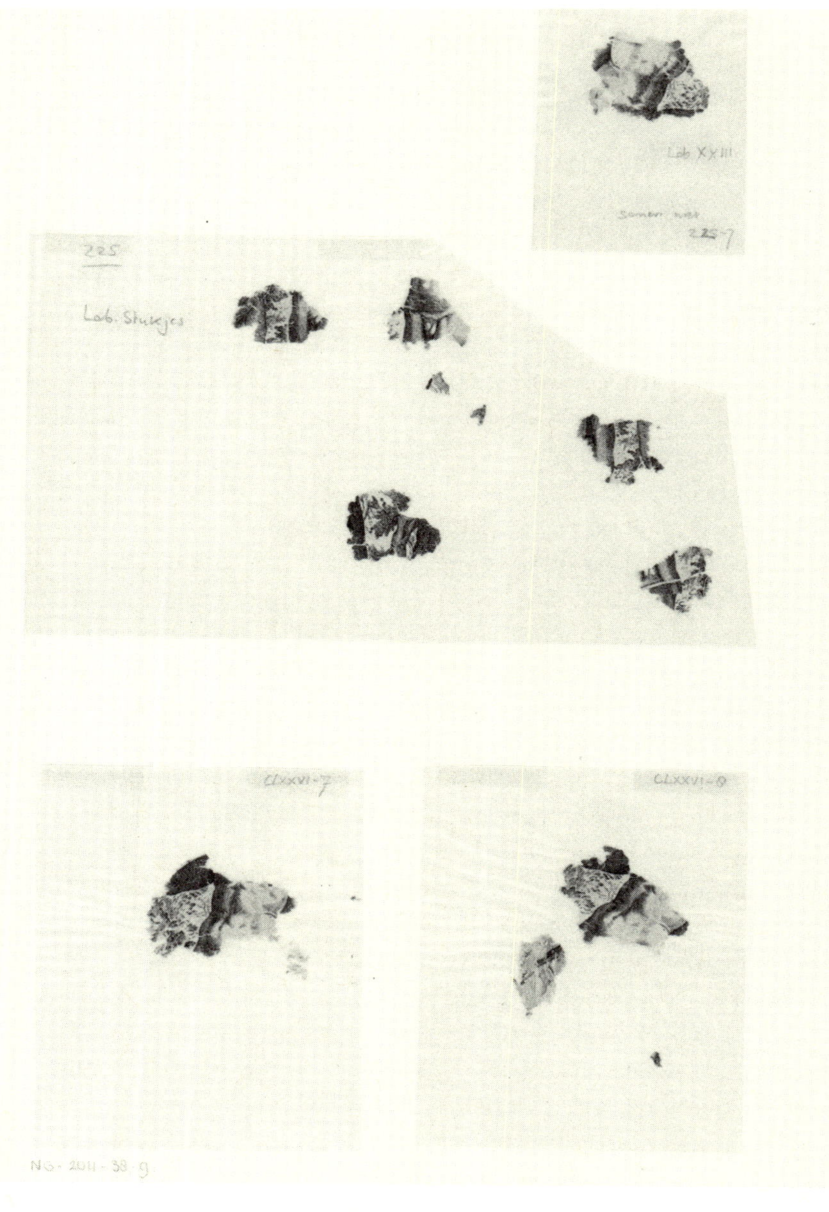

Figure 6.4. Anonymous after Bartholomeus Spranger and Hendrick Goltzius, published by Joos de Bosscher, *Adam and Eve*, 1585–1596, engraving, Rijksmuseum, Amsterdam, NG-2011-38-9.

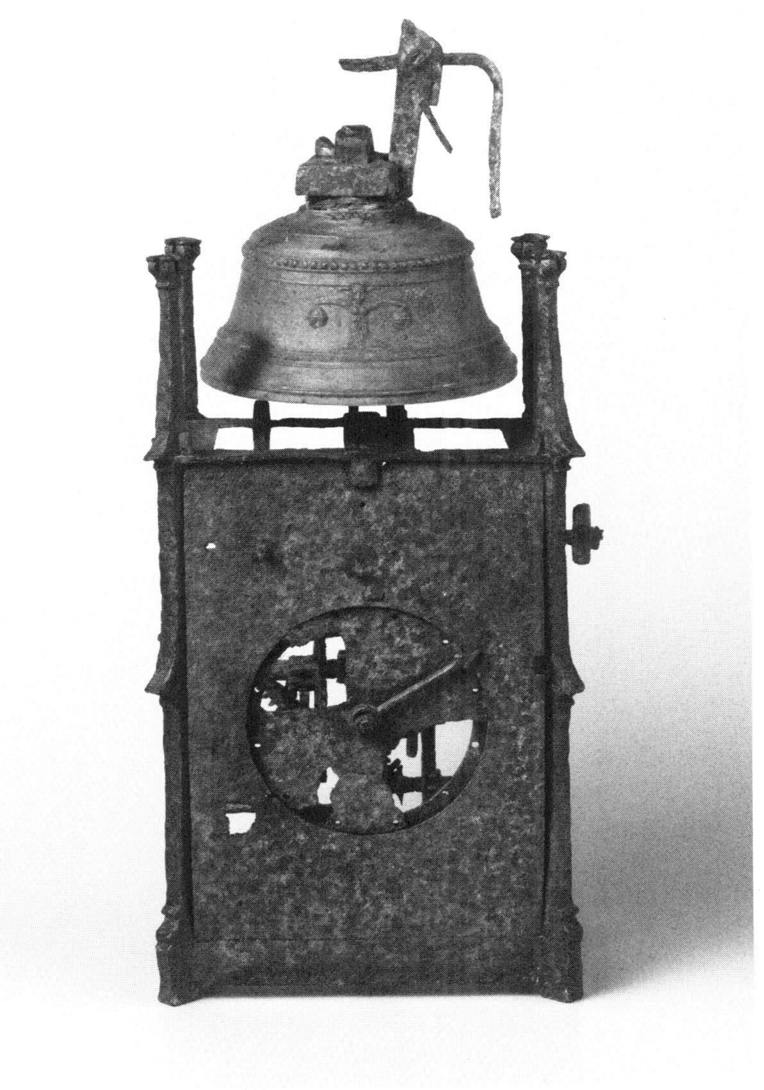

Figure 6.5. Anonymous, *Clock*, c. 1590–1596, iron, 38.9 x 20.5 x 16.4 cm, Rijksmuseum, Amsterdam, NG-NM-7687.

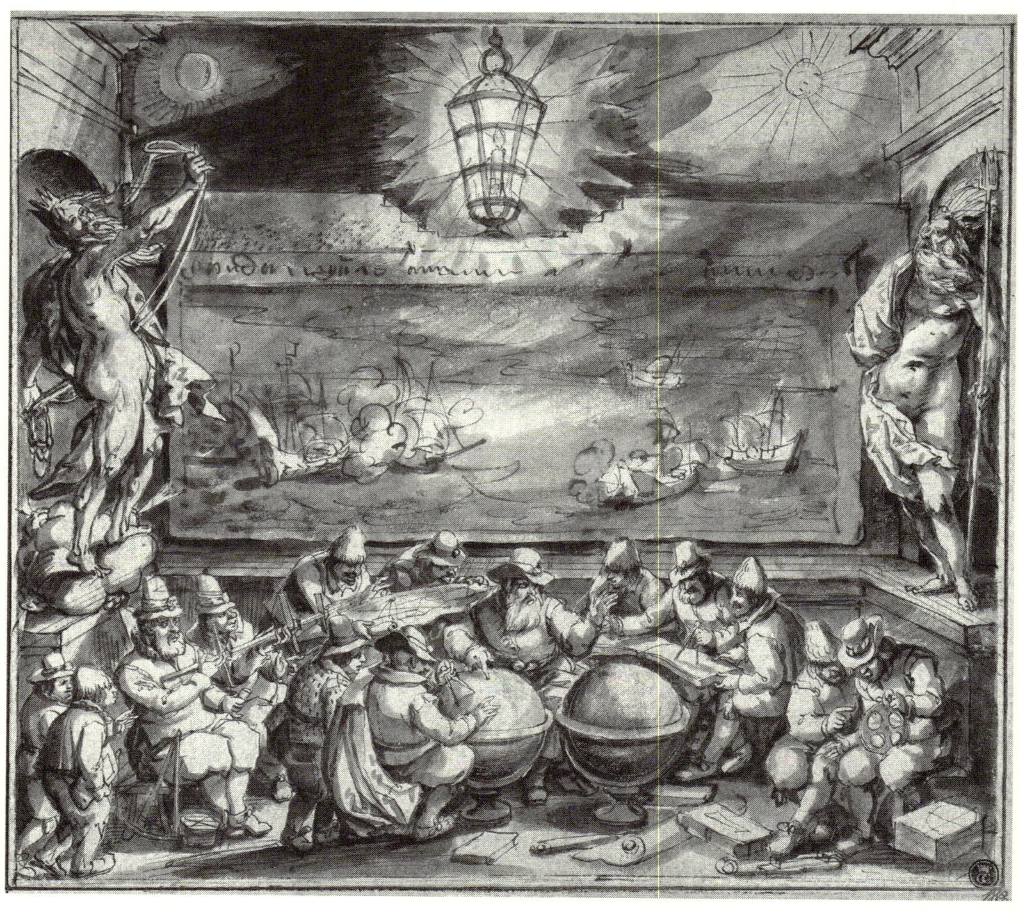

Figure 6.6. David Vinckboons, *Petrus Plancius Instructing Students in the Science of Navigation*, early seventeenth century, black and brown ink and wash, 26 x 28.6 cm, Metropolitan Museum of Art, Frits and Rita Markus Fund, 2003.

Apart from his interest in cosmography (Figure 6.6), Plancius was known to hold fervent anti-Catholic views. He preached in Amsterdam in the 1580s and was at one point brought before city officials to debate the doctrine of predestination.[15] And in his writings, Plancius often framed the quest for the Northeast passage as a kind of Calvinist crusade.

At the center of de Veer's written account, meanwhile, lay an improvised architecture: a giant hut crafted from found driftwood and ship parts (Figure 6.7). De Veer reports how the decision to build the structure came about at a crew meeting of September 11, 1596: "We took counsel together what were best to do according to the current situation in order that we might winter there and attend such adventure as God would send us; and after we had debated upon the matter, to keep and defend ourselves from the cold and wild beasts, we determined to build a house upon the land, to keep us therein as well we could."[16] This "Behouden Huys" (Safe House) as de Veer called it, was constructed on treeless land, and a few remains are still extant today. The account details the construction minutely: driftwood and bits of hull were assembled in cold so severe that nails froze in the mouths of hammering crewmen.[17] One of the book's illustrations shows a structure with chimney and sauna, crafted from planks of the trapped ship. The crew filled the lodge with some of the cargo intended for Asia — an hourglass, oil lamps, songbooks. Set against Vinckboons's later ink-and-wash drawing of Plancius (Figure 6.6), de Veer's engraving seems both model and cautionary example: the shipwreck that made the *Behouden Huys* necessary could have been avoided by proper navigation, now being taught by Plancius in a confined, illuminated space. Across the two (Arctic) images, interiority is a refuge and a guide.

In the *Waerachtighe beschrijvinghe*, the house became a metaphor for order in the wilderness. The book narrates what was essentially the story of an elaborate staying put; living off meat from trapped Arctic foxes and hunted polar bears, drinking melted snow and rationed wine and beer salvaged from the ship, the crew passed the time tending to the house itself. In essence, they were trying to territorialize an ice desert in conceptual as well as physical terms — to

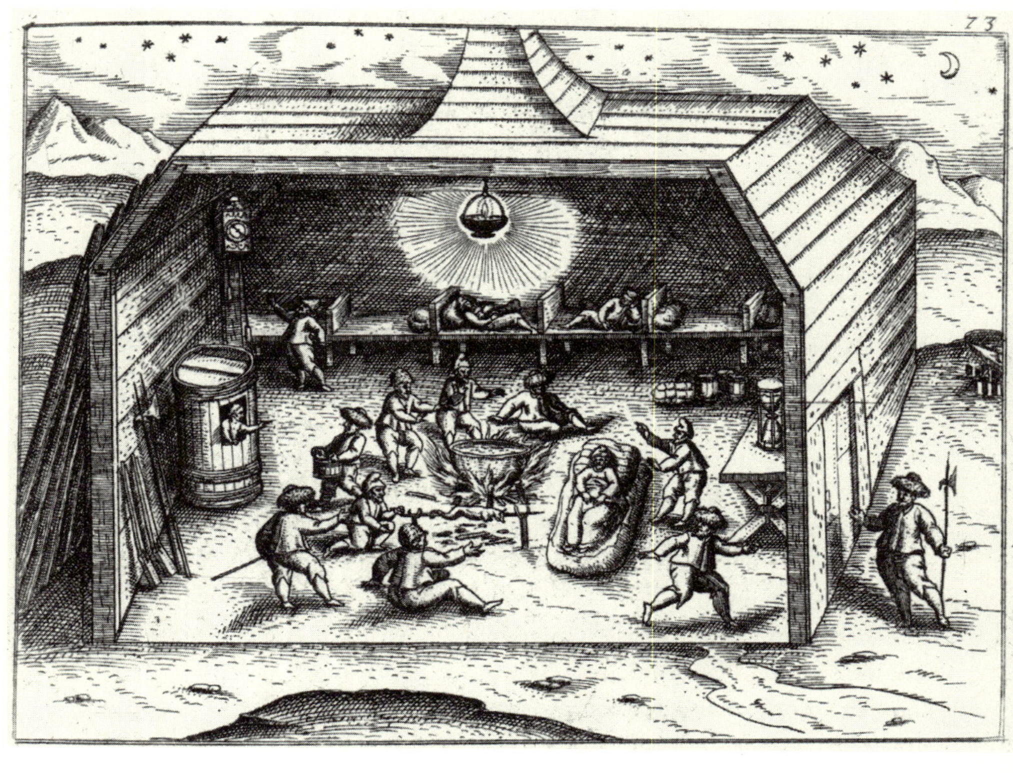

Figure 6.7. Gerrit de Veer, *Waerachtighe beschrijvinghe van drie seylagien, ter werelt noyt soo vreemt ghehoort...* (Amsterdam: Cornelis Claesz, 1598), plate 73.

fashion shiplike life atop an unbordered wasteland. The crew seemed
to have kept to a strict Calvinist calendar, with few saints' days and
frequent prayers. As in the English North, sensory bewilderment
was a constant foe. De Veer's entries, even before they describe the
shelter's construction, mingle the technical and the dire:

> 21 September: Clearing weather in the afternoon. The ice was not so strong
> in the sea as it had been before, but it was so cold that we had to bring our
> kitchen on deck.
>
> 22 September: sunny and quiet with a wind from the west, but very cold.
>
> 23 September: Quiet and misty weather with wind from the east northeast.
> We hauled two loads of wood and in the evening when we came on board our
> carpenter had died. He was from Purmerend.
>
> 24 September: we buried him in the cleft of a hill, near flowing water, since we
> could not dig up the earth by reason of the great frost and cold; and that day
> we went twice with our sleds to fetch wood.
>
> 25 September: dark weather, the wind blowing west and south west.[18]

The dispassionate *rhythm* of the entries gets at the consecutive effects
of the icy days, marked by a desperate clinging to the construct of
the calendar, the ship's log. Death and meteorology receive equal due.

For the logbook — artic and no — was a writing rooted in con-
cision.[19] Ships' notebooks had existed since antiquity, companions
to the prose medium of the late medieval "rutter" books (French
routier, from the Portuguese *rotiero*, or itinerary), which provided
navigational directions or descriptions (compare Figure 3.2).[20] These
were mechanistic affairs. Yet as Iberian and French vessels began
to venture farther afield — with long spans spent out of sight of
land — celestial navigation grew more important, and systematic
records of ships' positions became vital. Many Dutch forays also bred
elaborate logbook publications.[21] In 1597, the mathematician Adriaen Veen even published a guide to bookkeeping at sea, signaling
the growth of the practice among amateurs.[22] On English voyages,
the logbook would become standardized as a "literary" form; Hakluyt's (second edition) of *The principal navigations* deployed a tabular
form on one of its pages (Figure 6.8), a format Veen had linked to

cartography and banking. Quantitative data on windspeed and currents were combined with more fulsome paragraphs about anything exceptional. The logs were seen as supplementary (rather than alternate) species of nautical information, accompanying maps, and, as we have seen with Anthonisz.'s 1558 tract (see Figure 3.2), were often sprinkled with coastline features in profile that, captioned, fused narration and mapping. John Gatonbe's terse *Journal of a Voyage for the Discovery of a North-West Passage*, for example, offered a woodcut of a Greenland coastline segment with a note about its inaccessibility (Figure 6.9): "Cape Comfort rises thus, the heighth of the pole being 62°33, the smoothest land, and, best to look to of all the country of Greenland; yet we could not come near it for ice."[23]

On Nova Zembla, de Veer retained the logbook form as a testament to his observations' reliability. Describing phenomena totally novel to most readers, de Veer was surely aware that his narratives invited potential accusations of fraudulence. The logbook mode was familiar and trustworthy. And it served as a convenient metonym for the day-to-day of the marooning itself, just as the *Behouden Huys* sought to impose order upon a previously uncharted set of circumstances. Whiteout weather conditions and, once the sun had set in November, complete darkness, save for occasional illumination by the moon and stars, foisted blindness on the crew, and with it came disruptions of temporal and spatial orientation: the men "could not see out of their eyes, and were often led astray from the right path"[24] and "could not distinguish day from night by reason of the darkness."[25] And de Veer occasionally runs up against conditions in which he doubts his own eyewitnessing. Between January 24 and 25, a celestial phenomenon appeared in the dark midday sky that seemed, terrifyingly, to interrupt the chronological rubric steering the sailors' lives:

On the 24th of January it was faire, clear weather, with a wind from the west. With Jacob van Heemskerck and four others, I left the house for the seaside on the South Side of Nova Zembla: contrary to what we expected, there I saw a sliver of the sun. We sped back to house to relate the good news to Wilhelm Barents. However: wise and experienced pilot that he was,

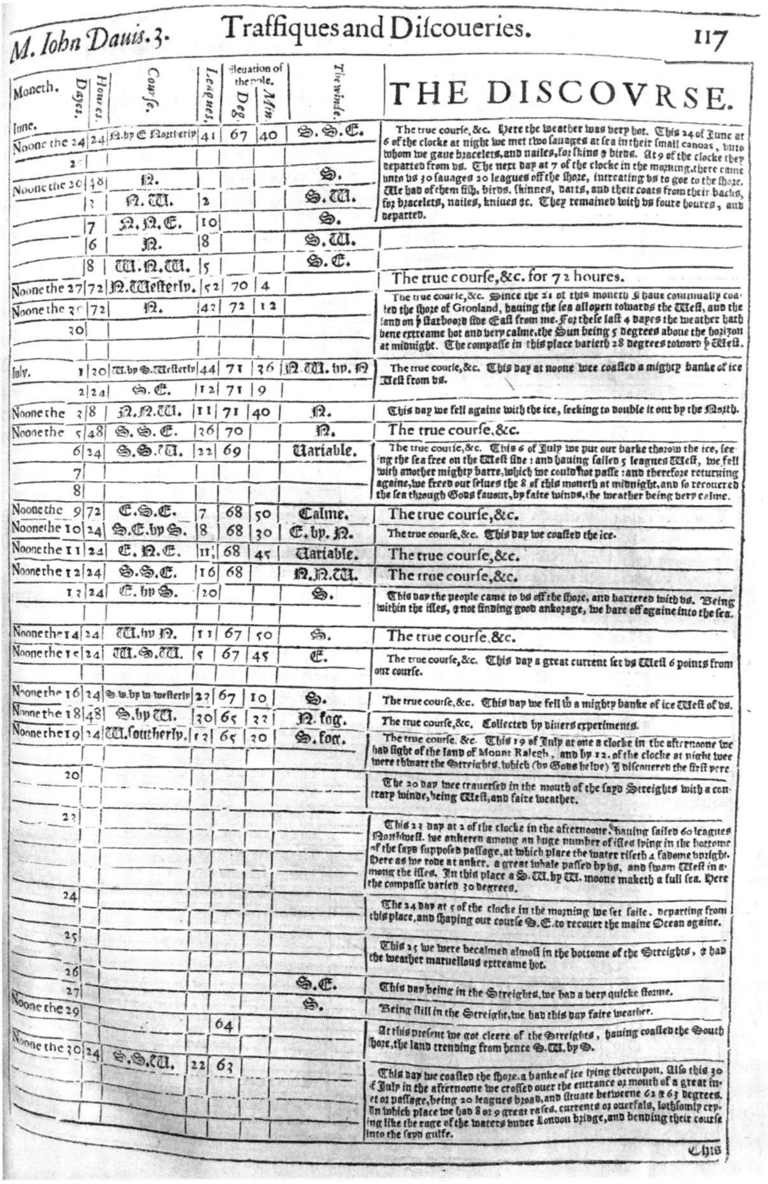

Moneth.	Dayes.	Houres.	Course.	Leagues.	Eleuation of the pole		The winde.	THE DISCOVRSE.
					Deg.	Min.		
Iune.	Noone the 24	24	N.by E Northerly	41	67	40	S.S.E.	The true course, &c. Here the weather was very hot. This 24 of Iune at 6 of the clocke at night we met two sauages at sea in their small canoas, vnto whom we gaue bracelets, and nailes, for skins & birds. At 9 of the clocke they departed from vs. The next day at 7 of the clocke in the morning, there came vnto vs 30 sauages 20 leagues off the shore, intreating vs to goe to the shore. We had of them fish, birds, skinnes, darts, and their coats from their backs, for bracelets, nailes, kniues &c. They remained with vs foure houres, and departed.
	25							
	Noone the 26	48	N.				S.	
		3	N.W.	2			S.W.	
		7	N.N.E.	10			S.	
		6	N.	8			S.W.	
		8	W.N.W.	5			S.E.	
	Noone the 27	72	N.Westerly.	52	70	4		The true course, &c. for 72 houres.
	Noone the 30	72	N.	42	72	12		The true course, &c. Since the 21 of this moneth I haue continually coasted the shore of Gronland, hauing the sea all open towards the West, and the land on ye starboord side East from me. For these last 4 dayes the weather hath bene extreame hot and very calme, the Sun being 5 degrees aboue the horizon at midnight. The compasse in this place varieth 28 degrees toward ye West.
	20							
Iuly.	1	20	W.by S.Westerly	44	71	36	N.W. by N	The true course, &c. This day at noone wee coasted a mighty banke of ice West from vs.
	2	24	S.E.	12	71	9		
	Noone the 3	8	N.N.W.	11	71	40	N.	This day we fell againe with the ice, seeking to double it out by the North.
	Noone the 5	48	S.S.E.	36	70		N.	The true course, &c.
	6	24	S.S.W.	22	69		Variable.	The true course, &c. This 6 of Iuly we put our barke thorow the ice, seeing the sea free on the West side: and hauing sailed 5 leagues West, we fell with another mighty barre, which we could not passe: and therefore returning againe, we freed our selues the 8 of this moneth at midnight, and so recouered the sea through Gods fauour, by faire winds, the weather being very calme.
	7							
	8							
	Noone the 9	72	E.S.E.	7	68	50	Calme.	The true course, &c.
	Noone the 10	24	S.E.by S.	8	68	30	E.by.N.	The true course, &c. This day we coasted the ice.
	Noone the 11	24	E.N.E.	11	68	45	Variable.	The true course, &c.
	Noone the 12	24	S.S.E.	16	68		N.N.W.	The true course, &c.
	13	24	E.by S.	20			S.	This day the people came to vs off the shore, and bartered with vs. Being within the isles, & not finding good ankorage, we bare off againe into the sea.
	Noone the 14	24	W.by N.	11	67	50	S.	The true course, &c.
	Noone the 15	24	W.S.W.	5	67	45	E.	The true course, &c. This day a great current set vs West 6 points from our course.
	Noone the 16	24	S.W.by W.westerly	22	67	10	S.	The true course, &c. This day we fell with a mighty banke of ice West of vs.
	Noone the 18	48	S.by W.	30	65	22	N. fog.	The true course, &c. Collected by diuers experiments.
	Noone the 19	24	W.Southerly.	12	65	20	S. fog.	The true course, &c. This 19 of Iuly at one a clocke in the afternoone we had sight of the land of Mount Ralegh, and by 12. of the clocke at night wee were thwart the Streights, which (by Gods helpe) I discouered the first yere.
	20							The 20 day wee trauersed in the mouth of the sayd Streights with a contrary winde, being West, and faire weather.
	22							This 22 day at 2 of the clocke in the afternoone, hauing sailed 60 leagues Northwest, we ankered among an huge number of isles lying in the bottome of the sayd supposed passage, at which place the water riseth 4 fadome vpright. Here as we rode at anker, a great whale passed by vs, and swam West in among the isles. In this place a S.W. by W. moone maketh a full sea. Here the compasse varied 30 degrees.
	24							The 24 day at 5 of the clocke in the morning we set saile, departing from this place, and shaping our course S.E. to recouer the maine Ocean againe.
	25							This 25 we were becalmed almost in the bottome of the Streights, & had the weather maruellous extreame hot.
	26							
	27						S.E.	This day being in the Streights, we had a very quicke storme.
	Noone the 29						S.	Being still in the Streight, we had this day faire weather.
					64			At this present we got cleere of the Streights, hauing coasted the South shore, the land trending from hence S.W. by S.
	Noone the 30	24	S.S.W.	22	63			This day we coasted the shore, a banke of ice lying thereupon. Also this 30 of Iuly in the afternoone we crossed ouer the entrance or mouth of a great inlet or passage, being 20 leagues broad, and situate betweene 62 & 63 degrees, in which place we had 8 or 9 great races, currents or ouerfals, lothsomly crying like the rage of the waters vnder London bridge, and bending their course into the sayd gulfe.

This

Figure 6.8. Richard Hakluyt, *The principal navigations, voiages, traffiques and discoueries of the English nation* (London: George Bishop, Ralph Newberie, and Robert Barker, 1600), p. 117, Houghton Library, Harvard University, Cambridge, HOU F STC 12626a.

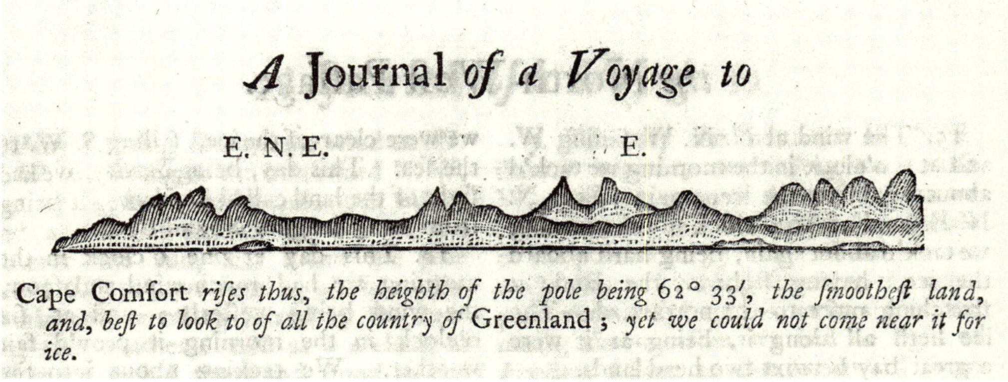

Figure 6.9. John Gatonbe, *Journal of a Voyage for the Discovery of a North-West Passage,* in *John Churchill, Collection of Voyages and Travels: Some Now First Printed from Original Manuscripts,* London, 1732, vol. 6, p. 248, Houghton Library, Harvard University, Cambridge, f *68-553.

> Barents didn't believe us, claiming that it was fourteen days too early for the sun to show itself where it did. We strongly asserted that the contrary was true . . . about such seemingly contradictory things we wondered and argued amongst each other, and said to one another that perhaps we had been wrong about the time.[26]

They were. Barents was correct. De Veer ventures rare introspection: "It was foul weather, with an extreme cold almost not to be endured, whereupon we looked pitifully [*en vreesden*] at one another, fearing that if it should grow colder we should die there."[27] Death would always haunt the archipelago. Much later, Nova Zembla would become the site of a Soviet gulag and then a thermonuclear testing site — posthumous layerings of other species of annihilation.[28]

As Anne Goldgar has described it, overcoming confusion became a great source of anxiety for Barent's crew. Nautical orderings of space and time — splitting hour from hour and inside from outside using hourglasses and doors — were transposed onto dry land.[29] De Veer's grid-like narrative attempts this kind of ordering, too, as do the anonymous illustrations which interrupt his account from time to time. In a rare painted page now in London (Figure 6.10), a treeless field of ice pyramids hems in fur-hatted men who pick their way toward a waterway edge, halberds and axes raised, as three others flee into the background. A polar bear, inquisitive, bobbing, and camouflaged at the water's edge, appears about to receive the musket shot of a single marksman, who has just discharged his weapon in a red burst of flame. Limning the sky and shoreline, bands of sunless blue signal horizon and water, between which the furious humans scrape, chop, and shovel an orthogonal ditch into the foreground. This is a struggle against the earth itself, the pulling and dragging of sleds, trees, and carcasses. "The way was full of ice and icebergs, and with great difficultly we worked," de Veer tells of the scene, "with chopping, throwing, pushing, digging."[30] This conflict against the nonhuman pivoted upon desperate demarcations of "us" versus "them." But the Arctic threat — and the Arctic norm — was

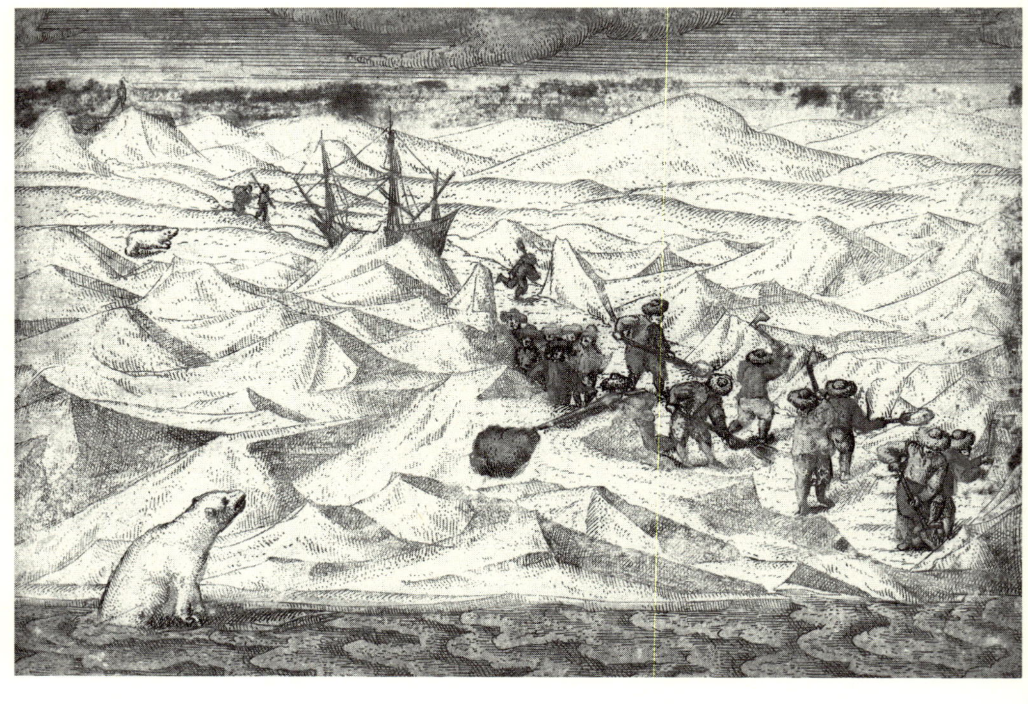

Figure 6.10. Gerrit de Veer, *Waerachtighe beschryvinghe van drie seylagien, ter werelt noyt soo vreemt ghehoort*... (Amsterdam: Cornelis Claesz., 1598), plate 106.

that these constructed polarities would always break down. On December 26, de Veer writes: "Our bunks were frozen, which made us behold one another with sad countenance."[31] As if a premonition of the clumped prints, the Arctic blurring of human and nonhuman corpora remained, in the Arctic, the most frightening prospect of all.

Unstuck

When discovered in the nineteenth century, the Barents engravings had been buried within soil that alternatively froze and melted (temperatures ranged from 5 degrees to minus 30 degrees Celsius in the Russian Arctic) for nearly three centuries. In terms of the excavated block, what had happened was clear: the animal sizing used to manufacture the paper (in these Netherlandish impressions, likely bone or fish sizing) had become wet, then dried, then frozen, over and over again as the seasons alternated.[32] The prints had become glued to one another, the paper fibers intermeshed. The result was, in effect, blocks of papier-mâché, the works succumbing to "the rhythm of geology," as one writer has put it.[33]

In 1977, a team of conservators under Peter Poldervaart at the Rijksprentenkabinet began to separate the sheets. Their process, to put it briefly, deployed the enzyme trypsin to dissolve giant protein molecules melding the sizing to itself.[34] The sheets were carefully unstuck, one by one, in ruined condition. This unpeeling took more than a year, after which the prints were washed and mounted on Japanese paper, in fragmentary form. The visual effect today is of cracking, tears, or fissures in the paper, not so much a loss as a breaking. (This is a procedure that —utterly irreversible— is unlikely to be performed today.[35]) "We wanted to see what was inside these stacks of prints that had turned to hard, blackened blocks," claimed Poldervaart.[36]

Today, the Rijksmuseum catalogue does not file the engravings as a discrete "Nova Zembla" cache. The Arctic history is there, if one cares to dig. But the engravings are basically listed as prints akin to others, with Hollstein numbers and states. They are, for example, simply "Goltzius" prints in distressed condition. But the "landscape" the prints used to inhabit has been largely scrubbed. The unique paper conservation, in this respect, perhaps marks an endeavor of return: the prints began life as two-dimensional, caked themselves into three-dimensions, and were rendered, via selective separation, as two dimensions once again. Thanks to the Arctic, the sheets had fallen out of the mode of figuration usually associated with Mannerist prints. The conservators' job was to bring them back, warding off their history of slow fusion with the ground itself, their settling into the time of the earth, durational time, their absorption in a geological cycle of seasons and darknesses.

Is this just a question of weird provenance? Apart from the damage, how different are the Nova Zembla engravings from other old master prints with afterlives of duress, even specifically subterranean duress?[37] The situation with the Siberian stuff might be, in fact, a material one — these prints, melded to the earth itself, marooned far from where we normally expect them, physically became part of an Arctic environment. (One of the many objects recovered from the shipwreck was a medallion engraved by the Frankfurt smith Hans Gelther, with, ironically, a relief of "Time that Uplifts Truth From the Earth.")[38]

In 2012, the artist Siân Bowen engaged the Nova Zembla cache while an artist in residence at the Rijksmuseum. Bowen created handmade books of drawings on vellum, pricked and dusted through with silver and palladium. She then embossed other sheets roughly, punching through premade drawings, working with her papermaker, Gangolf Ulbricht. The books were then installed alongside relics from the actual Barents exhibition — books and restored prints from the Siberian find (Figure 6.11). Bowen claimed to invoke slowness — a slowness she linked to the Arctic: "[My show] depicts a journey edging little by little through the frozen icepack. Many of the other works take time to take them in; in part due to the way that the light is reflected off or diffused through the surfaces."[39] The installation wrought a kind of repetition of the almost same, consistent with the marooned sailors' experience and with the seasonal cycles endured by the interred engravings. Poetic, to be sure. But like the restored Haarlem engravings, the surfaces remained fragile, but agitated, interrogating

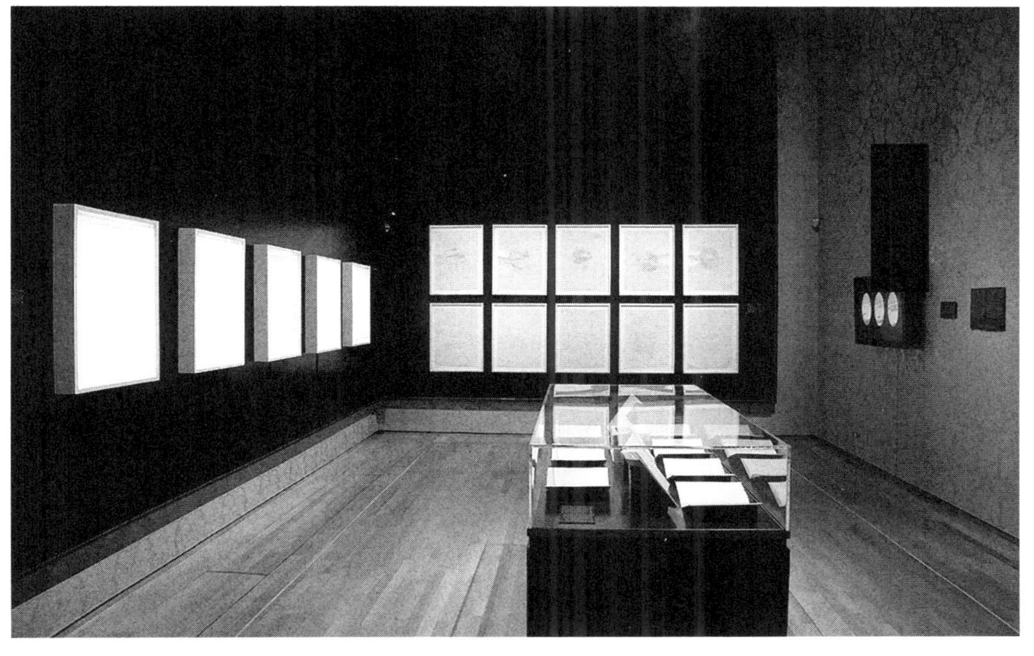

Figure 6.11. Siân Bowen, *Suspending the Ephemeral*, 2012, installation view, Rijksmuseum, Amsterdam.

the relationship between damage and creativity. At the end of the Amsterdam show, Bowen actually sent some of her handmade books to Nova Zembla with a meteorological expedition. There, in late 2014, they were physically buried in the soil and abandoned.

Bowen's Arctic project resonates with years of scholarly emphasis on matter in terms of time as well as place. Many such theorizations aim at the stoppage of narratives of speed — a deceleration of the neoliberal human in the name of the slow "being" of the thing. In the light, Bowen's practices here might seem to represent some neo-Romantic, "abstract" recoil into decelerated nature. But perhaps she is probing the opposite: a heterogeneous interest in technology and posthuman or prehuman histories — paper's capacity for endurance, to "carry" specific kinds of traces over time as well as space. These engagements remain at once contingent upon and questioning of paper media's capacity to "reveal."

Debatably, the print medium's ontological divorce from object modes rooted in the sacral (painting, sculpture), at least in the West, means that print bears a different responsibility to point away from itself (not just in terms of "secular" subject matter) either as information or image, to act as a window as much as a thing. To serve as an *imago contrafactum*, as we saw in the previous chapter, an image brandishes its neutral, eye-witnessed distance from something it shows — and therefore accrues truthfulness. But this can break down. Black and white, print never makes the same claims to mimesis as, say, painting, in terms of dissimulation. But at the same time, its potential for obduracy will always be limited by the medium's general associations with a public.

The material properties of paper, however, its relative portability, mean that print often bears a relatively stronger capacity to comingle or even collapse processes of physical versus perceptual conveyance: of delivery both as apparition and material.[40] In Nova Zembla, the physical movement of packaged engravings was vividly arrested by a cosmic act of displacement. And today, this jars. For the Amsterdam restorers, making the long-unseen prints viewable again — rendering them half-images, via a kind of enzyme-based iconoclasm

(Figure 6.4) was imperative. But why? On the one hand, we simply don't think about Goltzius engravings at the North Pole. On the other, we are not used to associating print dissemination — and with it, certain conceptions of the early modern global — with invisibility and stasis, rather than opticality and drift. But the printed image cannot be stabilized, any more than the *Behouden Huys* on Nova Zembla could indefinitely cleave inside from outside. Prints — personal in scale — have always fantasized about being peeled open, discovered, peered into. But when this actually happens, it is disfiguring.

Cold Weather and the Freedom of the Seas

In the wake of the Barents voyages, the Delft legal prodigy Hugo de Groot, known as Grotius (b. 1583), formulated his notion of the freedom of the seas. Grotius's manuscript of 1604, *De Jure Praedae* (On the law of prize and booty), included an essay entitled "Mare Liberum" that maintained that "navigation, by the law of nations, is free to all persons."[41] Grotius defended the idea of a stateless ocean where the right of sovereignty did not apply, not least because material conditions at sea made "landed" property impossible; like the air, "the sea is common to all, to wit, so infinite that it cannot be possessed and applied to all uses."[42]

The impetus for Grotius's work was the Dutch seizure of a ship off Singapore in 1603. (The sailor responsible for the capture, in fact, was Jacob van Heemskerck — a Barents lieutenant who survived Nova Zembla in 1596–97.)[43] By invoking nature as a rationale for mercantilist freedom, Grotius was abrogating sea claims made through war, fiat, or exploration, a collective case against the both Iberian dominion of the Atlantic and Pacific and, among others, English dominion over the North. In 1613, in fact, Grotius was called in specifically to support Dutch claims to hunt walrus in the "English" seas off Greenland.[44] But it was not just the fluidity of the seas (so claimed Grotius) that made them incapable of being demarcated or occupied, but also, as he put it in a later defense of his theory, their scale and "incomprehensibility": "That vigorous motion of the sea, as the untamed instinct in wild beasts, would make it impossible, even if occupation took place here, for possession to be continued, and ownership through possession, unless by a perpetual and close guardianship."[45]

What Grotius proposed, then, in the precise moment of the Dutch forays into the Far North, was the idea of a *legally* defined antithesis between sea and land. This suggested two new orders of capitalist existence: first, the space of territory and sovereignty, the space of property; second, the space of free mercantile movement, of freedom and enslavement. As Carl Schmitt pointed out, capitalism needs a model of maritime space that posits a clear distinction between earth and sea — the ocean as a place of free circulation and free trade, as opposed to the land, where goods and labor produced by (exploitative) polities can interact.[46] The idea of a *mare liberum* could also justify colonies, so that forces such as the English and Dutch could conquer land that was not contiguous with their European domains.[47] It was the discovery of the New Worlds of the North and South in the sixteenth century that prompted this theorization of a legal — as well as environmental — opposition of water and soil. Grotius, of course, was making a case less for freedom than for piracy, arguing against Spanish claims to dominion.

But then as now, climate seemed to trouble all of this. Around the moment of the "Mare Liberum," Grotius also wrote about ice in his native Netherlands, treating frozen water as a kind of middle state and social equalizer:

> Here [on the ice] no one inquires about rank; here all are frank and free. Here a peasant maid has a noble by her side. There my peasant lad goes along, leading the grand ladies. Over there I see a courtly fellow escorting a lady burgher. If one asks from the bottom of one's heart who is truly wise, then I say from the bottom of my heart, truly naught but ice.[48]

Ice, paradoxically, modeled a free sea. And such a state had become a new norm in North Europe. Climate historians have recorded abysmally cold winters during 1564–65, 1572–73, 1594–95, and 1607–1608, when freezes in France, Germany, and the Netherlands lasted more than eight weeks. A Dutch chronicler from Zeeland described how in 1608, "there had never been such a freeze in living memory . . . many people froze to death on 14, 15, and 17 January."[49] The "Little Ice Age" paralyzed canals and made shipping impossible. In some places, snow was more than two feet deep. Contemporary accounts from the second half of the sixteenth century describe the decline in temperature and, with it, predictability: "There is no real, constant sunshine, neither a steady winter nor summer," wrote the Stendal pastor Daniel Schaller.[50] A pamphlet published at Leipzig in 1562 describes the past season's "great cold followed by enormous snow, which brought many a poor man much woe."[51] And by 1600, a Lucerne apothecary named Renward Cysat (1545–1614) concluded that such extreme cold marked a new trend: "For some time, the years have shown themselves to be more rigorous and severe than in the past, and deterioration [*abnemmen*] among creatures, not only among mankind and animals, but also of the earth's crops and produce, has been noticed, in addition to extraordinary alterations [*verendrungen*] of the elements, stars, and winds."[52]

The temperature drop, which devastated rye and grapes in much of central Europe, was blamed, intermittently, upon Jews, straying Christians, or demons. Wolfgang Behringer has pointed to the striking correlation between deathly cold temperatures in France and England in 1586–87 and a rise in witchcraft trials.[53] The weather may have been diabolical, but its causality lay with sinful earth dwellers.[54] Barents's early in-freezing was certainly a result of this cold. Ever-firm in its belief in deliverance, de Veer's own account did at times wonder if the Arctic weather was a divine punishment.

Pictorially, this giant cold snap has been associated with the growth of the Netherlandish winter landscape tradition. In 1565, a giant ice mountain (*ysgebercht*) actually appeared in the river at Delfshaven and froze boats at their mooring, an occurrence that was described in a large panel by Cornelis Jacobsz van Culemborch, an artist about whom we otherwise know almost nothing (Figure 6.12).[55] The painting, arguably the first winter scene in the northern Netherlands, is a heaping of grays and whites. It is inscribed: "In the year 1565, on the afternoon of January the 2nd, an ice mountain came

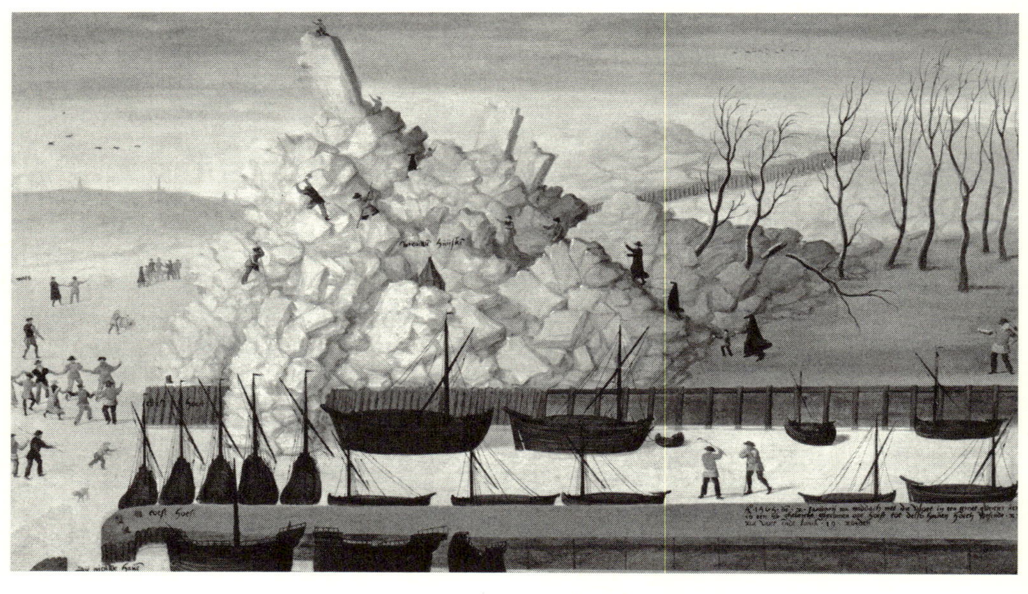

Figure 6.12. Cornelis Jacobsz van Culemborch, *Ice at Delfshaven*, 1565, oil on wood, 78 x 135 cm, Boymans Museum, Rotterdam, 11113.

in on the flood at Delfshaven pier in little more than a quarter of an hour, and measured 23 roods high and 17 long."[56] Yet more locally, 1565–66 was the same season that Pieter Bruegel painted *Hunters in the Snow* just down the coast in Antwerp (Figure 6.13), while next year, his chilly *Adoration of the Magi in the Snow* (Figure 6.14) would appear. These were the winters when the Scheldt River froze two feet thick.[57] Of course the winter genre did not arise simply as a reaction to low temperatures, a reading that assumes a rather positivist concept of how artists related to the climatological "real." But in both the Delfshaven painting and the Bruegel panels, cold weather emerges as a new kind of physical protagonist, all in a population quickly urbanizing and leaving agrarian pursuits behind.[58] And at the same time, the snow and ice (a natural form of Reformation white-wash) defamiliarized both city and country by masking them. "*Hic frigent artes*"[59] (Here the arts are freezing), famously wrote Erasmus of iconoclastic Basel in 1526, the same place where John Calvin would later deem it "cold and lifeless to represent God."[60]

"Cruelly Disfigured"

For Arctic cold resisted the opposition of sea and earth that Grotius sought to codify. All the while, polar conditions were severe enough to disrupt late medieval theories of temperature and survivalist strategies everywhere. John Davis, as we have seen, sailed in search of a Northwest Passage three times between 1585 and 1587, and conducted experiments in an improvised laboratory onboard.[61] He recorded these in the remarkable *Worldes hydrographical description*, believing, like Plancius, the idea of "the sea frysing" to be "ridiculous."[62] Both Davis's and Barents's Arctic voyages (along with the writing of Olaus Magnus) were described in Robert Boyle's 1665 *New Experiments and Observations Touching Cold* (Figure 6.15). The Nova Zembla sailors' experience, for Boyle, testified to the "power of cold, either to straighten the sphere of activity of fire or to hinder its wonted effects."[63] Boyle even cited Barents in his tables of temperature measurements.[64] In fact, published Arctic accounts had circulated so widely by Boyle's day that sailors often cross-referenced tales about Northern cold and peril. Edward

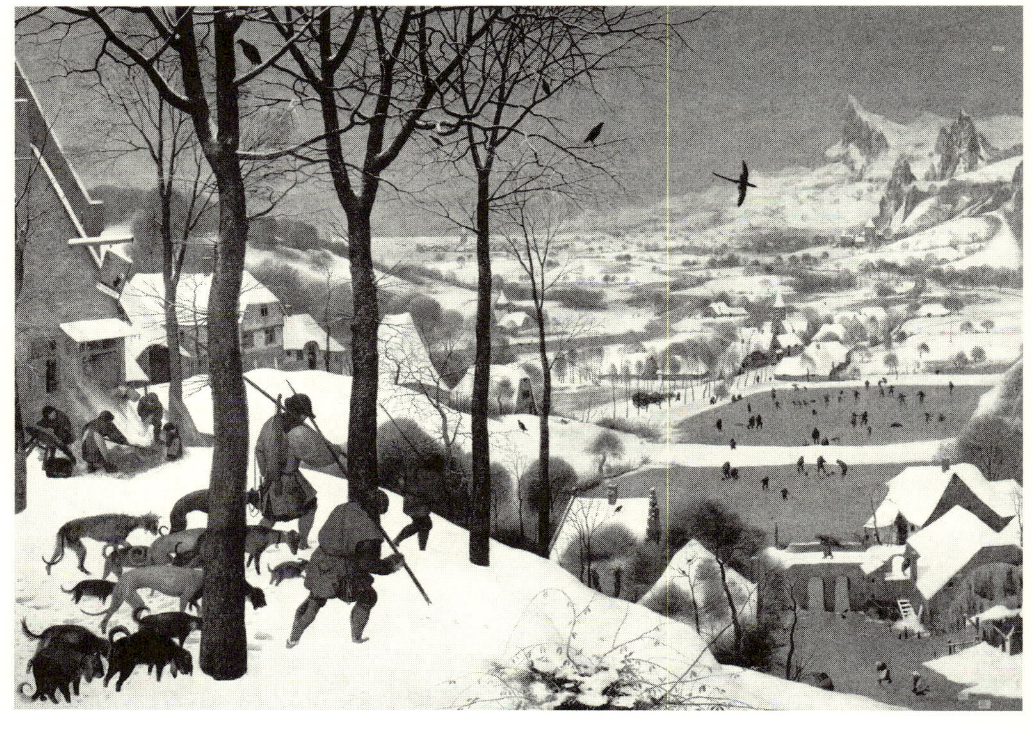

Figure 6.13. Pieter Bruegel the Elder, *Hunters in the Snow*, 1565, oil on panel, 117 x 162 cm, Kunsthistorisches Museum, Vienna.

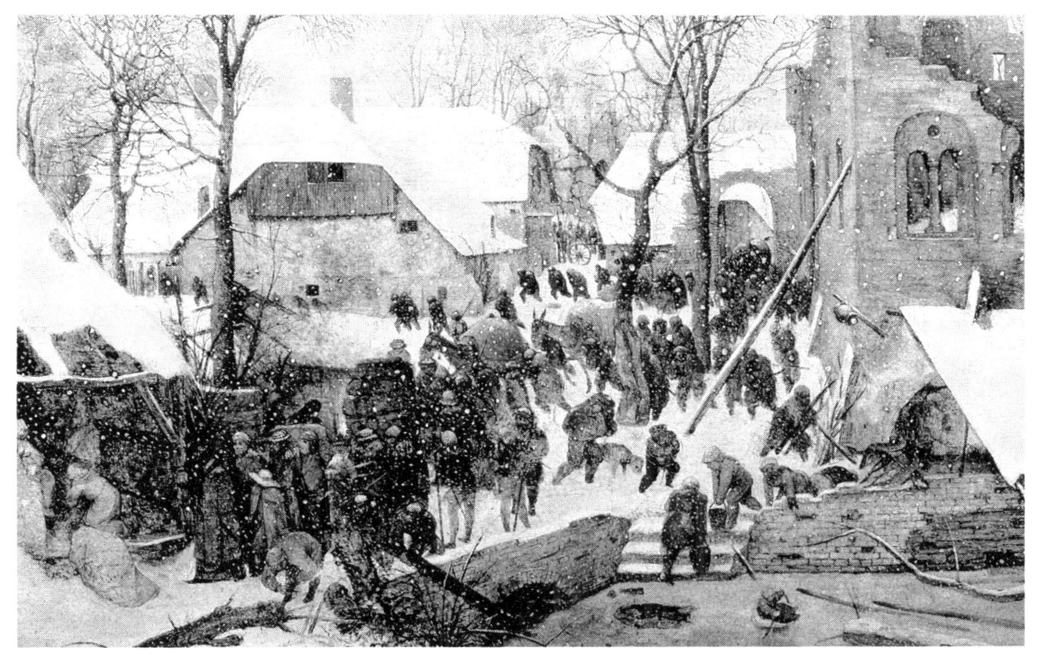

Figure 6.14. Pieter Bruegel the Elder, *Adoration of the Magi in the Snow*, 1567, oil on wood, 35 x 55 cm, Winterthur.

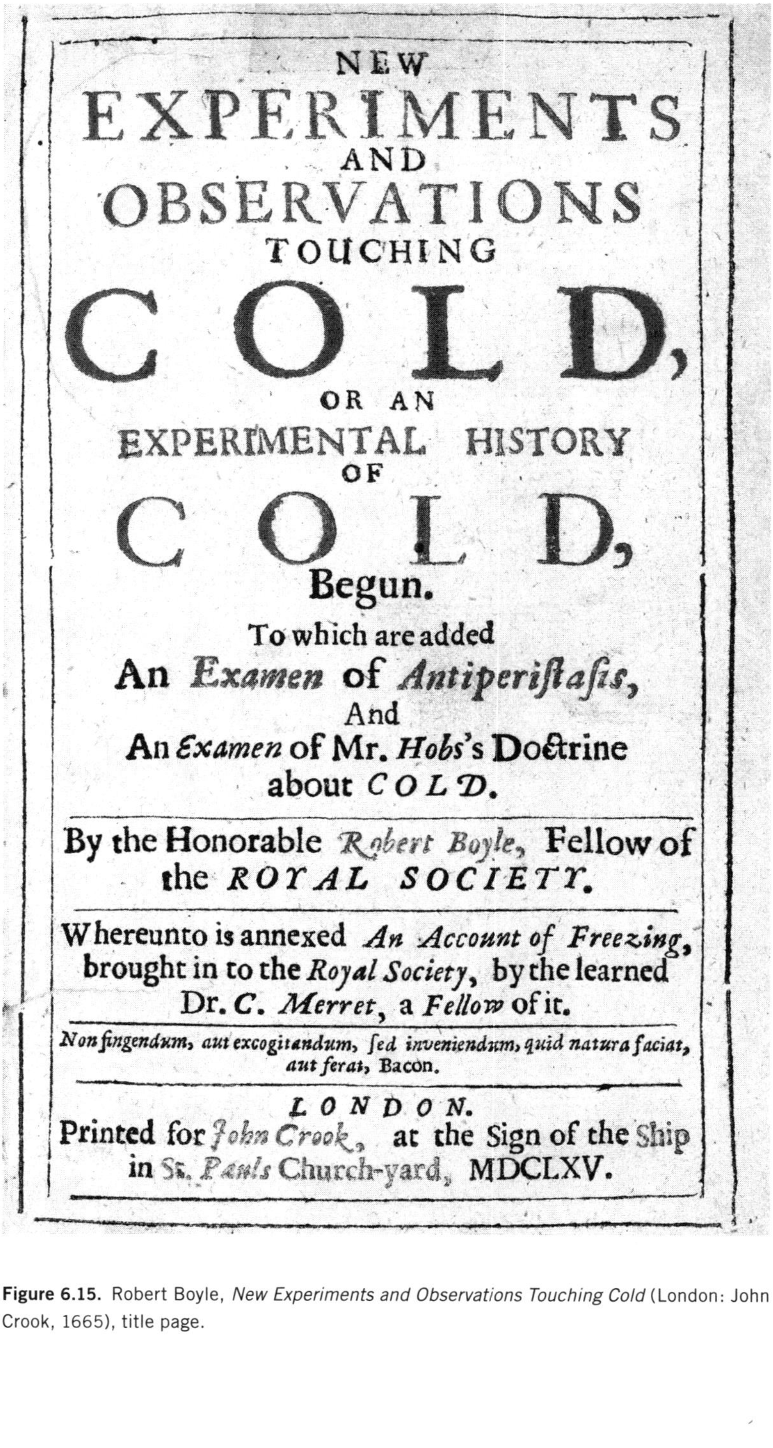

NEW
EXPERIMENTS
AND
OBSERVATIONS
TOUCHING
COLD,
OR AN
EXPERIMENTAL HISTORY
OF
COLD,
Begun.

To which are added

An *Examen* of *Antiperiſtaſis,*

And

An *Examen* of Mr. *Hobs's* Doctrine
about *COLD.*

By the Honorable *Robert Boyle,* Fellow of
the *ROYAL SOCIETY.*

Whereunto is annexed *An Account of Freezing,*
brought in to the *Royal Society,* by the learned
Dr. *C. Merret,* a *Fellow* of it.

*Non fingendum, aut excogitandum, ſed inveniendum, quid natura faciat,
aut ferat,* Bacon.

LONDON.
Printed for *John Crook,* at the Sign of the Ship
in St. *Pauls* Church-yard, MDCLXV.

Figure 6.15. Robert Boyle, *New Experiments and Observations Touching Cold* (London: John Crook, 1665), title page.

Pellham, trapped on Spitsbergen in Bottle Cove in 1631, recalled tales of dead crewmen from the previous century, Barents among them:

> who all dyed miserably upon the place, being cruelly disfigured after their deaths by savage Beares and hungry Foxes . . . these fearefull examples presenting themselves before our eyes, at this place of Bottle Cove aforesaid, made us, like amazed men, to stand looking one upon another, all of us, as it were, beholding in the present, the future calamities both of himself and his fellowes. . . . [So] stood wee with the eyes of pittie beholding one another.[65]

This scenario of self-regard, with shifting temporalities and the threat of bodies transformed *into* the Arctic landscape, could also take on a grisly material dimension. Hugh Willoughby, one of the founders of the Merchant Adventurers in London, vanished with his crew in Northern Muscovy in 1555. Their ice-choked ship was discovered one year later by an English rescue party. An official chronicler described what was found: "One man [was] frozen seated in the act of writing, pen still in hand, and the paper before them; others at table, platters in hand and spoon in mouth; others opening a locker, and others in various postures, like statues, as if they had been adjusted and placed in these attitudes."[66] *Like statues.* Willoughby's frozen corpses were even transported, at great difficulty, back to London and reburied in European soil, almost as if a premonition of the salvaged Nova Zembla prints.

For drowning, starvation, and exposure aside, marooning in the cold Arctic threatened death in forms previously little known. And sailors, stricken, knew this. The Danish aristocrat Jens Munk opened his account of a disastrous overwintering in Northern Canada, *Navigatio septentrionalis*, with a suicide:

> On the 18th of May, it happened, early in the morning, while we were sailing alone, that one of my men, as he was walking on the deck, suddenly jumped overboard at a distance of quite two fathoms and plunged his head underwater, without, however, as it appeared, sinking so quickly as he desired. But, as it blew hard, no one could save him, which I should much have wished. He therefore, went down and was lost.[67]

The voyage would breed more death: of Munk's crew of sixty-five that departed from Copenhagen, exactly three survived.[68] The agency of. the "free seas" in changing or ending the *mental* lives of humans was a constant even in this moment. One of the few verse poets to visit the Far North in the sixteenth century was the Buda-born, Oxford-educated Stephen Parmenius, who actually died there. Parmenius, driven out of Hungary by the Turks in 1579, sailed with Humphrey Gilbert to Newfoundland in the summer of 1583 as an official chronicler. He intended to write an epic Latin poem about the marvels of the New World. Spending a month near St. John's, however, Parmenius discovered only pine forests, grass, and fish. He dismayed at "nothing but wilderness,"[69] and bemoaned not seeing natives. When Parmenius's ship, the *Delight*, wrecked near Sable Island in a storm, the poet drowned.[70] Elsewhere, two vessels captained by Arthur Pet and Charles Jackman headed for the Kara Sea. A haunting, fire-damaged pen sketch made aboard Pet's ship in the Asian Arctic (Figure 6.16) shows clusters of small islands fronting blocked-in ships beset by, as an inscription notes, "infinite yse."[71] (Barents actually carried a manuscript version of Pet and Jackman's logbook to Nova Zembla.)[72] We know that one of the expedition's ships disappeared entirely, the crew allegedly wrecked and then killed by locals.[73]

For to perish in such terrain was not always to vanish, but to accrete, to become one with terrain. Pellham later recalled fear that his crew would become like Willoughby's men: "Metamorphosed into the ice of the Country."[74] Far from being a sea of freedom — and precisely because it was neither water nor land — the Arctic, such men feared, would imprison them, would *stop* them from moving. Or entomb them, like prints as so much admixed matter.[75]

Frozen Words

Barents's century was, in fact, rich in ice-bound discourse. In the fourth book of Rabelais's *Gargantua and Pantagruel*, a ship sails through waters so cold that speech freezes in midair, "congealed, frozen up, and not heard."[76] The diction's solidity is such that phrases

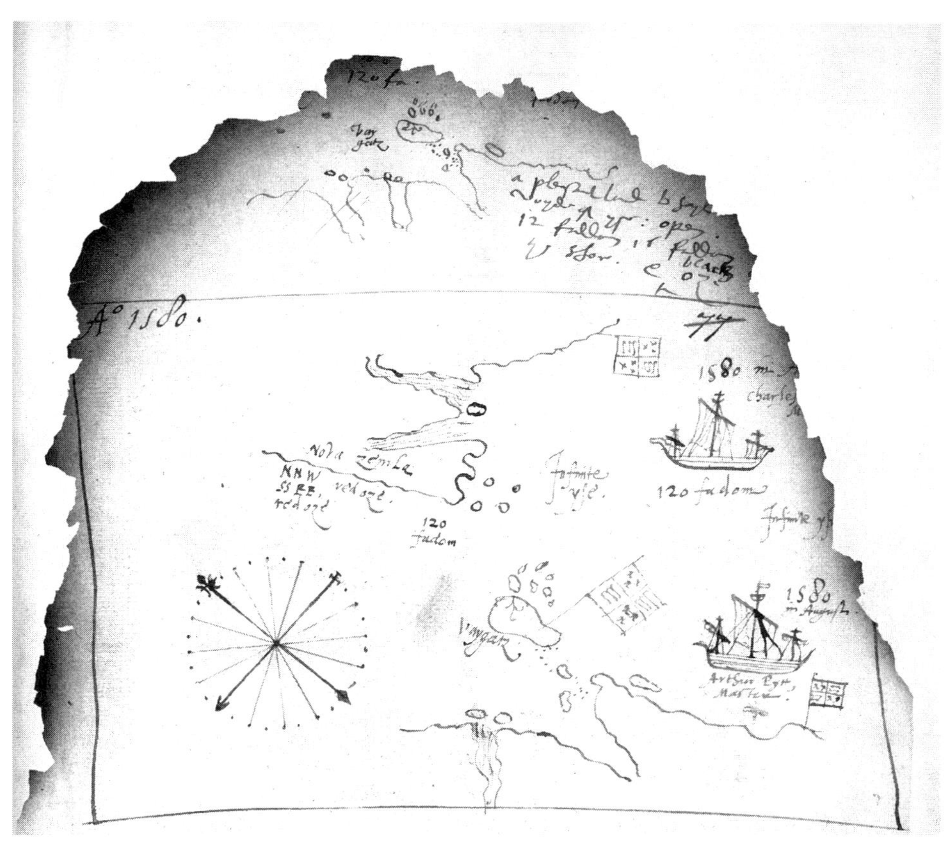

Figure 6.16. *Voyages of Pet and Jackman*, 1580, MS, British Library, Cotton MS. Otho E. VIII. f 78.

can be snatched by the giant Pantagruel and scattered on the ship's bridge, whereupon they hauntingly thaw (Figure 6.17):

> he threw three or four handfuls of them on the deck; among which I perceived some very sharp words, and some bloody words, which the pilot said used sometimes to go back and recoil to the place whence they came.... We also saw some terrible words, and some others not very pleasant to the eye. When they had been all melted together, we heard a strange noise, hin, hin, hin, hin, his, tick, tock, tack, lorg, bredelinbrededack, frr, frr, frr, bou, bou, bou, bou, bou, bou, bou, bou, track, track, trr, trr, trr, trrr, trrrrr, on, on, on, on, ouououon, gog, magog, and I do not know what other barbarous words.[77]

The sounds, the ship's captain finally explains, are noises from a long-past naval battle staged on the sea itself—the crash of swords, the creaking of masts, the shouts of men, chipped fragments of a great din, now released into the frigid air. "We listened, and with full ears sucked in the air as some of you suck oysters," Rabelais writes. The repetition and accumulation of the unfreezing sounds arrest Pantagruel's ship, literally and figuratively, as it does the readerly flow of the voyage; the crew, like us, is forced to reckon with an unsettling rain of Schwittersesque noise speech, language self-referring and concrete. We in fact know that when visiting Calais around 1545, Rabelais conferred with the Breton pilot Jacques Cartier, the same explorer who had sailed through the ice-choked waters off Newfoundland.[78]

The anecdote of the thawing of *paroles gélées* parodies a passage from Plutarch. Along with providing an eerie premonition of the Nova Zembla situation (among the other objects Barents rescued from the permafrost was a Flemish-French dictionary from 1589—frozen words indeed),[79] Rabelais here, as literally dozens of commentators from Bakhtin to MacPhail have pointed out, presciently models the contemporary notion of the contingency of language.[80] What is unfrozen is not just some "past," but rather decontextualized messages, broken down into disorderly fragments, delivered materially, but delayed. A 1710 English story by Joseph Addison, "Frozen Voices," even melded elements of Barents's account with those from Rabelais.[81]

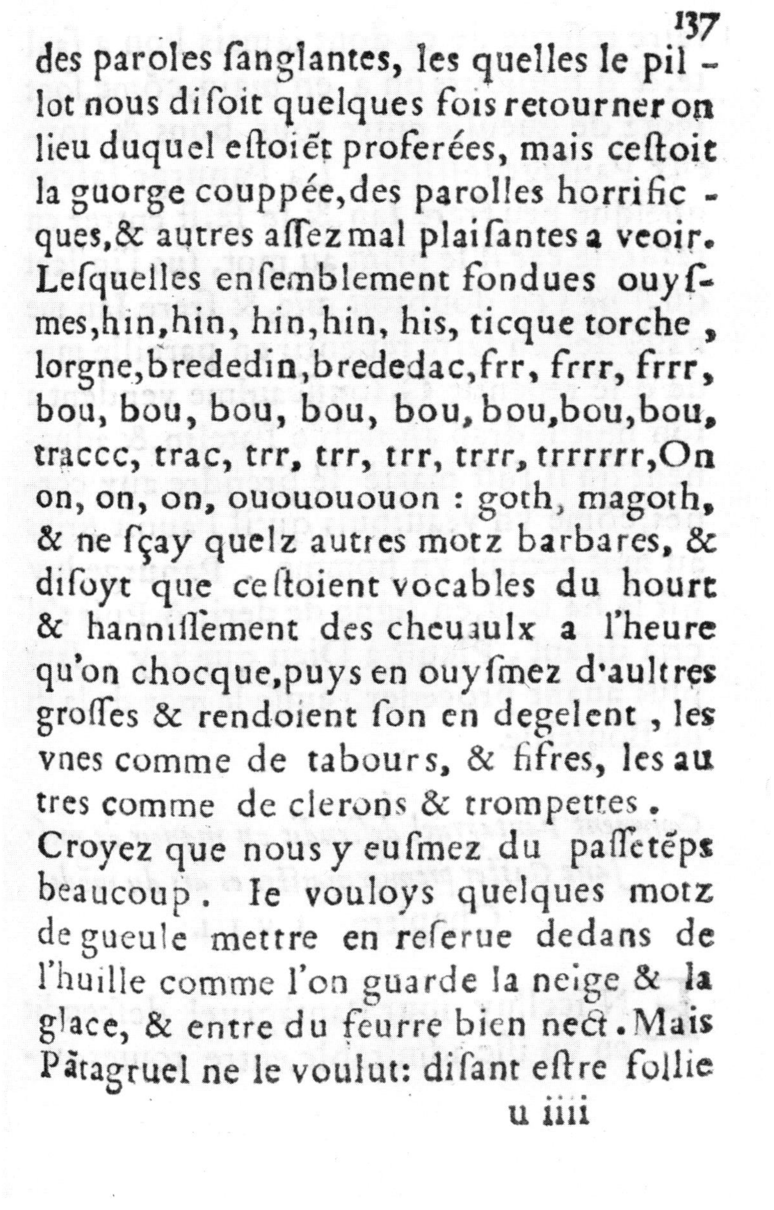

des paroles ſanglantes, les quelles le pil -
lot nous diſoit quelques fois retourner on
lieu duquel eſtoiēt proferées, mais ceſtoit
la guorge couppée, des parolles horrific -
ques, & autres aſſez mal plaiſantes a veoir.
Leſquelles enſemblement fondues ouyſ-
mes, hin, hin, hin, hin, his, ticque torche ,
lorgne, brededin, brededac, frr, frrr, frrr,
bou, bou, bou, bou, bou, bou, bou, bou,
traccc, trac, trr, trr, trr, trrr, trrrrrr, On
on, on, on, ouououon : goth, magoth,
& ne ſçay quelz autres motz barbares, &
diſoyt que ceſtoient vocables du hourt
& hanniſſement des cheuaulx a l'heure
qu'on chocque, puys en ouyſmez d'aultres
groſſes & rendoient ſon en degelent , les
vnes comme de tabours, & fifres, les au
tres comme de clerons & trompettes .
Croyez que nous y euſmez du paſſetēps
beaucoup. Ie vouloys quelques motz
de gueule mettre en reſerue dedans de
l'huille comme l'on guarde la neige & la
glace, & entre du feurre bien neɥt. Mais
Pãtagruel ne le voulut: diſant eſtre follie

u iiii

Figure 6.17. François Rabelais, *Le Quart livre des faicts et dicts héroïques du noble Pantagruel* (Lyon: Baltasar Aleman, 1552), 137r, Bibliothèque Nationale, Paris, RESERVE 8-BL-19595.

Arctic or not, Rabelais's unfreezing words are bewildering: "We really heard them, but could not understand them, for it was a barbarous gibberish." And in turn, Rabelais influenced at least one geographical account of the Arctic, that in André Thevet's *Cosmographie universelle*, published in 1575. Thevet transformed the frozen water into a metaphor: "When the sea is frozen there, and the ice breaks up, it makes a sound like a human voice."[82] And indeed, published accounts of Arctic exploration, as we have seen, presented particular problems of form and structure, not just because of the icy geographical situation of their contexts, but because of their subjects' relative unsuccess.

In the Arctic, environment and landscape — as with Frobisher's ice and Pantagruel's words — take on agency and become actors in their own right. This holds currency today. Many art-historical debates about materiality, it seems, are debates about mobility — conceptual as well as physical movement. The Nova Zembla engravings summon the issue of where it is — literally and figuratively — that art, in fact, *belongs*. Since the work of Elizabeth Eisenstein, print has often been understood as a placeless medium; its circulatory capacity in the early modern world was, perversely, what gave it authority to "fix" information, as Eisenstein put it.[83] If, as Alois Riegl claimed when talking about migration-era jewelry from Siberia, the "object" status of an artwork is most present when it moves around, then the "image" status emerges only when that artwork is allowed to rest.[84] Print has always borne the capacity to fly around the world in various multiples — this has become its role in many a historical discourse of frictionless, happy cultural circulation. And more so than other species of artwork, print might lend itself most readily to such physical rhetorics of animation — animation in the sense of making seemingly still things move, seemingly dead things come alive.

The Amsterdam print conservators sought this futile reclaiming of stillness, of *image* — the restoration of a clean vector of reference. And yet as with Pantagruel, this melting breeds disruption. We have a strange situation where to unfreeze, to unstick the prints from one another is, in more than chemical ways, an attempt to stabilize them, to ward off decay, to permit us to ponder, perhaps, their makers, their state, their iconography, their legible *information* far more immediately than their numinous itinerancy. It is a gesture of demystification, an almost iconoclastic act. In the afterlife of the Barents cache, frozen prints are unearthed and deposited away, just as frozen sailors are found and reburied. Nervously warded off is both spatial distance and ontological remove — imagistic "meaning" is restored, unstably, to what the Arctic rendered *dead.*

A Poetics of the Clump

Caspar David Friedrich's *The Sea of Ice* of 1823–24 (Figure 6.18) was poorly received when it was first exhibited in 1824. "An utterly lifeless, monotonous, and desolate view," wrote an anonymous journalist.[85] Friedrich had never visited the Arctic, of course (in 1811, he expressed an interest in travel to Iceland, however).[86] But the famous picture, based on floes that Friedrich studied on the Elbe, was known as *The Polar Sea* until about 1826.[87] (The Delfshaven painting from earlier in this chapter [Figure. 6.12], another portrait of European icebergs, seems an uncanny precedent.) We know that Friedrich followed reports of the expedition of William Edward Parry in 1819–20 avidly. As dramatic as the jagged shards of blue appear in the colossal painting's foreground, it is the ghostly second iceberg at left that suggests a more ominous future, a recurrence of the shipwreck at right.[88] Despite *The Polar Sea*'s historical enshrinement within the sublime, the lesser-known oil sketches of ice from around 1820–21 (Figure 6.19), on which the painting is based dispense with grandeur.[89] They demonstrate a fascination less with human hubris than with geological form. Spatially, we are welcomed into the *Sea of Ice*, as we are into Friedrich's *Northern Landscape* (see Figure 1.3), from around the same date. But the oil sketches' surfaces, in their very preliminarity, suggest a more hostile kind of nature: "Are these still landscapes, or something else?" a different Friedrich critic wondered in 1824.[90] The sketches, that is, perhaps conceptualize the cold landscape as debris, rather than theatre.

The Victorianist Adriana Craciun has indentified what she calls an "archipelagic" mode of experience at work in nineteenth-century Arctic words and images.[91] Before (say) Franklin, Arctic explorers of the American and Asian Far North never assumed that they were coming to a continent. Rather, they regarded the Arctic as a chain of islands within a large sea — an *archi-pelagus*, a place of passage. And they wrote and imaged it as such: George Best's miasmic North Atlantic of disassembled, "broken" points (see Figure 3.1) is one example, as is Ellis's iceberg (see Figure 1.1).[92] This, as Craciun suggests, marked a departure from a more traditional mode of discovery, one understood as cleanly "terrestrial or continental," with fixed self-other boundaries — as I / thou, here / there, conqueror / conquered.

The geophysical situation of the unsettled Arctic prompted a heterogeneity of representational form, one mimetic upon the broken Arctic landscape itself: "the land was not firme, as it was first supposed," wrote Best in 1578, "but all broken Ilandes in the manner of an Archipelagus, and so with other secret intelligence."[93] Throughout all of this, the Arctic remained a place ever tacking between a site of known experience and the realm of the imagination, something halfway "supposed" like Best's "Fyrmeland of America."[94]

The Barents sheets, superficially, allegorize this archipelagic condition. Seen now, the prints — illustrations from Ovid, depictions of New and Old Testament fables — resemble not so much weightless sheets of paper, but chunks of Arctic landscape themselves. In the few objects left unrestored (see Figure 6.1), we almost catch the sheets arrested in the process of reinterring itself in the earth. Even after treatment, the Arctic soil is not "on" these pages, something to be scraped off; it is intermixed with the paper at the level of fibers. The engravings are themselves a species of archipelago — they are indeed broken, and to a large extent, *land*.

De Veer's journal, illustrated with printed configurations of etched lines, did not just mimic the whites and thin blacks of the Arctic landscape, but mirrored the enterprises of both the merchant and the explorer that the Far North shut down. Lurking beneath it all, to borrow from Rosalind Krauss, might be the organizational yearning for the Arctic grid (see Figure 6.3), perhaps along the lines of Olaus's snowflake lattice (see Figure 5.2). "Unlike perspective, the grid does

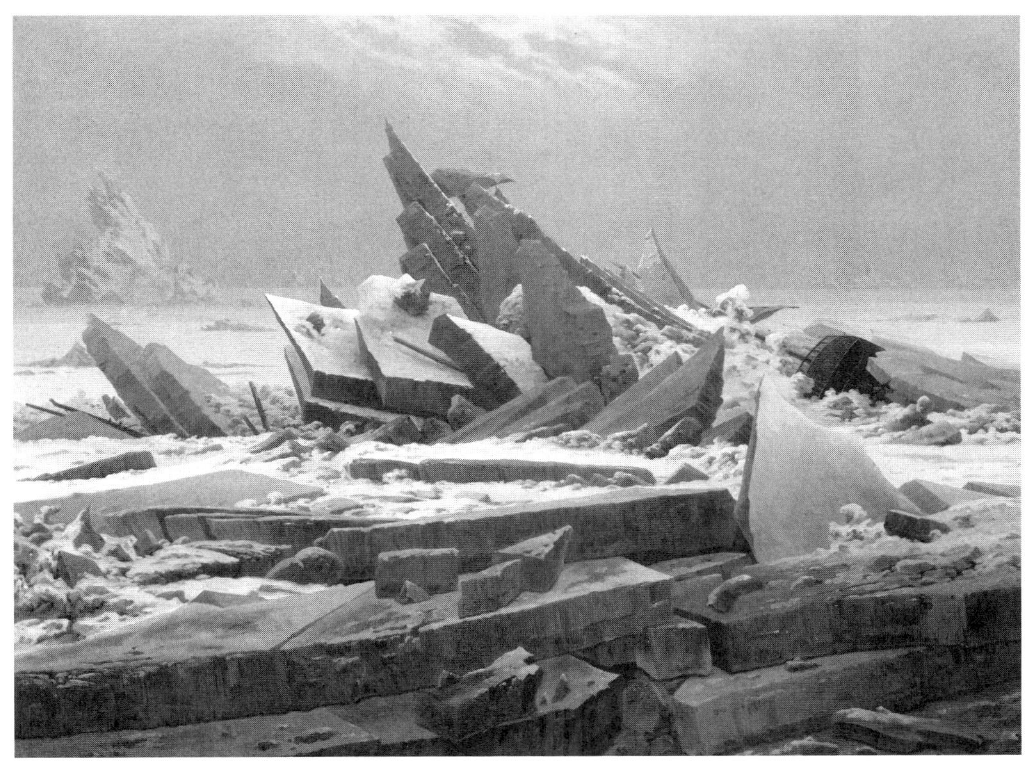

Figure 6.18. Caspar David Friedrich, *The Sea of Ice*, 1823-24, oil on canvas, 96.7 x 126.9 cm, Hamburger Kunsthalle, Hamburg, Inv. 1051.

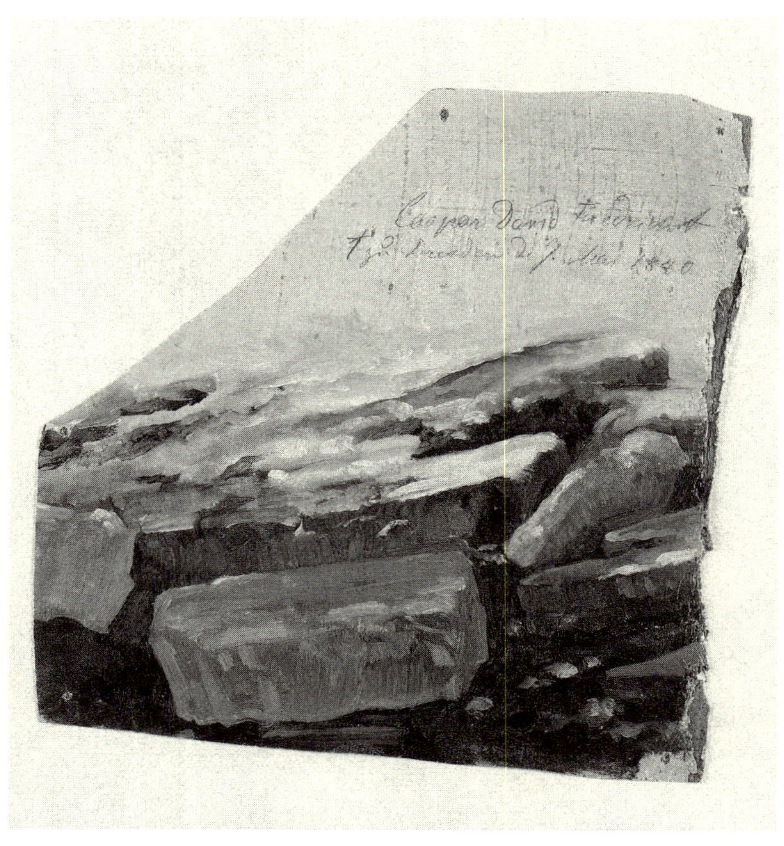

Figure 6.19. Caspar David Friedrich, *Study of Ice Floes on the Elbe River*, undated, oil on canvas, 14 x 18 cm, 17.2 x 16.5 cm, 15.2 x 20.5 cm, Hamburger Kunsthalle, Hamburg, Inv. nos. 41084; 41085; 41086.

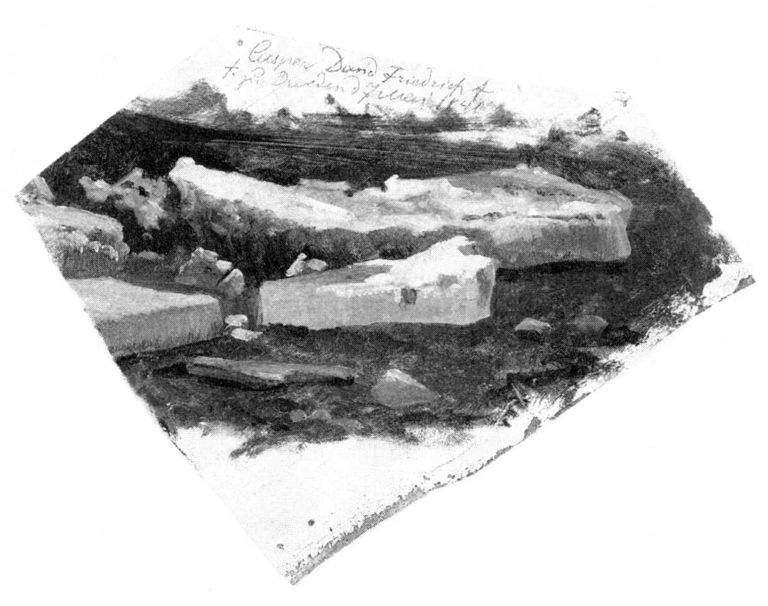

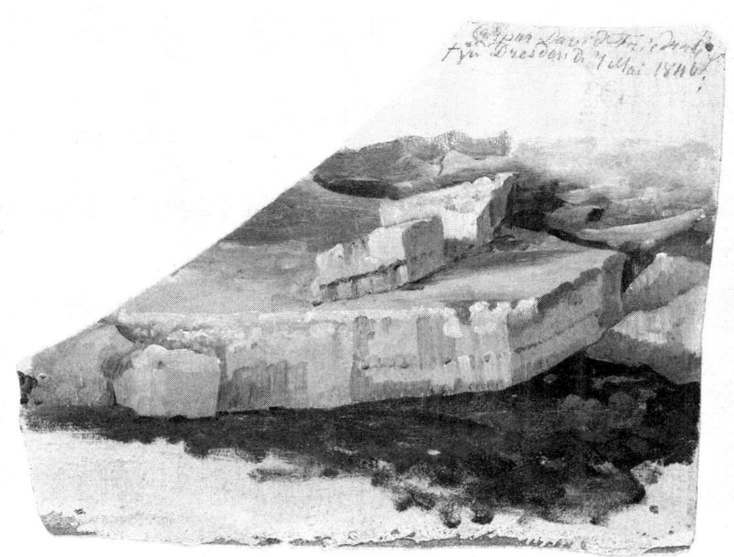

not map the space of a room or a landscape," Krauss writes. "It is a transfer in which nothing changes place . . . something that freezes and locks the self."[95] In the Arctic's case, broken paper grids — half ruined, half saved — summon a poetics of inertia, of trying to see in a cold that inevitably kills.

At the time of his death in 1969, Theodor Adorno was planning an essay on the subject of *Kälte*.[96] Coldness was bourgeois "indifference to the fate of others,"[97] which breeds both barbarism and, unexpectedly, survival within capitalism. Far from a nostalgia for intimacy and warmth, Adorno's theory advocated for the rejection of a culture of enjoyment. The necessary precondition of really knowing the world, for him, demanded "a consciousness of unhappiness both general and personal." Such coldness becomes an "authentic dignity," an ongoing renunciation of the false palliatives of the now, a way to exist: "Anyone who is not cold, who does not chill himself, must feel condemned."[98] Adorno's is a troubling proposal, to be sure, self-contradictory and of course not immune from capitalist absorption itself. (The negative has long been a sexy philosophical commodity in its own right.) But it has been argued that Adorno's very investment in a critical *Kälte* succeeds in one respect by deliberately failing. As it fails, its failure shows.[99] Adorno famously embraced "cold" art in general: Schoenberg, he claimed, wrought a "glacier landscape" in his expulsion of recognizable musical language.[100]

What might it mean, then, to think about early globalization before the Romantic period, about early modern cultural contact, in terms not of "hot" movement and exoticism, but of "cold" stasis and indifference? In some sense, Adorno's dialectic of alienation has always been there, within historicizations of commerce, disenchantment, information flow. But both within and without a certain Reformation poetics — one, we should note, in which the Dutch sailors on Nova Zembla were immersed — what was unseen was often more authoritative than what was externally visible — and individual experience often superior to that of the collective. "Those who are socialized into desperate isolation," writes Adorno about loneliness, "hunger for togetherness and band together in cold clumps [*kalten Haufen*]."[101] These congeal, as did the Barents prints, as fragments of what was subjugated: image turned to object and then, in the contemporary world, back to image again. "To rescue," writes Adorno, "means to love *things*."[102] In the same way, entrapment and risk in this early modern moment emerge as the *true* operations of capitalist life in the *mare liberum* we are now supposed to inhabit. Stasis — forever resisted by capital — remained the real mode, the alternate mode, by which the Nova Zembla prints interacted with the "global."

The geophysical realities of Nova Zembla account not just for allegories of broken passage. The prints reveal the material interruptions of transit that were critical modes of existence in the actual lives of "globally" intended artworks. Viewed from a shipwrecked distance, from what Hans Blumenberg termed the spectator's "nautical metaphorics of existence,"[103] Arctic maroonings challenged many norms within the then-emerging genre of the exploration travel narrative. The latter often told of sun-drenched indigenes and fabulous lands of treasure. Like perspective, such accounts famously nourished a poetics of "transport" to displace homebound readers and beholders virtually. By contrast, certain Arctic remnants of disaster halted the voices of the marvelous in favor of the mundane. They came to associate the exotic not with vivacity and abundance, but with stoppage and loss.

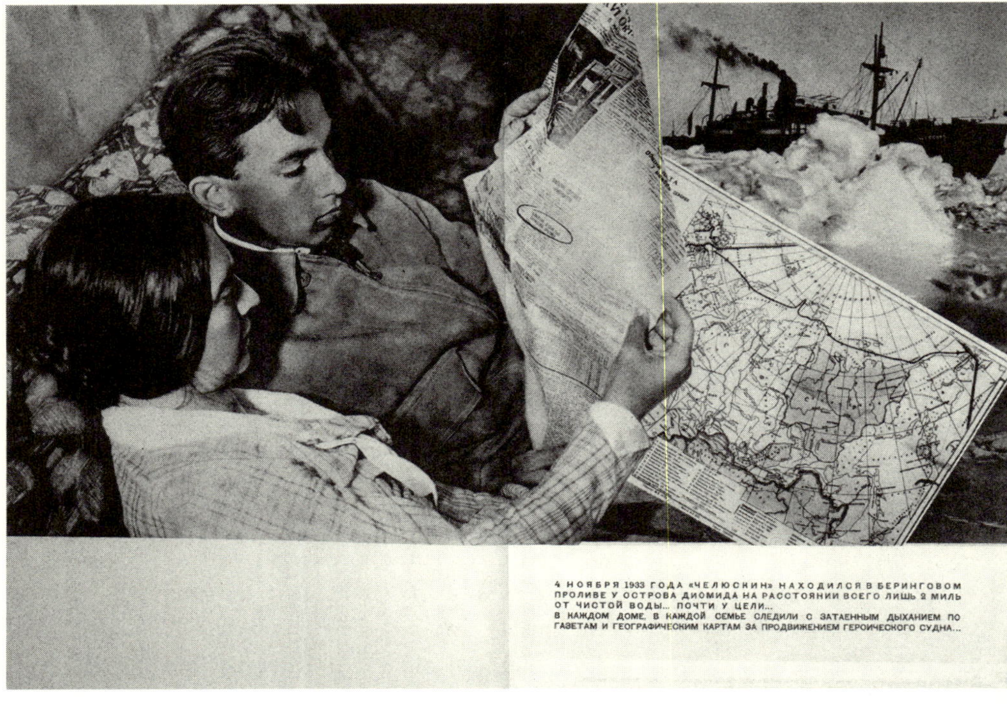

Figure 7.1. Sophie Küppers and El Lissitzky, *SSSR na stroike*, 1934, number 10, pp. 4–5, page 41.3 x 30 cm, Princeton University Library Rare Books.

CHAPTER SEVEN

There Are No Fortresses

It is another composite of views: a mother and child finger pages of *Pravda*, reclining on a flowered couch (Figure 7.1). We are in Moscow, in 1933, at the left half of a photomontage credited to Sophie Küppers and El Lissitzky. The image before us appears in the October 1934 issue of *SSSR na stroike* (USSR in construction).[1] Across the scene, we see a map of northern Siberia, laced by a black line running from Archangelsk to the Bering Strait. It tilts atop a photograph of a steamship in heaving ice. That trapped vessel, we learn from nearby text, is captained by the sitters' husband and father, the Arctic navigator Otto Yulyevich Schmidt. Curling off the page, the newspaper proffers a circled headline conveying the news that Schmidt's *Chelyuskin* icebreaker is now stuck, along with more than a hundred passengers, "in the middle of the Diomid Strait." The distressing news anchors the collage, moving us from the tense intimacy of the Soviet capital to the anonymity of the Bering Sea.

But the *Chelyuskin* story had a heroic end. In late August of 1933, the ship, indeed, foundered in ice 120 miles off the Siberian mainland. As the vessel quickly sank, more than two hundred crew members and passengers decamped to the ice along with food and supplies, taking with them scientific equipment, books, and, most importantly, a functioning radio transmitter. Makeshift tents were erected. Two months passed, during which strandees listened to records on a salvaged phonograph, published a camp newspaper, and held thrice-weekly courses in dialectical materialism.[2] In constant contact with Moscow, "Camp Schmidt" was soon located by air, and a rescue operation mobilized. Hundreds of Soviet airplanes airlifted the passengers to safety in an operation choreographed, the *SSSR na stroike* text tells us, by Stalin's central committee itself. Socialist ingenuity had bested the harshest of environments. "In the darkness of the polar night, the sun of human intellect now shines brightly," wrote Maxim Gorky the following year.[3]

Even before the *Chelyuskin* adventure, Socialist Realist mythologies of Arctic heroism were everywhere in the early 1930s: novels, expositions, radio programs, even theatrical plays.[4] Stalin himself had been incarcerated at the Siberian Arctic camp of Kureika between 1914 and 1916, and in 1934 actually delivered a speech at a polar conference in Moscow.[5] There, acting upon his alleged motto that "technology decides everything," Stalin turned to the idea of a Soviet national "Arctic" literature that would thematize human struggle against nature, forming a perfect analogue to the aims of the recently concluded Five-Year Plan.[6] "There are no fortresses the Bolsheviks cannot conquer!" Stalin had (allegedly) written in a telegraph that Lissitzky and Küppers later incorporated into a different *SSSR na stroike* photomontage.[7]

Many of these Soviet imaginings looked specifically to the sixteenth century. While the English navigator Richard Chamberlain had landed on the White Sea coast in 1553, the Russians themselves began their own push into the North and the East during the decades to follow; the Siberian cities of Tiumen and Tobolsk were settled in 1586–87, and in 1600, the trade port of Mangazeia, on the Taz river, was founded from scratch.[8] It was, again, the search for a passage — in this case, the Northeast Passage to the Pacific — that would come to define Russia's anguished cultural negotiations of the Arctic as a colony. In 1619, the tsardom of Michael I actually closed down the sea route to northern Siberia to prevent European officials and went so far as to falsify maps, rendering the Nova Zembla of Barents — an archipelago — as a spit of connected mainland.[9] And much later, because of the craze over the *Chelyuskin*, de Veer's account of the Barents overwintering, examined in Chapter 5, which had long been considered a secret document in the Soviet Union, was translated into Russian for the first time.[10] The book's Russian editor was Vladimir Yulyevich Vize, an explorer who himself had overwintered on the Northeast Passage. Vize wrote a popular history of the Russian Arctic (first published in 1932) that placed the earliest Slavic claims to the Far North back in, indeed, the sixteenth century.[11]

And yet, in 1934, Küppers and Lissitzky offered a visual metaphor of Arctic peril and togetherness. Home and away, close and far, the force of Soviet media — in this case, a copy of *Pravda* and, by extension, the published *SSSR na stroike* — fold the Arctic into domestic programs of technology besting terrain.[12] The montage positions us vertiginously over a domestic scene. Vast distances are collapsed: the caption tells us that "people followed the movements of the heroic vessel from the newspapers and maps."[13] This all was occurring, of course, as forces around Stalin were weaponizing the Arctic to destroy human beings. The Glavnoe Upravlenie Lagerei, the gulag system added more than five new camps in 1933 alone. Labor colonites throughout Siberia were constructed, including on the islands of Vaygach (home of Jan Huygen van Linschoten's idols) and even Nova Zembla. By the late 1940s, anywhere from 10 to 30 percent of labor camps in the system lay inside the Arctic Circle.[14] (It has been contended that a refusal of American help for the *Chelyuskin* operation in 1934 stemmed from concern that nearby gulag transport ships would be discovered.[15])

And yet: *SSSR na stroike*'s Arctic offered homebound individuals the possibility to contemplate alternative lifeworlds. Unlike the West, Russia never conceptualized the Arctic as a contest; even the tsars had no interest in the nineteenth-century race to the North Pole that enthralled America and Europe. The Western fervency for heroism and speed, the tundra mastered by adventuresome gentlemen, was matched after 1917 by the quiet organization of Soviet polar research institutes and scientific expeditions. The Institut po izucheniyu Severa (Institute of Northern Studies), for example, the oldest of its kind, was founded in 1925.[16] (Lenin's central committee actually issued conservation decrees for Arctic forests and White Sea coast as early as 1920.)[17] Soviet forays probed meteorological conditions, tested air and soil, founded pack ice stations, and erected radio transmitters. These were projects often overlapping with gulag construction; long, mundane undertakings organized from afar. State publications emphasized this bureaucratic Arctic in their very design: Lissitzky and Küppers's *Chelyuskin* issue of *SSSR na stroike*, for example, paired airbrushed photos of huddled conferences in Moscow with action shots of the icebound castaways (Figure 7.2). Photomontage here mattered insofar as it was factographic (akin to the *contrafactum*), while at the same time, invested in counterfactuals being plotted back in the warm Kremlin by actors thinking through what was not (yet) real. The Soviet Arctic was a bureaucratic Arctic, a space (as presented to the public) conquered by work and debate.

There was an audacity to all of this. Ruth Gruber, an American photojournalist who was shown inchoate settlements at Igarka and Murmansk in 1935, maintained that only socialism could develop the Far North in proper terms. Touring a research outpost on the Kara Sea, Gruber wrote: "Only a government, unstinting and farsighted, would build a settlement like [this], complete with bathhouse and school and pigsty. No private firm would have the funds or resources or desire to invest billions in a scheme that to private enterprise would seem apocryphal."[18] Gruber, to be sure, was being shown a Potemkin project. But in general, the USSR adopted a far slower, protocol-driven approach to Arctic vastness than contemporaries in the West. Soviet culture heroized explorers, to be sure, but also monumentalized the Far North as a kind technologized grayness, a colossal architecture of science, energy, and terror. Unexpectedly, it is *this* Soviet Arctic that looks back to the earliest Northern voyages. And it is this Arctic that might summon the working mode of certain art practices today.[19]

Bad Activism

Olafur Eliasson and Minik Rosing's beloved *Ice Watch Paris* was installed in November 2015 (Figure 7.3). The work consisted of twelve

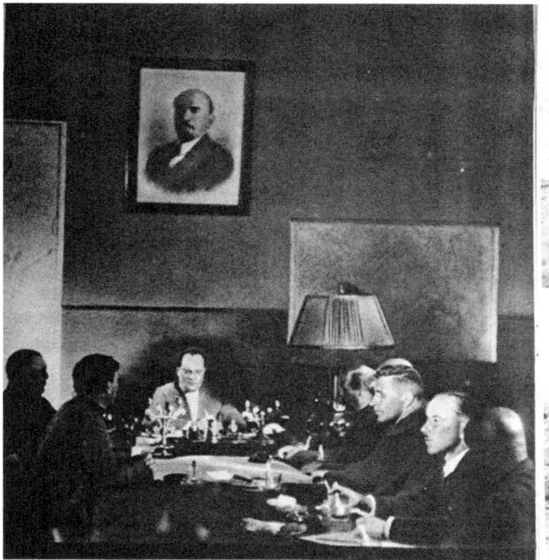

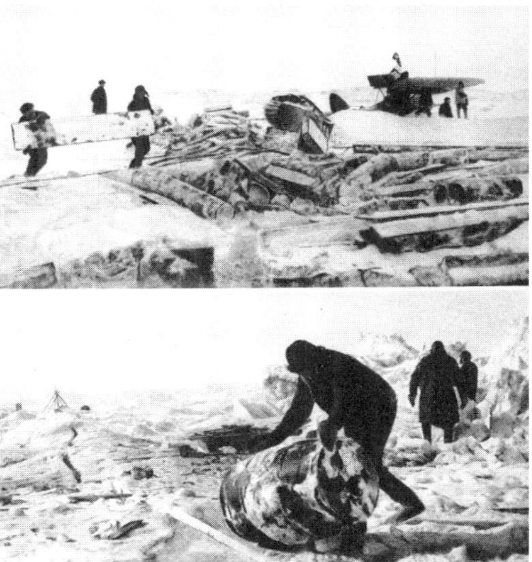

Figure 7.2. Sophie Küppers and El Lissitzky, *SSSR na stroike*, 1934, number 10, pp. 8-9, page 41.3 x 30 cm, Princeton University Library Rare Books.

large blocks of ice harvested from the sea off eastern Greenland. The shards were towed through the North Sea, loaded on freezer trucks, driven to Paris, and then arranged on the Place du Panthéon. The installation coincided with the United Nations Climate Change Conference of 2015. The shards — giant, cumbersome, militantly sculptural — were meant to melt away over time. The ice was arranged in a Stonhenge-like circle, "like a compass," wrote Eliasson, "…It leaves navigation to the people who are inside it. It is a mistake to think that the work of art is the circle of ice — it is the space it invents." This "space" of course, changed materially from day to day *for* the individual beholder. *Ice Watch*, Eliasson's fans claimed, mounted a bold refutation of the efficacy of "data" alone regarding climate change discussion, proffering instead in a kind of phenomenological happening.

Yet as we have seen, in the Far North, cleavages between ideas of environment as an either / or proposition of quantitative experience rarely hold.[20] Eliasson's Paris work entered something of a canon of melting ice as artwork: projects by Francis Alÿs, Rafael Ferrer, and others.[21] Yet the *Ice Watch Paris* installation, of course, was different. Its appearance coincided with the Paris terrorist attacks of November 13–14, 2015. The Place du Panthéon became redoubled as a pilgrimage site, as the melting ice accrued (for some) a poignancy of loss and tears, the fragility of bodies, of spilled blood — the social centrality of such phenomena — all while cleaving to its stated intent of making climate change sensible. Eliasson spoke of the work: "Let's appreciate this unique opportunity — we, the world, can and must act now. Let's transform climate knowledge into climate action. … I hope it will inspire shared commitment to taking climate action."[22] And indeed, for a paralyzed Paris, Eliasson's literalism was romantic and hopeful, the intimacy of a desperate local and global situation made viscerally clear. Over the course of five weeks, the imported sculptures disappeared — a foil to the preservational gesture of the Pantheon nearby. Michael Bloomberg's foundation (which sponsored Eliasson's project in part) lauded the piece as "a great example of how public art can spur people to action."[23] Ecoliterary theorist Timothy Morton

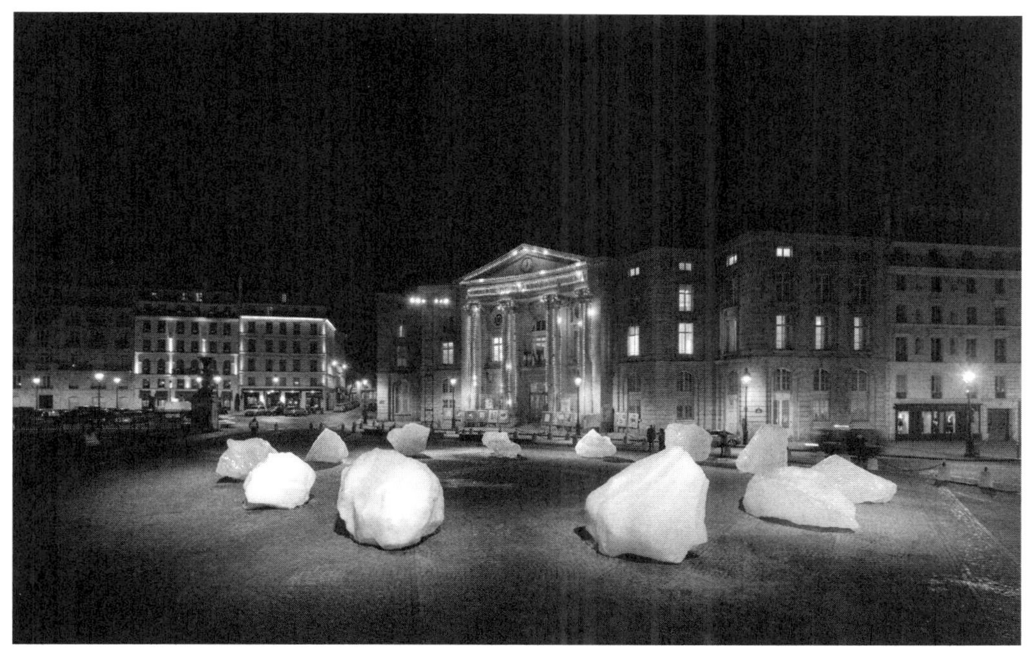

Figure 7.3. Olafur Eliasson and Minik Rosing, *Ice Watch Paris*, 12 blocks of glacial ice, installation view, Place du Panthéon, Paris, 2015.

championed *Ice Watch Paris*'s potential to "start a conversation" about the earth.[24]

But a conversation among whom? What would the actual actions that people might be "spurred" to take look like? One critic pointed out that "the carbon footprint resulting from *Ice Watch Paris* is 30 metric tons (~33 US tons) of carbon dioxide . . . largely based on the transportation of the 12 blocks of ice, weighing a total of 80 metric tons (~88 US tons), from the Nuup Kangerlua fjord outside Nuuk to Paris."[25] Eliasson's piece somewhat inaccurately universalized the idea of the "human" who is actually behind Anthropocene warming. Climate change, of course, affects all spheres of the human differently, a factor that often drops out of much traditional environmentalism's rhetoric of self-righteousness, its mostly First World proclamations about "us." Jason Moore diagnoses this with his concept of the Capitalocene, a paradigm for thinking about the politics of environmentalism that refuses to let neoliberalism universalize global warming's agents.[26] And this might be how any "activist" angle for *Ice Watch Paris* needs rethinking: at the level of spectatorship and production, the piece tended to pivot on a rhetoric wherein the (Arctic) environment is something for or against a broadly "human" self. Even as the piece patronized bourgeois bad conscience, its grandiosity literalized capital's unbudging commitment to overconsumption and waste.

To be crassly schematic: a work such as *Ice Watch Paris* marks a neo-*materialist* turn in Arctic art practice. Current work ostensibly about the poles, as about other environmental precarities, often rehearses certain speculative realist tendencies or object-oriented ontologies. With this there seem to be two main issues at stake. On the one hand, art is manifesting alternatives to (and retrenchments of) mainstream environmental activism — the kind to which we saw Lippard gesturing in 1969. On the other, in the face of climate emergency, practices are querying the real-life place of ecological concerns while hoping, naïvely, that hegemonic capital will "come to its senses." In Eliasson, humans' ontological continuity with things or matter is taken for granted. Not much is specifically asked of us — "being," a kind of theology, replaces epistemology.[27] This is all well intentioned, but ultimately results in a kind of environmental kitsch: we know in advance what these pieces want us to feel. The effect is a kind of extravagant slacktivism.

These are dynamics that have been institutionalized across artcritical discourse. Arguably, they retain special relevance to "environmental" practice — Arctic or otherwise — concerned as it is so concretely with the symbolic qualities of matter *qua* matter. Conspicuous, for example, in all the Inuvik artworks from the *Place as Process* artists from 1969 we examined in Chapter 3 was the relative silence about indigenous presence, and the outright polluting of an environment later understood as fragile. Lippard stopped short of presenting any of the 1969 Inuvik pieces as political in any overt sense, but she did attend to the nominally "ecological" slant (her words) of NETCo's pieces, specifically, vis à vis the Arctic surroundings. The "intricate balances of organisms and their environments"[28] are particularly well queried in the Far North, Lippard wrote. The ruined social and physical state of Inuvik's town fabric was inseparable from ecological concerns, an effect that Lippard, writing in 1969 on the heels of the American civil rights movement, saw as an upshot of economic inequality. The town of Inuvik, in fact, was an "instant" site built by the Canadian government in the 1950s, manned by a transient white executive class and a disenfranchised Inuit population living in appalling housing conditions. A disgusted Lippard described the settlement as "one of Canada's newest slums ... a miserable conglomeration of lean-tos, tents, and shacks."[29]

Here the "Arctic" designated a zone of relative indifference, as it did for Frobisher's crews. As much as a physical landscape to be occupied by conceptual practice, Lippard's 1969 writing cast the Arctic as a terrain of the *social*, a dire and riven one, to be sure. And it was one acquiring new visibility just as it became less different than the rest of the industrialized world. The *Place as Process* works were interested in the tension between lived site and myth. But Lippard's *Hudson Review* piece found itself unexpectedly distracted by the real-world exigencies of Arctic sites outside the gallery. Arctic "dematerializa-tion," after such an experience, was a process within art *and* life.

Like Ellis's chunky woodcut (see Figure 1.1), both Lippard's black-and-white photos and the *SSSR na stroike* layouts *constructed*, rather than patly *documented* the various situations staged in and by the Arctic via information networks. There might be an unexpected historicity here, but also a paradox: material such as Eliasson's in Paris helps mobilize a public in its icy actuality and metacommentary about it. But as much as bits of Greenland expensively dragged to Paris reveal an inconvenient truth, they also franchise critique and then largely walk away.

The state of Eliasson's piece summarizes the situation facing most works dealing with climate change today: art's capacity either to "raise awareness" about the (Arctic) crisis — often by seeing a bunch of stuff that is supposed to change our minds (struggling polar bears, speeding Greenpeace Zodiac boats) — or to interrogate its actual existing (and unevenly distributed) effects upon social spheres. Works in the former category, such as Eliasson's project, retain only the best intentions, but they often fail to develop any kind of new critical language to connect a concrete work and an ostensible cause. Instead, we get a miasma of "moving" Arctic experiences that almost look back to Friedrich — that rely upon a very traditional sublime. While sincere, such works remain content to leave unplumbed the idea of what we are supposed to do next, keeping it business as usual in the (art) world.

However, efforts to query the Arctic environment in more complex ways exist. In 2006, the Center for Land Use Interpreta-tion (CLUI) staged *Ultima Thule*, a fixed-video installation set in extreme Northern Greenland on a radar surveillance base (Figures 7.4 and 7.5). In an arrangement of photographs and videos at the National Museum in Nuuk, the Center traced networks of listen-ing devices from the giant air base that monitor everything from missiles to debris in the earth's upper atmosphere. Less about the Arctic than about its militarization, the document-heavy instal-lation was viewed by only a few hundred people. It agnostically framed the Cold War as a conflict of the unseen — radar, submarines, radio transmissions, front lines across the North Pole. The project decentered expressive argument, instead aggregating data and photodocumentation. What emerged was a quiet vision of how a site-specific, static Cold War Arctic of missiles and lines had given way to a Warm War Arctic of supertankers and underwater land claims.[30] What emerged, perhaps, was an Arctic of urgency without pathos.

Defining itself as a "research organization involved in exploring, examining, and understanding land and landscape issues," CLUI has quietly pursued the interpretation not of the earth, but of specific human interventions *with* the earth across various landscapes since the 1990s. As with Greenland's Arctic tundra, the Center looks not at places that are conventionally beautiful, but at places where people actually work and live. CLUI intends dead-serious social practices for a world in which, as one critic puts it, "the ability to change people's minds through argument [is] seen as [an] exhausted mode."[31] As with the *Ultima Thule* piece, most CLUI work is not blatantly critical either of the human alteration of the earth or of its preservation, as director Matthew Coolidge points out: "Humans are a part of nature and nature shouldn't be something considered exclusive of humans."[32] Discarded with this practice are ecologies simply of mankind versus environment, or humans "in" nature. These pairs are exchanged for ecologies of politics, ecologies of information, ecologies of capital, and ecologies of history. "There is something performative in how the Center refuses to allow their activities to be categorized exclusively as art, geology, land reclamation, or political activism," states historian Cornelia Butler, "preferring instead an amalgam of these."[33] The Center deploys an archival aesthetic — maybe even like that of Olaus Magnus. Yet CLUI's *Ultima Thule* installation turns the idea *of* the archive on its head. Offered a reading of the Arctic landscape that dispenses with both the tragic and the scenic, we are spurred to rethink what, in fact, we understand the object of "environmental" activism to be. And work such as the Center's *Ultima Thule*, that is, might compel because it doesn't brandish itself as art — at least not

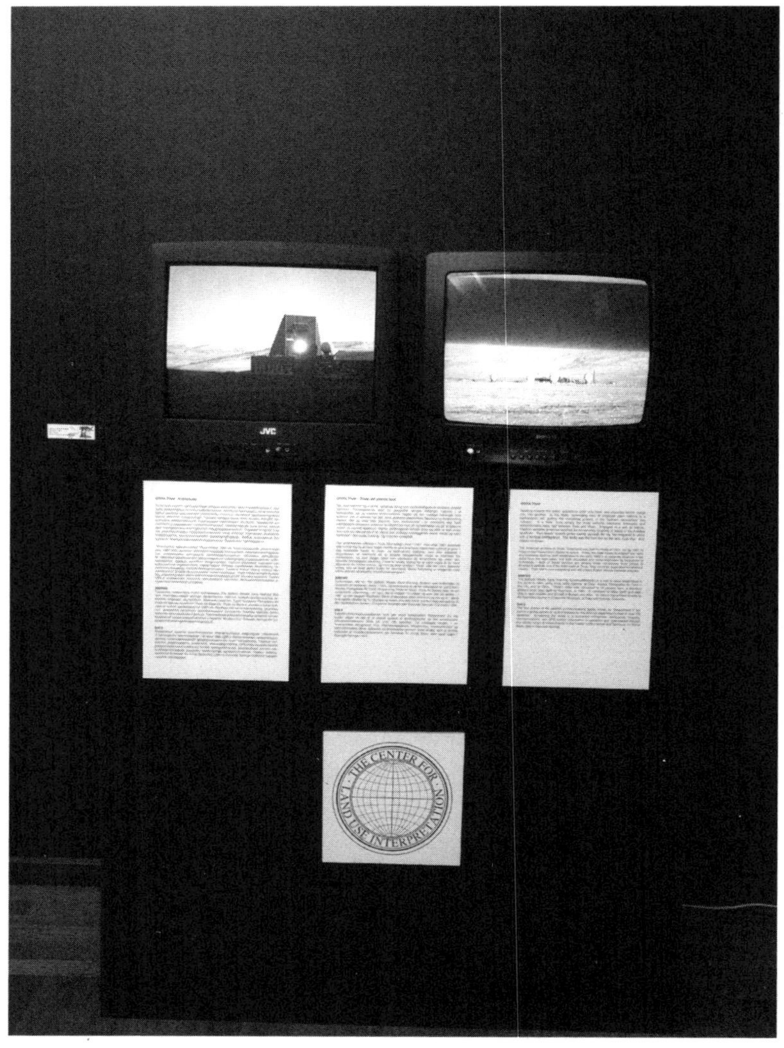

Figure 7.4. Center for Land Use Interpretation, *Ultima Thule*, 2006, installation view, two videos on podium, each a two-minute loop from *Rethinking Nordic Colonialism: A Postcolonial Exhibition Project in Five Acts* (2006, Greenland National Museum and Archives, Nuuk) curated by Kuratorisk Aktion.

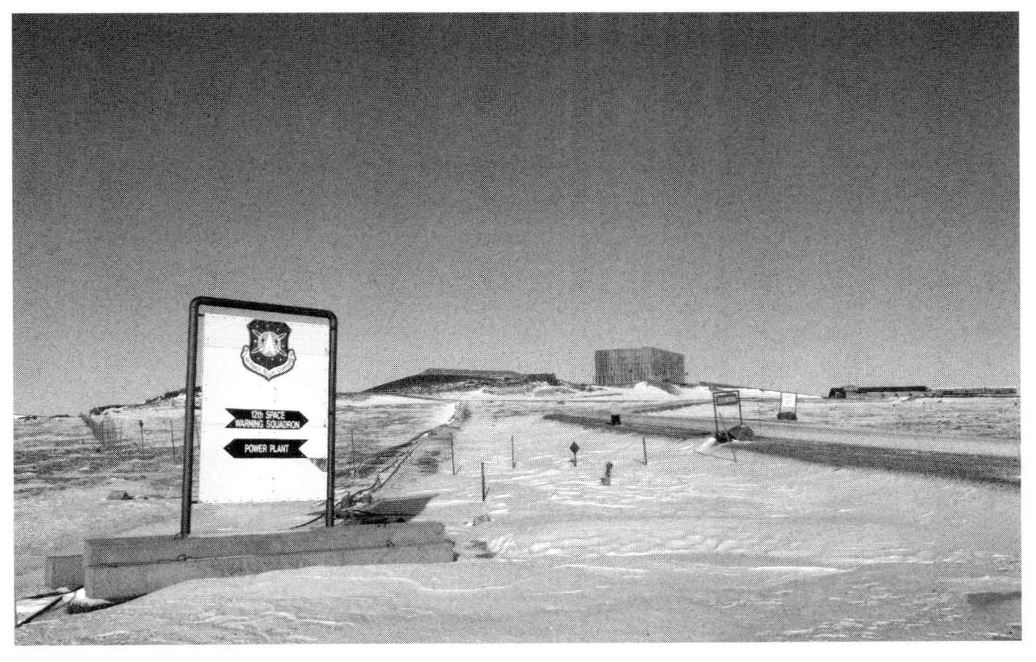

Figure 7.5. Center for Land Use Interpretation, *Ultima Thule* (detail).

in the conventional way. It suggests that the critical work of "Arctic" art is not making stuff (even tragic stuff) visible and *meaningful*, but is, perhaps, in interrogating the *limits* of Arctic visibility, of Arctic meaning, via practices that academia and the art world (as complicit in polar melting as any other capital-based forces today) cannot easily frame.

In comparison with *Ice Watch Paris*'s Greenland, the Greenland we get in CLUI's *Ultima Thule* is remote, softly anonymous, decentered, hard to get to, unironically bureaucratic, oriented toward the permanent. It is kind of boring. But it might be far more environmentally sensitive than Eliasson's installation. Sensitive not just in the sense of far fewer natural resources used (no tankers or flat-bed trucks here, only fifty-eight photographs and a website), but in its disavowal of any aesthetic of profundity. Like other CLUI projects, *Ultima Thule* is invested in tactical knowing of the naturescape, swapping out romantic sentiment for what we might call an "administrative sublime."[34] The arctic project, Coolidge claims, is concerned with something as unsexy as "preparedness." "As we know that what we anticipate," CLUI claims, "we in some way manifest," Of course, such studied ambiguity runs the risk of sounding a lot like miasmic neoliberal shrugging at intellectual commitment of any kind. And yet the center rigorously complicates any fetishization of "place" as a site of Heideggerian intimacy with the local. As with its other works, CLUI often reads sites such as the Arctic as networks, ones that can fail, decay, disconnect. In its sprawling collection of photographs, CLUI charts the environmentally unexceptional: shopping malls, sewer pipes, and water towers. Through the Center's practice, we think about land such as that of the Arctic, less as experience than as archive — again, like Olaus Magnus. CLUI's is a preservation operation, yes, but one far more engaged with the notion of nature as something everyday, rather than an excursionary respite.

Strange Things to Men

A century ago, Kazimir Malevich had imagined a tenser relationship between geography and critique. In April of 1919, five of Malevich's

White on White paintings appeared at the Tenth State Exhibition in Moscow (Figure 7.6). In an accompanying essay, Malevich wrote of "a new color realism . . . a system, cold and durable . . . mobilized unsmilingly by philosophical thought."[35] The white in his pictures, Malevich explained, is the serious "representation" of infinity — a floating of forms in colored space.[36] This bleached materiality insisted upon the idea of welcoming escape and airborne flight: "Swim into the abyss. I have set up the semaphores of Suprematism. I have overcome the lining of the coloured sky, torn it down and into the bag thus formed, put colour, tying it up with a knot. Swim in the white abyss, infinity is before you," he declared.[37] Suprematism, as Malevich presented it, was the ultimate imagining of situations unknown: "I have come out into the white. Follow me," he wrote.[38] The white pictures instrumentalized color as an immediate, homespun force buffered by the real world, a "semaphore" of earthly potentialities outside of bourgeois legibility. Malevich, that is, embraced a metaphor of transcendence through works that remained physically brute and frozen: heavy, obdurate stoppages. As he put it in 1916, replying to a critic: "What does warmth have to do with creative work? Can one really not create in the cold, and coldly create?"[39]

In fact, in the chilly and differently iconoclastic Flemish 1560s, Pieter Bruegel once finished a landcape composition by flecking it with hundreds of white spots, representations of snow (see Figure 6.14). These falling flakes all but blocked out the New Testament scene beneath.[40] As in Malevich, the poetics of apparent blanking here summoned a new lifeworld, rather than cancelling one out. In Moscow, the *White on White* works brandished their status as objects smeared with chunky rifts of blanched pigment, heavy varnish layered over preexisting compositions.[41] This white — "cold and durable," as Malevich put it — offered a material invitation, not to a mystical neverland of reference or expression ("the scum of interiority" was a Malevich phrase), but, in true revolutionary fashion, to the transplanting of some elsewhere *here*.[42]

But by 1933, it had fallen to Malevich's pupil Lissitzky to dramatize a different kind of chill. A montage from *SSSR na stroike* that year

Figure 7.6. Kazimir Malevich, *Suprematist Composition: White on White*, 1918, oil on canvas, 79.4 x 79.4 cm, The Museum of Modern Art, New York, 1935. Acquisition confirmed in 1999 by agreement with the Estate of Kazimir Malevich and made possible with funds from the Mrs. John Hay Whitney Bequest (by exchange), 817.1935.

depicts an island landscape in the Barents Sea, now photographed from ground level (Figure 7.7). We again confront a small map inset in shadow, a wall of ice eerily dark, its foreground pushed up against the periodical page. The photograph, as a tiny caption at lower right tells us, was taken by geophysicist Rudolf Samoylovich (b. 1881), a veteran of more than twenty Arctic expeditions, including one by airship. In a strange echo of Barents, Samoylovich was among the crew of the Soviet icebreaker *Krasin*, which, in the same body of water as Nova Zembla, had to overwinter. Samoylovich was one of the many Soviet explorers to reflect, in writing, on the psychological effects of the Far North. As he said to a US reporter in the 1920s, "The Arctic does strange things to men."[43] And Samoylovich ultimately underwent a grimly typical Soviet Arctic experience. He fell afoul of one of Stalin's undersecretaries. Five years after his photograph for *SSSR na stroike*, Samoylovich was tried for вредительство ("wrecking") and sent to a Northern camp at Kolyma.[44] In 1938, he was sentenced to a decade of hard labor. In 1940, he was shot.[45]

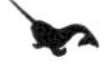

One might say that two of the most significant Arctic technologies of the twentieth century were Soviet — the icebreaker and the gulag, paired engineerings of motion and confinement, metaphors of struggle against and instrumentalization of an impossibly hostile environment. And these technologies insisted that Arctic failure and success, punishment and liberation, murder and salvation, perversely and necessarily coexist. So many early modern explorers' accounts — from Ellis's to Frobisher's — read as reflexive struggles to separate the human and the environmental realms from one another (in the case of Barents's *Behouden Huys* and the Rijksmuseum paper project, literally). The sixteenth-century Europeans' continued faith in technology's ability to keep them apart from hostile weather and seas was based on a denial. It sustained a full century of human investment and loss. And it bred a negative pictorialism that no longer trusted the (Platonic) idea of the image as a pat semblance, imitation,

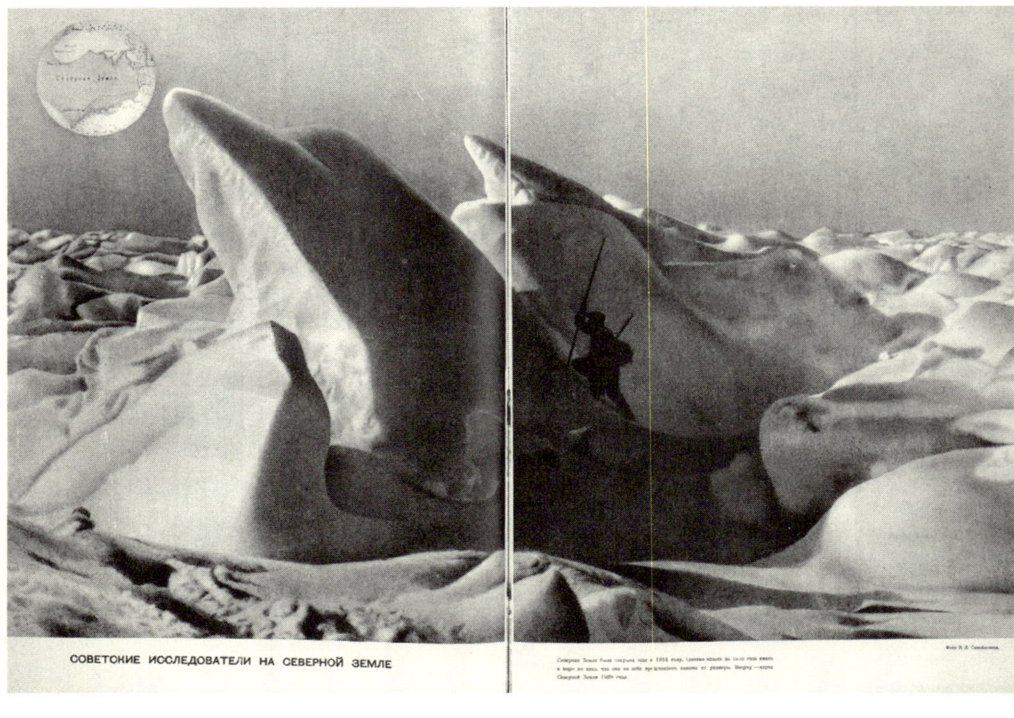

Figure 7.7. Sophie Küppers and El Lissitzky, *SSSR na stroike*, 1933, number 9, pp. 22-23, page 41.3 x 30 cm, Princeton University Library Rare Books.

or optical counterpart to some world — a doubling, that is, of something else. Of course, this unconscious pictorialism had always been there. The Reformation was just one more resuscitation of Old Testament anxieties. Yet Arctic exploration — of North America, Asia, and Europe — laid bare an entire *world* of violently disfigured sight. It cast into Reformation Europe (quietly) an environmental situation whose *physical* unsettledness strangely summoned the same *conceptual* disarray of the senses that iconoclasm was opening out. It was visible, but in a realm of degraded visibility. It was this terrifying — but hopeful — condition that both Soviet and later European Arctic culture embraced.

By summoning formal trends and transitions that occur between various conditions of the nonfigural around the Arctic, from Bruegel to Malevich, I mean not to chart some ineluctable (painterly) trajectory of formal abstraction. Rather, I seek to dispute the characterization of the early modern era as a homogeneous, unconflicted image culture that the nineteenth century is often alleged to fragment. This is hardly new. In the wake of other investigations of the "dead" image in late medieval Europe, the preceding has tried to look beneath an early modern episteme synonymous with easy visibility.[46] Strange trees, wondrous animals, and bountiful waterways — *lively* things — tend to be the things we talk about when we talk optimistically about a global Renaissance. And these were bright and desirable constituents of New World encounters. But naturally dead places were equally important. Put into this light, the lavish story of Renaissance curiosity is just one among many. For the Arctic was a place of difficulty. The Arctic image is awkward. It might be more cognate with what Hito Steyerl calls the "poor image" of today, the bastardized, uncertain, quasi-readable "blur" that, in a rich, hi-res world, "insists upon its own imperfection." But its speed is glacial rather than breathless. The Arctic image formed a crucial part of early narratives of art and exploration precisely because, as a kind of fugitive poetics, "it is a visual idea in its very becoming," to use Steyerl's words; hardly, that is, "an image at all."[47]

Much of the outrage characterizing the tone of environmental advocacy today, while well placed, participates in the mythic sense of Arctic nature as a sanctuary — something pristine and demarcated. While adoration of natural experiences "away from it all" remains an arguably American obsession,[48] perhaps it is the Romantic idea of awestruck human *separateness* from the Far North that imputes the Arctic (and elsewhere) an undeserved foreignness that once nourished wonder (think Frederic Church) and now licenses exploitation (Prudhoe Bay, for example).[49] This nature / culture fissure might also have particular import for the history of art in neoliberalism, with its compulsive need always to rebrand the very idea of wilderness.[50] Once the image of the Far North was that of a featureless expanse, an abstraction that is all but measurable, speaking to a language of colonization. In more recent years, that image has (again) come to abet corporate resource extraction, which continues to benefit from the myth of some Nordic tabula rasa, as if keeping alive Frobisher's quest for ore. Maybe today, "Arctic" is better imagined as an artistic condition, practice, or mode, rather than as a physical place or a cold feeling. Understanding the Far North as something different from a "landscape" — that is, paradoxically — might undo this dream of its otherness, might move its understanding away from purely ethnographical or ecological discourses, both from past times and today.

Consciousness of the unseen — not as secret, but as tool — has always remained vital to the various fashionings and betrayals of New Worlds. The Arctic, like the Soviet or the Protestant future, can often be presented only by a vision born of a forced blindness.[51] It is unnecessary to point out that our contemporary Arctic is not so passive a foe. From Houston to Shanghai, it is polar water that now acts as a real-life *material* invader. (It is estimated that if all the Arctic land ice in the Nuuk shelf melted, as it continues to do, the earth's seas would rise twenty-six feet.)[52] Yet the Arctic's attritional lethality is undramatic, of a slowness that capital's ceaseless need for visibility is reluctant to engage.[53] And where the Arctic once swallowed up travelers in Spitsbergen, in Baffin Island, in Nova Zembla, in Kolyma, far away, the Arctic today engages in a quiet, irrevocable advance, everywhere, meltingly unformed. It is, as Ellis realized, literally impossible to fix in a single view.

The early moderns were prescient in their fears and hopes for the Far North, as were later nations in their realization that, in terms of the Arctic, there are no fortresses. The fact that there are now forest fires in Greenland is wearingly unsurprising.[54] No longer Ellis's "perplexitie" or even Malevich's "white abyss," the Arctic today can no longer be imaged in any stable sense as some passive realm "out there," some far-off utopia or hell. The former ice is physically here, right now. It is all too late. The Arctic is coming for *you*.

Acknowledgments

Jonathan Crary believed in this project when it seemed lost, and Hal Foster first set the book on its path to Zone. I remain humbled by the sustained confidence of both.

Jan de Hond generously allowed me full access to the Barents prints and archives in the Rijksmuseum, and offered many invaluable suggestions. Anne Goldgar corrected errors and unselfishly shared her own (far superior) writing on Nova Zembla. Susan Dackerman, Joseph Koerner, and Amy Powell — whose own work shaped the book's thinking about absences and images in many ways — offered key suggestions at a Getty gathering in early 2017. The office of Gloria Culver of the College of Arts and Sciences at the University of Rochester graciously supported image rights for the whole project. And because of Rachel Haidu, this book came to mark a beginning, rather than an end.

Meighan Gale, effortlessly, transformed my verbiage into a real book, and Bud Bynack saved me from many mistakes. Gina Broze is the reason any images here exist. Julie Fry designed a cover that is hushedly perfect. Michael Gaudio, Jennifer Roberts, and Rebecca Zorach suffered through the entire manuscript and helped everything — everything — sound less tired. I am indebted to those audiences who took time to critique early versions of this material, in Bergen, Hamburg, Helsinki, Los Angeles, Madison, Montreal, Munich, New Orleans, Saõ Paulo, and Williamstown. Alexander Marr and David Young Kim made vital editing time possible at Cambridge and Penn. Kimberley Ann Deal and Charles Thompson IV influenced the book's earliest formation, albeit indirectly. Many conversations, over many years, quietly impacted this book's content. I am grateful to Mieke Bal, Janet Berlo, Rachel Burke, Lauren Cannady, Jalen Chang, Matthew Coolidge, Ashton Fancy, Caroline Fowler, Marius Hauknes, Anne Heuer, Barbara Heuer, Jared Heuer, Robert Heuer II, Schuyler Heuer, Elizabeth Alice Honig, Lucy Lippard, Gillian Mackenzie, Abigail Newman, Fernanda Pitta, Larry Silver, Michael Sullivan, Angela Vanhalen, and above all, Stephanie Porras. Elizabeth Anne Monroe facilitated the project in ways she does not know. Shira N. Brisman gave more of herself to this book than it ever deserved.

Matthew Jesse Jackson, Nina Dubin, Sarah Jane Jackson, John Spelman, Lisa Conathan, Elizabeth Spelman, and Everett Spelman made the final writing of the manuscript an unexpected joy; Matthew, particularly, deserves thanks for salvaging the book's Soviet content, and this author's sense of worth. Michael Ann Holly and Keith Moxey constantly assured me that the project was not, in fact, a terrible idea. Over and over again, they opened to it their many doors.

Daniel Pearson modeled my writing. And, more than anyone, Jeehee Hong reminded me, in the best way, that one need not be settled to live, think, and love.

This book may seem bleak, bearing the imprint of darkened, uncertain years. Yet it was always guided by a happy star. I dedicate it to Helen Natalie Frances, *lux mea in tenebris*.

Notes

CHAPTER ONE: WE COULD NOT SEE OUT OF OUR EYES

1. Thomas Ellis, *A true report of the third and last voyage into Meta incognita: achieued buy the worthie Capteine, M. Martine Frobisher Esquire* (London: Thomas Dawson, 1578), fol. A7v. The sole intact copy of this tiny book is in the Huntington Library, San Marino, CA, inv. HEH 18070. On the various other accounts of the third Frobisher voyage, see James McDermott, "Frobisher's 1578 Voyage: Early Eyewitness Accounts of English Ships in Arctic Seas," *Polar Record* 32.183 (1996), pp. 325–34. Aside from this book, nothing is known of Thomas Ellis himself.

2. British Library, London: Landsdowne MS, 100/1, fol. 9r.

3. Sharat K. Roy, "The History and Petrography of Frobisher's 'Gold Ore,'" *Geological Series of Field Museum of Natural History* 7.2 (May 1937), pp. 21–38.

4. Ellis, *A true report of the third and last voyage into Meta Incognita*, fol. 1r. The iceberg woodcut and its accompanying description were cut out of the better-known transcription of Ellis that appears in Richard Hakluyt, *The principal navigations, voiages, traffiques and discoueries of the English nation* (London: George Bishop, Ralph Newberie and Robert Barker, 1600), pp. 630–35. (Hereafter *PN.*)

5. Tzvetan Todorov, *The Conquest of America: The Question of the Other*, trans. Richard Howard (Norman: Oklahoma University Press, 1984), esp. pp. 247–54.

6. Arthur Hall (1539?–1605), *A letter sent by F. A. touchyng the proceedings in a priuate quarell and vnkindnesse betweene Arthur Hall, and Melchisedech Mallerie gentleman . . .* [H. Bynneman for Arthur Hall, 1576?], fols. F2r–F2v.

7. C. C. A. Gosch (ed.), *Danish Arctic Expeditions, 1605 to 1620, in Two Books. Book I. The Danish Expeditions to Greenland in 1605, 1606, and 1607: To Which is Added Captain James Hall's Voyage to Greenland in 1612; Book II. The Expedition of Captain Jens Munk to Hudson's*

Bay in Search of a North-West Passage in 1619–20, 2 vols. (London: Printed for the Hakluyt Society, 1897), vol. 1, p. 30.

8. George Best, "The thirde Voyage," p. 28, in *A True Discourse of the late voyages of discoverie, for the finding of a passage to Cathaya, by the Northvveast, vnder the conduct of Martin Frobisher Generall deuided into three books* (London: Henry Bynnyman, 1578).

9. *Ibid.*, p. 21.

10. See J. C. H. King and Henrietta Lidchi (eds.), *Imaging the Arctic* (Seattle: University of Washington Press, 1998).

11. Angela Byrne, *Geographies of the Romantic North: Science, Antiquarianism, and Travel* (London: Palgrave, 2013), p. 6.

12. Ernest B. Gilman, *Iconoclasm and Piety in the English Reformation* (Chicago: University of Chicago Press, 1986), p. 190.

13. Stephen Greenblatt, "Shakespeare Bewitched," in Jeffrey Cox and Larry Reynolds (eds.), *New Historical Literary Study: Essays on Reproducing Texts, Representing History* (Princeton: Princeton University Press, 1993), p. 121.

14. Mary Fuller, "The Poetics of a Cold Climate," *Terrae Incognitae* 30 (1998), pp. 41–53.

15. Stephen Greenblatt, *Marvelous Possessions* (Chicago: University of Chicago Press, 1991), p. 116.

16. Eric Wilson, *The Spiritual History of Ice: Romanticism, Science, and the Imagination* (New York: Macmillan, 2003), p. 8.

17. Bernd Roeck, *Der Morgen der Welt: Geschichte der Renaissance* (Munich: Beck, 2017), p. 918.

18. J. F. W. Negendank, C. Brüchmann, and U. Kienel, "Die 'kleine Eiszeit' und ihre Abbildung im Klimaarchiv Binnensee," in *Die "Kleine Eiszeit": Holländische Landschaftsmalerei im 17. Jahrhundert*, exh. cat. (Berlin: SMzBPK, 2001), pp. 55–63; Christian Pfister, "The Little Ice Age: Thermal and Wetness Indices for Central Europe," *Journal of Interdisciplinary History* 10.4 (Spring 1980), p. 685.

19. But see Robert Rosenblum's often overlooked and not entirely unproblematic *Modern Painting and the Northern Romantic Tradition: Friedrich to Rothko* (London: Thames and Hudson, 1975). On Minimalism's quite different aesthetic of emptiness, see Robert Slifkin, "The Empty Room and the Ends of Man" in *Experience*, ed. Alexander Nemerov (Chicago: Terra Foundation, 2017), pp. 156–87.

20. Chauncey C. Loomis, "After the Arctic Sublime," in C. Knoepflmacher and G. B. Tennyson (eds.), *Nature and the Victorian Imagination* (Berkeley: University of California Press, 1977), p. 99.

21. Terry Eagleton, *Ideology of the Aesthetic* (London: Blackwell, 1991), p. 54.

22. Jason W. Moore, "Nature and the Transition from Feudalism to Capitalism," *Review* 26.2 (2003), pp. 97–172.

23. Jeffrey Knapp, *An Empire Nowhere: England, America, and Literature from Utopia to the Tempest* (Berkeley: University of California Press, 1992); Mary C. Fuller, *Remembering the Early Modern Voyage: English Narratives in the Age of European Expansion* (New York: Palgrave Macmillan, 2008); Peter Mancall, *Nature and Culture in the Early Modern Atlantic* (Philadelphia: University of Pennsylvania Press, 2017).

24. David B. Quinn, "Columbus and the North: England, Iceland, and Ireland," *William and Mary Quarterly*, 3rd ser., 49 (January 1992), pp. 278–92.

25. Michael Gaudio, *Engraving the Savage: The New World and Techniques of Civilization* (Minneapolis: University of Minnesota Press, 2008).

26. "Arthur Barlowe's Discourse of the First Voyage" in David Beers Quinn (ed.), *The Roanoke Voyages*, 2 vols. (London: Hakluyt Society, 1955), vol. 1, p. 100; on Barlowe, see also Mark Koch, "Ruling the World: The Cartographic Gaze in Elizabethan Accounts of the New World," *Early Modern Literary Studies* 4.2 (September 1998), pp. 1–39.

27. Ellis, in *PN*, p. 632.

28. Robert Boyle, *New experiments and observations touching cold, or, An experimental history of cold begun: to which are added an examen of antiperistasis and an examen of Mr. Hobs's doctrine about cold* (London: John Crook, 1665).

29. Joyce E. Chaplin, *Technology, the Body, and Science on the Anglo-American Frontier, 1500–1676* (Cambridge, MA: Harvard University Press, 2003).

30. Christopher Jacob Ries, "The Arctic One-to-One?" *Arctic* (Esbjerg: Louisiana Museum of Modern Art, 2013), p. 40.

31. See Mark Monmonier, *Rhumb Lines and Map Wars* (Chicago: University of Chicago Press, 2004), pp. 8–9.

32. See, for example, Grete K. Hovelsrud, Birger Poppel, Bob Van Oort, and James D. Reist, "Arctic Societies, Cultures, and Peoples in a Changing Cryosphere," *Ambio* 40 (2011), pp. 100–110.

33. Alexander Kluge, *Wer sich traut, reißt die Kälte vom Pferd* (Frankfurt: Suhrkamp, 2010), p. 4.

34. Lisa Jardine, *Worldly Goods: A New History of the Renaissance* (New York: W. W. Norton, 1998); Lisa Jardine and Jerry Brotton, *Global Interests: Renaissance Art between East and West* (Ithaca: Cornell University Press, 2000); Jerry Brotton, *Trading Territories: Mapping the Early Modern World* (London: Reaktion, 1997). Critiques of this global claim have come

from art-historical and environmental voices, among others. See, for example: Amanda Cohen-Aponte, "Decolonizing the Global Renaissance: A View from the Andes," in Daniel Savoy (ed.), *The Globalization of Renaissance Art: A Critical Review* (Leiden: Brill, 2017), pp. 67-94, and Jason W. Moore, *Capitalism in the Web of Life* (London: Verso, 2015).

35. Tim Ingold, "Matter against Materiality," *Archaeological Dialogues* 14.1 (2007), pp. 1-16.

36. Shira Brisman, *Albrecht Dürer and the Epistolary Mode of Address* (Chicago: University of Chicago Press, 2016).

37. Ken Hiltner, *What Else Is Pastoral?: Renaissance Literature and the Environment* (Ithaca: Cornell University Press, 2011); James Nisbet, *Ecologies, Environments, and Energy Systems in Art of the 1960s and 1970s* (Cambridge, MA: MIT Press, 2014).

CHAPTER TWO: THE STARS DOWN TO EARTH

1. J. L. Berggren, R. S. D. Thomas (eds.), *Euclid's Phaenomena: A Translation and Study of a Hellenistic Treatise in Spherical Astronomy* (London: Mathematical Society, 2006), p. 44. On the practical importance of a geometric Arctic and Antarctic for the construction of globes in antiquity, see Otto Neugebauer, *A History of Ancient Mathematical Astronomy*, 3 vols. (Berlin: Springer, 1975), vol. 2, pp. 582, 733, 865-66.

2. Margaret Small, "From Jellied Seas to Open Waterways: Redefining the Northern Limit of the Knowable World," *Renaissance Studies* 21.3 (2007), p. 317.

3. Alois Schlachter, *Der Globus, seine Entstehung und Verwendung in der Antike nach den literarischen Quellen und den Darstellungen in der Kunst* (Leipzig: B. G. Teubner. 1927), p. 46.

4. Strabo, *Geography* 2.2.2, in *The Geography of Strabo*, trans. Horace Leonard Jones, 8 vols. (Cambridge, MA: Harvard University Press, 1917-1932), vol. 2, p. 365.

5. Roman coins from the third century ce have been found in eastern Iceland. See Duane W. Roller, *Through the Pillars of Hercules: Greco-Roman Exploration of the Atlantic* (New York: Routledge, 2006), p. 83 n. 194.

6. Strabo, *Geography* 2.4.1; Pytheas fragment 7a; the textual fragments of Pytheas appear in Christina Horst Roseman, *Pytheas of Massila: On the Ocean* (Chicago: Acres Publishing, 1994). On these, see Richard Hennig, *Terrae Incognitae: Eine Zusammenstellung und kritische Bewertung der wichtigsten vorkolumbischen Entdeckungsreisen an Hand der darüber vorliegenden Originalberichte*, 2nd ed., 4 vols. (Leiden: Brill, 1936), vol. 1, pp. 120-36.

7. Small, "From Jellied Seas to Open Waterways," p. 321. The literature on Pytheas's (purported) journey is extensive. For an overview, see R. Chevallier, "The Greco-Roman Conception of the North from Pytheas to Tacitus," *Arctic* 37.4 (December 1984), pp. 341-46,

and Germain Aujac, "L'Île du Thulé, de Pythéas à Ptolémée," in Monique de Pelletier (ed.), *Geographie du monde au Moyen Âge et à la Renaissance* (Paris: CTHS, 1989), pp. 181–90. For hypothetical retracings of Pytheas's route, potentially though the Shetlands and the Faroes, see J. Oliver Thomson, *History of Ancient Geography* (Cambridge: Cambridge University Press, 1948), pp. 143–51.

8. Herodotus, *The Histories* 4.18.3. *Erēmos alēthōs* also can designate a "desert that has never been crossed." See the excellent James S. Romm, *The Edges of the Earth in Ancient Thought: Geography, Exploration, and Fiction* (Princeton: Princeton University Press, 1992), pp. 36–38.

9. Herodotus, *The Histories* 4.31.

10. Plato, *Phaedo* 112b.

11. Walter Benjamin, "The Mummerehlen," in Howard Eiland and Michael W. Jennings (eds.), *Walter Benjamin: Selected Writings, Volume 3: 1935–1938* (Cambridge, MA: Harvard University Press, 2006), pp. 390–92. Adorno speaks about Benjamin's fascination with snow globes: "Small glass balls containing a landscape upon which snow fell when shook were among his favorite objects." See Theodor W. Adorno, *Prisms*, trans. Samuel and Shierry Weber (Cambridge, MA: MIT Press, 1981), p. 233. Benjamin was purchasing Schneekugeln in Paris as early as 1926; see Gershom Scholem and Theodor W. Adorno (eds.), *The Correspondence of Walter Benjamin, 1910–1940*, trans. Manfred R. Jacobson and Evelyn M. Jacobson (Chicago: University of Chicago Press, 1994), p. 297.

12. Roller, *Through the Pillars of Hercules*, pp. 61–62.

13. Strabo, quoted in Susan Stephens and John J. Winkler (eds.), *Ancient Greek Novels: The Fragments* (Princeton: Princeton University Press, 1995), pp. 106–107.

14. Antonius Diogenes, *Incredible Things Beyond Thule*, in Stephens and Winkler (eds.), *Ancient Greek Novels*, p. 107.

15. *The Letters of Synesius of Cyrene*, trans. Augustine Fitzgerald (London: Oxford University Press, 1926), p. 244.

16. "Testimonia," in Stephens and Winkler (eds.), *Ancient Greek Novels*, pp. 120–21, doc. 4.

17. Tacitus, *Germania* 2.1, in *Tacitus*, vol. 1, trans. M. Hutton (Cambridge MA: Loeb Classical Library, 1970), p. 130.

18. Tacitus, *Agricola*, 10, quoted in Romm, *The Edges of the Earth in Ancient Thought*, p. 148.

19. Monique Mund-Dopchie, "L'ultima Thulé' de Pytheas dans les textes de la Renaissanceet du XVIIe siecle," *Humanistica Lovaniensia* 41 (1992), pp. 134–58; Mund-Dopchie, "La survie littéraire de la Thulé de Pythéas [Un exemple de la permanence des schémas antiques dans la culture européenne]," *L'antiquité classique* 59 (1990), pp. 79–97.

20. As sourced through Pliny; see J. Goropius Becanus [Jan van Gorp van der Beke], *Origines Antwerpianae, sive Cimmeriorum Becceselana novem libris complexa* (Antwerp: Christoffel Plantin, 1569), p. 66.

21. My thanks to Jeanne Nüchterlein for clarifying how this fixing occurred. Personal correspondence, April 26, 2017.

22. Mund-Dopchie, "L' L'ultima Thulé' de Pytheas," pp. 154–57.

23. Hennig, *Terrae Incognitae*, vol. 4, pp. 94–96. For the original Greek, see Jerker Blomqvist, "The Geography of the Baltic in Greek Eyes — from Ptolemy to Laskaris Kananos," in Bettina Amden et al. (eds.), *Noctes Atticae: 34 Articles on Graeco-Roman Antiquity and Its Nachleben: Studies Presented to Jøergen Mejer on His Sixtieth Birthday, March 18, 2002* (Copenhagen: Lund Unversity Press, 2002), pp. 45–47.

24. Vienna, Österreichische Nationalbibliothek, hist. gr. 113, fol. 175r, translated in: T. Hägg, "A Byzantine Visit to Bergen: Laskaris Kananos and His Description of the Baltic and North Sea Region," *Graeco-Arabica* 9–10 (2004), p. 186.

25. Thule, the period of cosmography

> Doth vaunt of Hecla, whose sulphureous fire
>
> Doth melt the frozen clime and thaw the sky;
>
> Trinacrian Etna's flames ascend not higher:
>
> These things seem wondrous, yet more wondrous I,
>
> Whose heart with fear doth freeze, with love doth fry.

Thomas Weelkes, *Madrigals of 5 and 6 parts: apt for the viols and voices* (London: Thomas Morley, 1600), fols. D1v–D2r.

26. The phrase appears in the writing of the Roman geographer Pomponius Mela (d. 45 CE), among others. See Romm, *The Edges of the Earth in Ancient Thought*, p. 151.

27. See Denis Cosgrove, *Apollo's Eye* (Baltimore: Johns Hopkins University Press, 2001), pp. 69–73.

28. Little has been written about this curious little book. For its publication history, see Karl Schottenloher, *Die Landschuter Buchdrucker des 16. Jahrhunderts, mit einem Anhang: Die Apianusdruckerei in Ingolstadt* (Mainz: Gutenberg-Gesellschaft, 1930), p. 72, nos. 19–21.

29. Petrus Apianus, *Cosmographia* (Ingolstadt: Apianus, 1533), fol. 14r–v. More fully: "Zonarum discrinem belle Probus grammaticus, ait, è manu accipi posse, si leuam contra ora nostra in ortum solis versa digitis expansis introspeximus: ut ubi pollex est, ibi zonam esse arcticà, que et septentrionalis vocatur, intelligamus nimio rigore inhabitabilem. Pollici proximo digito temperatam nostram, quam aestivalem nominant, indicari. Ut medius digitus aequino et ali adustae, et inhabitabili secundum vetustos respondebit.

Quartus alteram temperatam ostendet, quam hyemalem Probus nominat, quòd Sol in eam inclinans nobis hyenem relinquit, sicut in nostrum ascendens, aestatem aperit, diesq; longiores facere solet. Digitus minimus quintam zonam referet, Notiam et Australem dictam ob gelu perpetuum, et sicut septentrionalis nostra, inhabitabilem."

30. Tom Conley, "A Topographer's Eye: From Gilles Corrozet to Peter Apian," in Walter Melion (ed.), *Early Modern Eyes* (Leiden: Brill, 2010), p. 62.

31. Apianus, *Cosmographia*, ch. 28.

32. The following section reprises comments which first appeared in Christopher P. Heuer, *The City Rehearsed* (Oxford: Routledge, 2009), pp. 165–66.

33. *Hollstein's German Engravings, Etchings and Woodcuts ca. 1400–1700*, no. 112; Bartsch XVIII, no. 152.

34. Erwin Panofsky, *Perspective as Symbolic Form*, trans. Christopher S. Wood (New York: Zone Books, 1993), pp. 28–29.

35. David Summers, *Real Spaces: World Art History and the Rise of Western Modernism* (London: Phaidon, 2003), pp. 414–15. On perspective as nonfiction, see Yi-Fu Tuan, *Space and Place: The Perspective of Experience* (Minneapolis: University of Minnesota Press, 1977), esp. pp. 85–100.

36. Quoted in David Beers Quinn, with Alison M. Quinn and Susan Hillier (eds.), *New American World: A Documentary History of North America to 1612*, 5 vols. (New York: Arno Press, 1979), vol. 1, p. 180. On the propagandistic value of this "waie of the Northe" to the English crown, see Helen Wallis, "England's Search for the Northern Passages in the Sixteenth and Early Seventeenth Centuries," *Arctic* 37.4 (December 1984), p. 453.

37. George Wateson, *The cures of the diseased, in Remote Regions: Preventing mortalitie, incident in forraine attempts, of the English nation* (London: Felix Kingston, 1598), fol. B1r. On this phenomenon, see Karen Ordahl Kupperman, "Fear of Hot Climates in the Anglo-American Colonial Experience," *William and Mary Quarterly*, 3rd ser., 41.2 (April 1984), pp. 213–40.

38. John F. Pound, *Poverty and Vagrancy in Tudor England* (London: Routledge, 2014), esp. pp. 37–75.

39. It possibly was meant as a portable travel globe; see Daniela Roberts, *"Imago Mundi": Eine ikonographische und mentalitätsgeschichtliche Studie, ausgehend von Hans Holbein d. J. "The Ambassadors"* (Hildesheim: Georg Olms, 2009), p. 146. On possible changes to the globe by later restorers (including, perhaps, its handle), see Elly Dekker and Rudolf Schmidt, "The Globes in Holbein's Painting 'The Ambassadors,'" *Der Globusfreund* 47–48 (1999), pp. 19–52.

40. See the related globe by Johannes Schöner, discussed in Johannes K. W. Willers (ed.), *Focus Behaim Globus: Germanisches Nationalmuseum, Nürnberg, 2. Dezember 1992 bis 28.*

Februar 1993, exh. cat., 2 vols. (Nuremberg: Germanisches Nationalmuseum, 1992), vol. 2, pp. 673-74. The Holbein identification appears in Elly Dekker and Kristen Lippincott, "The Scientific Instruments in Holbein's Ambassadors: A Re-Examination," *Journal of the Warburg and Courtauld Institutes* 62 (1999), pp. 93-125.

41. On the company's formation, see S. van Brakel, "Die Entwicklung und Organisation Der Merchant-Adventurers," *Vierteljahrschrift Für Sozial- Und Wirtschaftsgeschichte* 5.3 (1907), pp. 401-32.

42. Eric H. Ash, "'A Note and a Caveat for the Merchant': Mercantile Advisors in Elizabethan England," *Sixteenth Century Journal* 33.1 (2002), pp. 1-31, esp. pp. 10-11.

43. William Scott, *The Constitution and Finance of English, Scottish and Irish Joint-Stock Companies to 1720*, 3 vols. (Cambridge: Cambridge University Press, 1910-1912), vol. 1, p. 39.

44. *Ibid.*

45. *Ibid.*, p. 42.

46. Jeanne Nuchterlein, *Translating Nature into Art: Holbein, the Reformation, and Renaissance Rhetoric* (University Park: Pennsylvania State University Press, 2011), p. 169. See also Richard Helgerson, "The Folly of Maps and Modernity," in Andrew Gordon and Bernhard Klein (eds.), *Literature, Mapping, and the Politics of Space in Early Modern Britain* (Cambridge: Cambridge University Press, 2001), pp. 249-50.

47. Petrus Apianus, *Eyn Newe unnd wolgegründte underweysung aller Kauffmanß-Rechnung in dreyen büchern, mit schönen Regeln un[d] fragstucken begriffen* (Ingolstadt: Georg Apian; , 1527). In the 1530s, the methods detailed in the open page in Holbein's painting would have been quite advanced; they relied upon abstract symbols, rather than abacus-based calculation. See Jessica Buskirk, "Portraiture and Arithmetic in Sixteenth-Century Bavaria: Deciphering Barthel Beham's *Calculator*," *Renaissance Quarterly* 66.1 (Spring 2013), pp. 35-80.

48. See Nate Probasco, "Cartography as a Tool of Colonization: Sir Humphrey Gilbert's 1583 Voyage to North America," *Renaissance Quarterly* 67.2 (Summer 2014), pp. 425-72.

49. The inscription appears in a cartouche on a 1592 terrestrial globe designed by Emery Molyneux, a cartographer who may have sailed to the Arctic himself between 1585 and 1587 in the voyages of John Davis. See Helen M. Wallis, "The First English Globe: A Recent Discovery," *Geographical Journal* 117.3 (September 1951), pp. 275-90. The original Latin from the globe's title cartouche: "Nec non et Anglicorum aliquot hominum excellentium probatissimas geographicas descriptiones in Septentrionalibus huius globi delineandis partibus summa cum fide, diligentia summaque cura incitati sumus." (In drawing the northern areas of the globe we have copied with the greatest faithfulness and diligence

the geographical description of many outstanding Englishmen, which [themselves] have an excellent reputation.)

50. Fernand Hallyn, "Holbein: La mort en abyme," *Gentse bijdragen tot de kunstgeschiedenis* 25 (1978–1980), pp. 1–13. On the broader phenomenon, see Michael Schuyt, *Anamorphosen: Ein Spiel mit der Wahrnehmung* (Cologne: DuMont, 1990); Kyung-Ho Cha and Markus Rautzenberg, "Im Theater des Sehens. Anamorphose als Bild und philosophische Metapher," in *Der entstellte Blick: Anamorphosen in Kunst, Literatur und Philosophie* (Paderborn: Wilhelm Fink, 2008), pp. 7–22.

51. Georges de Selve, for one, made a personal plea for a confessionally united Europe in his *Remonstrances addressant aux Alemans*, fragments of which can be found in Jean-Louis Ferrier (ed.), *Hans Holbein, "Les Ambassadeurs": Anatomie d'un chef d'oeuvre* (Paris: Denoël-Gonthier, 1977), pp. 84–105.

52. Kenneth Charlton, "Holbein's Ambassadors and Sixteenth-Century Education," *Journal of the History of Ideas* 21.1 (January–March 1960), pp. 99–109.

53. Susan Foister, *Holbein and England* (New Haven: Yale University Press, 2004), p. 214.

54. Jacques Lacan, *Four Fundamental Concepts of Psychoanalysis*, trans. Alan Sheridan (New York: W. W. Norton, 1978), p. 88.

55. On anamorphosis's critical unleashing of perspective's "disruptive possibilities," see Jonathan Crary, *Techniques of the Observer: On Vision and Modernity in the Nineteenth Century* (Cambridge, MA: MIT Press, 1990), p. 33; also Giancarlo Maiorino, *The Portrait of Eccentricity: Archimboldo and the Mannerist Grotesque* (University Park: Pennsylvania State University Press, 1991), p. 37.

56. Antonio de Torquemada, quoted in Mary Floyd-Wilson, "English Epicures and Scottish Witches," *Shakespeare Quarterly* 57.2 (Summer 2006), p. 157, n. 101.

57. "Les païs que les Demons hantent ordinairement sont situez vers Septentrion, où Satan a estably son throne pour s'esgaler, en ce qu'il peut au Tout-puissant, mais pourtant ils ne laissent d'estre encore és pays où Dieu n'est reconnue & sa religion est ignore, & où le people qui a les yeux fillez d'erreur court après l'idolotrie, & adore de nouveaux Dieux." In Pierre le Loyer, *Discours et histoires des spectres, visions et apparitions des esprits, anges, démons . . . divisez en huict livres*, 2nd ed. (Paris: Nicolas Buon, 1605), p. 326.

58. Robin B. Barnes, *Astrology and Reformation* (Oxford: Oxford University Press, 2015), pp. 140–52.

59. Weibke Schwartz, *Nordlichter: Ihre Darstellung in der Wickiana* (Münster: Waxmann, 1999), p. 49 n. 201. And see Euan Cameron, *Enchanted Europe: Superstition, Reason, and Religion, 1250–1750* (Oxford: Oxford University Press, 2010), pp. 183–87.

60. Walter L. Strauss, *The German Single-Leaf Woodcut, 1550–1600*, 3 vols. (New York: Abaris Books, 1975), vol. 2, p. 665, no. 2.

61. Absolon Pederssøn Beyer, *Dagbok og Oration om Mester Geble*, ed. Ragnvald Iversen, et al., 2 vols. (Oslo: Universitetsforlaget, 1963), vol. 1, fol. 107r; text on p. 65.

62. Cornelis Gemma, illustration from *De naturae divinis characterismis; sev, raris & admirandis spectaculis, causis, indiciis, proprietatibus rerum in partibus singulis vniuersi, libri II* (Antwerp: Plantin, 1575), p. 63.

63. Heinrich Bullinger, *A commentrary upon the seconde epistle of S. Paul to the Thessalonians*, trans. R. H. (London: Nicolson, 1538), fols. 48v–49r.

64. "Legere est in Libro de Inventione Fortunatie sub Polo Arctico Rupem esse excelsam ex lapide magnete 33 milliarum Germanorum ambitum. Hanc complectitur mare sugenum fluidum instar vasis aquam deorsum per foramina emettentis. Circum insulae sunt 4 equibus incoluntur duae, ambiunt autem has insulas contini montes vasti latique dietis 24 quibus negat hominum habitation . . . . Hic compassus navium non tenet nec naves qui ferrum tenent revertere valent." Transcribed in E. G. R. Taylor, "A letter dated 1577 from Mercator to John Dee," *Imago Mundi* 13 (1956), p. 62. On the map's peripatetic history, see Donald L. McGuirck, "Ruysch's World Map: Census and Commentary," *Imago Mundi* 41 (1989), pp. 133–41.

65. The best biobibliography of Mercator appears in Robert W. Karrow, *Mapmakers of the Sixteenth Century* (Chicago: Newberry Library, 1993), pp. 376–406.

66. Ingrid Kretschmer, "Mercators Bedeutung in der Projektionslehre (Mercatorprojektion)," in Manfred Büttner & René Dirven (eds.), *Mercator und Wandlungen der Wissenschaften im 16. und 17. Jahrhundert* (Bochum: Universitätsverlag Dr. N. Brockmeyer, 1993), pp. 151–74.

67. P. B. Beresford, "Map Projections Used in Polar Regions," *Journal of the Institute of Navigation* 6.1 (1953), pp. 29–37.

68. Taylor, "A Letter," p. 60.

69. Mark Monmonier, *Rhumb Lines and Map Wars* (Chicago: University of Chicago Press, 2004), pp. 8–9.

70. See also the offshoots from Mercator's projection discussed in Richard Ruggles, "The Cartographic Lure of the Northwest Passage: Its Real and Imaginary Geography." in Thomas H. B. Symons, *Meta Incognita: A Discourse of Discovery. Martin Frobisher's Arctic expeditions 1576–1578*, 2 vols. (Hull Canadian Museum of Civilization, 1999), vol. 1, pp. 179–256.

71. Marijke Spies, "Humanist Conceptions of the Far North in the Works of Mercator and Ortelius," in Marcel van den Broecke (ed.), *Abraham Ortelius and the First Atlas* (Tuurdijk: HES Publishers, 1998), p. 312 n. 19.

CHAPTER THREE: "A STRANGE QUANTITY OF ICE"

1. Thomas Crammer (1489–1556), quoted in W. K. Jordan, *Edward VI: Young King* (Cambridge, MA: Harvard University Press, 1968), p. 67.

2. Edward Peacock (ed.), *Inventarium monumentorum superstitionis: English Church Furniture, Ornaments and Decorations, at the Period of the Reformation; As Exhibited in a List of the Goods Destroyed in Certain Lincolnshire Churches, AD. 1566* (London: J. C. Hotten, 1866), p. 51. Peacock is transcribing anonymous manuscript documents from 1566 listing "such articles of church furniture . . . considered by the authorities to be superstitious or unnecessary" (p. 9).

3. Joseph Leo Koerner, *The Reformation of the Image* (Chicago: University of Chicago Press, 2004), pp. 83–136. On the English context, see Ann Kibbey, *The Interpretation of Material Shapes in Protestantism* (Cambridge: Cambridge University Press, 1986), pp. 74–77.

4. Hugh Latimer, *Sermons by Hugh Latimer* [1555], ed. G. E. Corrie (Cambridge: Cambridge University Press, 1844), p. 76: "These be the blanchers, that hitherto have stopped the word of God." On the "critical realism" of a different tradition of whitewash, see Angela Vanhalen, *The Wake of Iconoclasm: Painting the Church in the Dutch Republic* (University Park: Pennsylvania State University Press, 2012), pp. 177–78. On subsequent Reformations and actual painting and engraving practices, see Graham Parry, *The Arts of the Anglican Counter-Reformation, Glory, Laud, and Honour* (Woodbridge: Boydell Press, 2006), pp. 105–109 and 199.

5. John Weever, *Ancient Funerall Monuments* (1631), reprinted in *Ancient funeral monuments, of Great-Britain, Ireland, and the islands adjacent With the Dissolved Monasteries Therein Contained* (London: W. Tooke, 1767), p. 50.

6. "Nous susmes à la grande Eglise où il n'y a rien de considerable, elle est assez grande et toute blanchie par dedans." Balthasar de Monconys, *Journal des voyages de Monsieur de Monconys* (Lyon: Horace Boisat and Georges Remeus, 1666), p. 131. Italics added.

7. Thomas Tenison, *Of idolatry: a discourse, in which is endeavored a declaration of, its distinction from superstition, its notion, cause, commencement, and progress . . .* (London: Francis Tyton, 1678), p. 267.

8. Paul Emmons, "Size Matters: Virtual Scale and Bodily Imagination in Architectural Drawing," *Architectural Research Quarterly* 9, nos. 3–4 (2005), pp. 227–35.

9. Walter A. Kenyon, *Tokens of Possession: The Northern Voyages of Martin Frobisher* (Toronto: University of Toronto Press, 1975), pp. 3–15.

10. John Dee owned a black obsidian Aztec mirror. See Hugh Tait, "'The Devil's Looking Glass': The Magical Speculum of Dr. John Dee," in Warren Hunting Smith (ed.), *Horace*

Walpole: Writer, Politician and Connoisseur: Essays on the 250th Anniversary of Walpole's Birth (New Haven: Yale University Press, 1967), pp. 195–212.

11. George Best, quoted in David Beers Quinn, "The Northwest Passage in Theory and Practice," in John Logan Alle (ed.), *North American Exploration*, 3 vols. (Lincoln: University of Nebraska Press, 1997.), vol. 1, pp. 311–12.

12. Aside from Ellis's, there are the written accounts of George Best and Thomas Wiars (both published in Hakluyt's *The principal navigations*) and the narratives of Charles Jackman, Edward Fenton, and Edward Selman (in manuscript, British Library, Harlean MSS 167/40). See Michael Householder, *Inventing Americans in the Age of Discovery* (Aldershot: Ashgate, 2010), p. 82 n. 5. On the assemblage quality of these texts, see Colm MacCrossan, "Framing 'the English Nation': Reading between Text and Paratext in *The Principal Navigations*," in Daniel Carey and Claire Jowitt (eds.), *Richard Hakluyt and Travel Writing in Early Modern Europe* (Aldershot: Ashgate, 2012), pp. 139–52, and Mary C. Fuller, *Experiments in Reading Richard Hakluyt's* Principal Navigations (London: Hakluyt Society, 2017), pp. 7–15.

13. George Best, *A True Discourse of the late voyages of discoverie, for the finding of a passage to Cathaya, by the Northvveast, vnder the conduct of Martin Frobisher Generall deuided into three books* (London: Henry Bynnyman, 1578), preface.

14. Thomas Ellis, *A true report of the third and last voyage into Meta incognita: achieued by the worthie Capteine, M. Martine Frobisher Esquire* (London: Thomas Dawson, 1578), fol. A8v.

15. George Best, "The thirde voyage," pp. 12–13, in *A True Discourse of the late voyages of discoverie*.

16. Best, "The First Booke of the Voyage," p. 13, in *A True Discourse of the late voyages of discoverie*.

17. Best, "The Printer's Preface," *ibid.*, n.p.

18. Best "The First Booke of the Voyage," pp. 12–13, *ibid.*

19. Cornelis Anthonisz., *Onderwijsinge vander zee, om stuermanschap te leeren* ... (Amsterdam: Jan Ewoutzoon, 1558), on which see Arend W. Lang, Die "Caerte van oostlant" des Cornelis Anthonisz., 1543 (Bremerhaven: Deutsches Schiffahrtsmuseum, 1986), pp. 77–87. More broadly on the Dutch navigational publications in Britain, see Thomas Randolf Adams (ed.), *English Maritime Books Printed before 1801: Relating to Ships, Their Construction and Their Operation at Sea* (Providence, RI: John Carter Brown Library, 1995).

20. Anthonisz., *Onderwijsinge*, F1v.

21. Lang, *Die "Caerte van oostlant" des Cornelis Anthonisz.*, p. 58.

22. Best, "The Thirde Voyage," p. 17, in *A True Discourse of the late voyages of discoverie*.

23. *Ibid.*, p. 18.

24. *Ibid.*, p. 40.

25. Wayne Franklin, *Discoverers, Explorers, Settlers* (Chicago: University of Chicago Press, 1978), p. 141. While Atlantic icebergs—caused naturally by the seasonal calving of polar ice—were described in medieval legends, little discussion of them existed in Europe before the seventeenth century. See Mariana Gosnell, *Ice: The Nature, the History, and the Uses of an Astonishing Substance* (Chicago: University of Chicago Press, 2007).

26. English navigator John Davis (1550–1605), describing Greenland, quoted in Richard Bevis, *The Road to Egdon Heath: The Aesthetics of the Great in Nature* (Montreal: McGill–Queen's University Press, 1999), p. 16.

27. Cf. medieval English pilgrimage accounts of North Africa, such as the tale of Richard Eden: "The lande is barren, and the carriage or conveyance of fruits, vegetables, and other necessities, is incommodious . . . such regions lyve ever in continual wandering from place to place." See Gerhardt B. Ladner, "Homo Viator: Medieval Ideas on Alienation and Order," *Speculum* 42.2 (April 1967), pp. 233–59, and, more broadly, Yi-Fu Tuan, "Desert and Ice: Ambivalent Aesthetics," in Salim Kemal and Ivan Gaskell (eds.), *Landscape, Natural Beauty and the Arts (Cambridge Studies in Philosophy and the Arts)* (Cambridge: Cambridge University Press, 1993), pp. 139–57.

28. Thomas Nashe (1567–ca. 1601), quoted in Herbert Wright, "The Elizabethan Englishman's Concepts of Northern Europe," *Edda* 25 (1921), p. 290.

29. John Davis, quoted in Richard Hakluyt, *The principal navigations voiages, traffiques and discoueries of the English nation* (London: George Bishop, Ralph Newberie and Robert Barker, 1600), pp. 630–35. (Hereafter *PN*), p. 777.

30. "Caeterum quid narrem . . . quando praeter solitudinem nihil video?" Original from *Hakluyt's Collection of the Early Voyages, Travels, and Discoveries*, 4 vols. (London: R. H. Evans, 1809–1812), vol. 3, p. 204.

31. Report of an unnamed Franciscan friar on New Mexico, quoted in David Beers Quinn, with Alison M. Quinn and Susan Hillier (eds.), *New American World: A Documentary History of North America to 1612*, 5 vols. (New York: Arno Press, 1979), vol. 1, p. 410, doc. 217.

32. For example: "There appeared a shadow of land to us East Northeast, and so we ran with it the space of 2. houres, and then perceiving that it was but fogge, we hald along Southeast." From Hugh Smith, *The discoverie made by M. Arthur Pet and M. Charles Jackman, of the Northeast parts, beyond the Island of Vaigats with two Barkes: the one called the George, the other the William, in the yeere 1580*, in *PN*, p. 291.

33. *PN*, p. 784.

34. Edward Hayes, quoted in Quinn, Quinn, and Hillier (eds.), *New American World*, vol. 4, p. 23.

35. *PN*, p. 582.

36. Best, *A True Discourse of the late voyages of discoverie*, p. 13.

37. The first English maps to include scale rulers appeared in 1540; see P. D. A. Harvey, *Maps in Tudor England* (Chicago: University of Chicago Press, 1993), p. 8.

38. *Oxford English Dictionary*, s.v. "scale." The legibility aspect is noted by Gunnar Olsson, *Abysmal: A Critique of Cartographic Reason* (Chicago: University of Chicago Press, 2007), p. 442 n. 15.

39. Antoni Malet, "Renaissance Notions of Number and Magnitude," *Historia Mathematica* 33 (2006), pp. 63–81.

40. *Filarete's Treatise on Architecture: Being the Treatise by Antonio Di Piero Averlino, Known as Filarete*, trans. John R. Spencer, 2 vols. (New Haven: Yale University Press, 1965), vol. 1, p. 82 (book 7, 47r.).

41. Leon Battista Alberti, *On Painting: A New Translation and Critical Edition*, trans. Rocco Sinisgalli (Cambridge: Cambridge University Press, 2011), pp. 22 and 38.

42. Edward Worsop, *A discoverie of sundrie errours and faults daily committed by landmeaters* (London: Henrie Middleton, 1582), B2v. On the book, see M. A. R. Cooper, "Edward Worsop: From the Black Art and Sundrie Errors to True Geometricall Demonstration," *Survey Review* 32 (April 1993), pp. 67–79.

43. Andrew McRae, *God Speed the Plough: The Representation of Agrarian England, 1500–1660* (Cambridge: Cambridge University Press, 1996), p. 171.

44. A copy of Mercator's chart was included in Frobisher's personal ship's library during his first voyage to the Arctic in 1576 as "a great mappe universall of Mercator in prente." See David Watkin Waters, *The Art of Navigation in England in Elizabethan and Early Stuart Times* (New Haven: Yale University Press, 1958), p. 531, appendix 10, C, (k).

45. On "scalar failure," see Benjamin Morgan, "Scale as Form: Thomas Hardy's Rocks and Stars," in Tobias Menely and Jesse Oak Taylor (eds.), *Anthropocene Reading: Literary History in Geologic Times* (University Park: Pennsylvania State University Press, 2017), pp. 132–49; Mary C. Stiner, et al. "Scale," in Andrew Shyrock and Daniel Lord Smail (eds.), *Deep History: The Architecture of Past and Present* (Berkeley: University of California Press, 2012), pp. 242–72.

46. Hernán Cortés, *Letters from Mexico*, trans. and ed. Anthony Pagden (New Haven: Yale University Press, 1971), p. 104.

47. Alessandra Russo, "Cortés's Objects and the Idea of New Spain," *Journal of the History of Collections* 23.2 (2011), pp. 229–52.

48. Peter Martyr, *De orbe novo: The Eight Decades of Peter Martyr d'Anghara*, 2 vols. (New York: Putnam's, 1912), vol. 2, p. 308.

49. Cortés, *Letters from Mexico*, p. 104.

50. Monotony was a facet often echoed in the actual tone of the travel accounts themselves, both of the Arctic and elsewhere. See Mary C. Fuller, "His Dark Materials: The Problem of Dullness in Hakluyt's Collections," in Carey and Jowitt (eds.), *Richard Hakluyt and Travel Writing*, pp. 231–42.

51. C. C. A Gosch (ed.), *Danish Arctic Expeditions, 1605 to 1620, in Two Books. Book I. The Danish Expeditions to Greenland in 1605, 1606, and 1607: To Which is Added Captain James Hall's Voyage to Greenland in 1612; Book II. The Expedition of Captain Jens Munk to Hudson's Bay in Search of a North-West Passage in 1619–20*, 2 vols. (London: Printed for the Hakluyt Society, 1897), vol. 1, p. 119.

52. *PN*, p. 629.

53. John Davis, *The Voyages and Works of John Davis the Navigator*, ed. Albert Hastings Markham, 2 vols. (London: Hakluyt Society, 1880), vol. 1, p. 24.

54. Dionyse Settle, *A true reporte of the laste voyage into the west and northwest regions, &c. 1577. worthily atchieued by Capteine Frobisher* (London: Henrie Middleton, 1577), fol. A7r. On this passage, see also Howard Mumford Jones, "O Strange New World" in Robert D. Marcus and David Burner (eds.), *The American Scene: Varieties of American History, Volume 1* (New York: Meredith, 1971), p. 19. Cf. Mary Fuller, "The Poetics of a Cold Climate" *Terrae Incognitae* 30 (1998), p. 41: "Cabot and Columbus happened upon two utterly different Americas . . . a formidably northerly America of foggy seas, ice-scarred lands, and punishing winters [and a] tropical America, a paradisiacal America of green-covered islands and perpetual warmth."

55. On the individual as new measure in early modern travel writing, see Mary B. Campbell, *The Witness and the Other World* (Ithaca: Cornell University Press, 1988), pp. 3–13.

56. Magdalene College, Cambridge, Pepys Library, MS 1125 ("Fenton Journal"), fol. 10. See Walter Kenyon, "The Canadian Arctic Journal of Captain Edward Fenton, 1578," *Archivaria* 11 (Winter 1980–81), p. 173.

57. Roland Mushat Frye, "Ways of Seeing in Shakespearean Drama and Elizabethan Painting," *Shakespeare Quarterly* 31.3 (Autumn 1980), pp. 323–43.

58. Best, *A True Discourse of the late voyages of discoverie*, p. 51.

59. *Ibid.*

60. Sophie Lemercier-Goddard, "George Best's Arctic Mirrors: *A True Discourse of Late Voyages of Discoverie . . . of Martin Frobisher* (1578)," in Frédéric Regard (ed.), *The Quest for*

the Northwest Passage: Knowledge, Nation, and Empire, 1576–1806 (London: Pickering and Chatto, 2013), p. 69.

61. Rhordri Liscombe, "Modernist Ultima Thulé," *Revue d'art canadienne* 31.1–2 (2006), pp. 64–80.

62. Lucy R. Lippard, "Art within the Arctic Circle," *Hudson Review* 22.4 (Winter 1969–1970), pp. 665–74. The Edmonton show was organized by Iain and Ingrid Baxter. See Nancy Shaw, "Siting the Banal: The Extended Landscapes of the N.E. Thing Company," in John O'Brian and Peter White (eds.), *Beyond Wilderness: The Group of Seven, Canadian Identity, and Contemporary Art* (Montreal: McGill-Queen's University Press, 2007), pp. 63–68, and Grant Arnold and Karen Henry, *Traffic: Conceptual Art in Canada, 1965–1980* (Vancouver: Vancouver Art Gallery, 2012), pp. 73–74.

63. Matthew Farish and p. Whitney Lackenbauer, "High Modernism in the Arctic: Planning Frobisher Bay and Inuvik," *Journal of Historical Geography* 35.3 (July 2009), pp. 517–44.

64. Lippard, "Art within the Arctic Circle," pp. 672–63. Cf. a late nineteenth-century anecdote of Arctic exploration: "A Swedish explorer had all but completed a written description in his notebook of a craggy headland with two unusually sculptural valley glaciers, the whole of it part of a large island, when he discovered what he was looking at was a walrus." Retold in Barry Lopez, *Arctic Dreams* (New York: Vintage, 1986), p. 239.

65. Benjamin Buchloh, "The Posters of Lawrence Weiner," in *Avant-Garde and Culture Industry* (Cambridge, MA: MIT Press, 2003), p. 567.

66. Lucy R. Lippard, "Escalation in Washington" (1968), reprinted in *Changing: Essays in Art Criticism* (New York: Dutton, 1971), pp. 237–54.

67. Lippard, "Art within the Arctic Circle," p. 665.

68. *Ibid.*, p. 666.

69. *Ibid.*, pp. 672–73.

70. Lawrence Weiner, quoted in Sabine B. Vogel, "Lawrence Weiner 'Kunst ist ein Spielzug für Intellektuelle': Ein Gespräch mit dem Künstler," *Artis* 42.3 (March 1990), p. 37.

71. Lawrence Weiner, "Section 2," *Artforum* 20.9 (May 1982), p. 65. This and other (unresolved) statements by Weiner on the dynamics of language as material are discussed in Birgit Pelzer, "Disassociated Objects: The Statements / Sculptures of Lawrence Weiner," *October* 90 (Autumn 1999), pp. 76–108.

72. Virginia Dwan, "On Changing Boundaries," in Philip Kaiser and Miwon Kwon (eds.), *The Ends of the Earth: Art of the Land to 1974*, exh. cat. (Los Angeles: LACMA, 2012), pp. 93–94.

73. James Nisbet, Ecologies, *Environments, and Energy Systems in Art of the 1960s and 1970s* (Cambridge, MA: MIT Press, 2014), p. 93; see also Nisbet, "Coast to Coast: Land Work Between the N.E. Thing Co. and Lucy Lippard," *Archives of American Art Journal* 47.1–2 (Spring 2008), pp. 58–65.

74. Charity Mewburn, *Sixteen Hundred Miles North of Denver* (Vancouver: Belkin Art Gallery, UBC, 1999), pp. 26–28.

75. Clement Greenberg, letter of March 10, 1963, to Keith Lockhard, quoted in David Howard, "From Emma Lake to Los Angeles: Modernism at the Margins," in John O'Brian (ed.), *The Flat Side of the Landscape* (Saskatoon: Mendel Art Gallery, 1989), pp. 41–51.

76. Ross Fox, "The Greenberg Factor," in *The Canadian Painters Eleven* (1953–1960) (Amherst: Mead Art Gallery, 1994), pp. 26–37.

77. Kenneth Olwig, *Landscape, Nature, and the Body Politic: From Britain's Renaissance to America's New World* (Madison: University of Wisconsin Press, 2002), pp. 43–61.

78. Michael O' Connell, *The Idolatrous Eye: Iconoclasm and Theatre in Early Modern England* (New York: Oxford University Press, 2000), pp. 116–18; Matthew Milner, *The Senses and the English Reformation* (Aldershot: Ashgate, 2013), pp. 163–206.

79. Louis-Jacques Dorais, *The Language of the Inuit: Syntax, Semantics, and Society in the Arctic* (Montreal: McGill-Queen's University Press, 2014), pp. 106–108.

80. "The Second Voyage Attempted by John Davis," in Richard Hakluyt, *The principal navigations voiages, traffiques and discoueries of the English nation* (London: George Bishop, Ralph Newberie and Robert Barker, 1600), vol. 3, p. 104.

81. *Ibid.*

82. *Ibid.*, vol. 3, p. 100.

83. Henk Nalis (comp.), Ger Luijten and Christiaan Schuckman (eds.), *New Hollstein Dutch and Flemish Etchings, Engravings and Woodcuts, 1450–1700: The van Doetecum Family*, vol. 4 (Rotterdam: Sound and Vision, 1998), no. 982.

84. Jan Huyghen van Linschoten, *Voyagie, ofte schip-vaert, Jan Huygen van Linschoten, van by Noorden om langes Noorvvegen de Noortcaep, Laplant, Vinlant, Ruslandt, de VVitte Zee, de custen van candenoes, Svvetenoes, Pitzora* . . . (Franeker: Gerard Ketel, 1601), fols. 11r–11v: "Op den uytersten hoeck, aen de zuijdt-zijde van dit Eylandt staen wel drie ofte vier hondert houten Afgoden, soo cleyn als groot, ende zijn ghesneden van hout, qualick en plomp ghefatsoneert, soo dat men passenlicken can vermercken, datse naer menschen ghestaltenis ghesneden zijn: legghen wat schuyn opgheheven teghens een steunsel aen, met het aenghesicht nae 't oosten ghewent, ende hebben rondtsom haer een groote mennichte van Rheen ofte Rhinnen hoornen, die sy, soo 't schijnt, aldaer moeten voor een offerhande brenghen,

welcke hoornen ende Afgoden ons van verre scheenen Cruycen te wesen... Jck en can niet vermoeden hoe dat daer so grooten menichte van Beelden by den anderen, ende op een over hoop gheleyt zijn, dan is te dencken, dat soo dickwils als daer een sterft, alhier in de plaetse van den dooden, een Beeldt ghebracht wordt, ende schinjt alsoo waer te wesen om dies wille dat wy daer Beelden vonder, die van ouderdom vermollemt ende versleten waren, ende somminghe noch gantsch nieu, en niet langhe ghemaeckt: Oock mede dat de sommighe waren als Mans, andere als Vrouwen, ende ettelicke als Kinderen, eenighe Man ende Vrou aen den anderen: Jnsghelijcks stocken van vier, vijf, jae seven, acht, ende meer aenghesichten onder den anderen, als van een gheheel Huysghesin: Ofte moet wesen, dat sy daer t'eenighen tijde van 't Jaer in Beevaert comen, ende alsdan een yeghelick sijn ghelijckenisse ende Beeldt daer by leyt. Saghen daer oock bynaest t' fatsoen van een bare ofte berry, hebbende de stijlen van ghelijcken met ghesneden aensichten, daer sy, nae te presumeeren is, de Beelden in Processie mede moeten omdraghen. Wy meenden eerst dat het een Kerck-hoff ende begraeffenisse moeste wesen: Maer en vernamen daer gheen apparentie van graeven ofteghebeenten, anders dan de voorsz. Rhinnen hoornen, die daer hoop-werck waren. Andere teyckenen van huysen ofte Menschen en conden daer tot noch toe niet vernemen, al hoe wel wy 't landt een stuck weeghsover en weer over liepen. Doch by dese Beelden ende Afgoden is het ghenoech kennelick dat daer Menschen woonen: Maer waer dat sy hun onthouden, en wisten tot noch toe niet t' ontdecken."

85. Rafael Karsten, *The Religion of the Samek* (Leiden: Brill, 1955), pp. 11–23 and 106–12.

86. O. V. Ovsyannikov and N. M. Terebikhin, "Sacred Space in the Culture of the Arctic Regions," in David Carmichael, et al. (eds.), *Sacred Sites: Sacred Places* (London: Routledge, 1994), pp. 56–60.

87. T. I. Itkonen, *Heidnische Religion und späterer Aberglaube bei den finnischen Lappen* (Helsinki: Suomalais-ugrilainen seura, 1946), pp. 309-11.

88. Adam Olearius (Adam Ölschläger), *Gottorffische Kunst-Kammer: worinnen aller-hand ungemeine Sachen, so theils die Natur, theils künstliche Hände hervor gebracht und bereitet* (Schleswig: Gottfried Schultzens Kosten, 1674), 2nd ed., fol. A3r–A3v: "Solche gemahlte heilegen muss jeglicher in seiner Stuben und Kammer haben / und vor denselben stehend beten und gar offt neigen. Und wenn jemand zu ihnen ins Haus kommt / muss er zuvor ehe er jemand / vor solchen Bilde seine devotion thn / wird als ein Gott geheret... und muss niemand als von ihres Glaubens genossen gemeldet werden sehen aus ob sie schon ganz neue als wenn sie ein Jahr im Rauche gehangen. Werden also auf einen absonderlichen Gotter-Markt verkaufft oder nur wie sie reden um Geld vertausche und was der Kramer fordert muss der Kaufer geben."

89. Transcribed in A. E. Nordenskiöld, *Voyage of the Vega Round Asia and Europe, with a Historical Review of Previous Journeys* (London: Macmillan, 1882), p. 80. On the survival of the tradition on Vaygach, see Noel D. Broadbent, *Lapps and Labyrinths: Saami Prehistory, Colonization and Cultural Resilience* (Washington, DC: Smithsonian, 2010), pp. 184–86.

90. Pietro Martire d'Anghiera, translated in Richard Eden, *The decades of the newe worlde or west India: conteynyng the nauigations and conquestes of the Spanyardes, with the particular description of the moste ryche and large landes and ilandes lately founde in the west ocean perteynyng to the inheritaunce of the kinges of Spayne . . . Wrytten in the Latine tounge by Peter Martyr of Angleria, and translated into Englysshe by Rycharde Eden* (London: Edwarde Sutton, 1555), fol. 150v.

91. See William Pietz, "The Problem of the Fetish, I," *Res* 13 (Spring 1987), pp. 23–45, esp. pp. 39–42, on the reactions of Pieter de Marees to what he encountered on the West African coast in 1602.

92. Carlos M. N. Eire, *War Against the Idols: The Reformation of Worship from Erasmus to Calvin* (Cambridge: Cambridge University Press, 1989), p. 84.

93. Peter Mancall, "The Raw and the Cold: Five English Soldiers in Sixteenth-Century Nunavut," *William and Mary Quarterly* 70.1 (January 2013), p. 11. On the importance of analogous thinking in New World representation, see Anthony Pagden, *The Fall of Natural Man: The American Indian and the Origins of Comparative Ethnology* (Cambridge: Cambridge University Press, 1982), pp. 1–4, and Campbell, *The Witness and the Other World*, pp. 90–91 and 189.

94. Robert Heath, *Paradoxical assertions and philosophical problems full of delight and recreation for all ladies and youthful fancies* (London: Printed by R. W., 1659), pp. 46–48.

95. Jess Edwards, *Writing, Geometry and Space in Seventeenth-Century England and America: Circles in the Sand* (London: Routledge, 2006).

96. For example: Percy G. Adams, "The Discovery of America and European Renaissance Literature," *Comparative Literature Studies* 13.2 (June 1976), pp. 100–15; Stephen Greenblatt, *Marvelous Possessions* (Chicago: University of Chicago Press, 1991); Russell West, *Spatial Representations and the Jacobean Stage: From Shakespeare to Webster* (Basingstoke: Palgrave, 2002); Peter C. Mancall, "Richard Hakluyt and the Visual World of Early Modern Travel Narratives," in Carey and Jowitt (eds.), *Richard Hakluyt and Travel Writing*, pp. 87–101.

97. Michael Gaudio, "The Space of Idolatry: Reformation, Incarnation, and the Ethnographic Image," *Res* 41 (Spring 2002), pp. 73–91.

98. On early modern exploration as a kind of a perspectival act, see Daniela Bleichmar, *Visual Voyages: Images of Latin American Culture from Columbus to Darwin* (New Haven: Yale University Press, 2017), pp. 5–26.

99. *Hakluyt's Collection of the Early Voyages, Travels, and Discoveries of the English Nation [1598–1600]: A New Edition, with Additions,* 5 vols. (London: R. H. Evans, 1810), vol. 3, p. 40.

100. Archivo General de Simancas, Valladolid, Sección Estado, L831, ff. 267. See Bernard Allaire and Donald Hogarth. "Martin Frobisher, the Spaniards and a Sixteenth-Century Northern Spy," *Terrae Incognitae* 28.1 (2013), pp. 45-46.

101. Josiah Blackmore, *Manifest Perdition: Shipwreck Narrative and the Disruption of Empire* (Minneapolis: University of Minnesota Press, 2002), pp. 21–22.

102. On the little-studied circumstances of the lecture's first delivery, see Emily J. Levine, *Dreamland of Humanists: Warburg, Cassirer, Panofsky, and the Hamburg School* (Chicago: University of Chicago Press, 2013), p. 163.

103. I owe this brilliant suggestion to Michael Gaudio. For Panofsky, perspective wrought "a purely formal and not a substantial reality," See Erwin Panofsky, *Perspective as Symbolic Form*, trans. Christopher S. Wood (New York: Zone Books, 1991), p. 30.

CHAPTER FOUR: THE SAVAGE EPISTEME

1. Broadsheet, 40 x 36 cms., Zentralbibliothek, Zürich, PAS II 7:4; Wolfgang Harms and Michael Schilling (eds.), *Die Sammlung der Zentralbibliothek Zürich: Kommentierte Ausgabe,* 2 vols. (Tübingen: Max Niemeyer, 2005), vol. 1, no. VI.148, pp, 290–91; Franz Obermeer, "Die frühen illustrierten Einblattdrucke zu Amerika und ihre Verbreitung im zeitgenössischen Pressewesen," *Wolfenbütteler Notizen zur Buchgeschichte* 1-2 (2003), pp. 16–17; David Beers Quinn, "Le femme et l'enfant Iunk de Nuremberg, 1566," *Recherches Amérindiennes au Quebec* 11.4 (1981), pp. 311–13; F. W. Sixel, "Die deutsche Vorstellung von Indianer in der ersten Hälfte des 16. Jahrhunderts," *Annali del Pontificio Museo Missionario Etnologico* 30 (1966), pp. 22, 68, 137. The sheet's date of "MDL VII" is from the Julian calendar, still in use at the time in the Holy Roman Empire. On the captives' time in the Spanish Netherlands, see William C. Sturvesant and David Beers Quinn, "This New Prey: Eskimos in Europe in 1567, 1576, and 1577," in Christian F. Feest (ed.), *Indians and Europe: An Interdisciplinary Collection of Essays* (Aachen: Rader Verlag, 1987), pp. 61–140.

2. As reported by an eyewitness on the scene. See *Chronycke van Antwerpen Sedert Het Jaer 1500 tot 1575* (Antwerp: J. p. van Dieren, 1843), p. 65: "Coorts daer naer in deselve maendt quam t'Antwerpen een schip aen vuyt Indien ende Canarien, dat in hadde een wilt wyff met haer kindt, diese gevangen hadde daer te lande int geberechte, al naeckt synde, eetende nyet dan menschenvleesch; dese sach men oock tAntwerpen om gelt."

3. J. G. Taylor, "Historical Ethnography of the Labrador Coast," *Handbook of North American Indians* 5 (1984), pp. 508–21. One copy of the print, we know, was acquired by the

Zurich canon Jacob Wick, collector of broadsheets on other strange natural phenomena: comets, earthquakes, and monstrous births.

4. Bernadette Driscoll, "The Iunk Parka," in *The Iunk Amautik*, exh. cat. (Winnipeg: Winnipeg Art Gallery, 1980), pp. 11–20.

5. Bruno Weber (ed.), *Das Porträt auf Papier* (Zürich: Zentralbibliothek, 1984), no. 125, pp. 122–24. Cf. Johannes Fabian, *Time and the Other: How Anthropology Makes Its Object* (New York: Columbia University Press, 2003), p. 67, which describes how anthropological observation "calls for a native society that would, ideally at least, hold still like a tableau vivant."

6. Walter L. Strauss, *The German Single-Leaf Woodcut, 1550–1600*, 3 vols. (New York: Abaris Books, 1975), vol. 1, p. 201. There are two other editions of the same broadsheet, see *ibid.*, vol. 1, pp. 135 and 376.

7. Peter Parshall, "*Imago Contrafactum*: Images and Facts in the Northern Renaissance," *Art History* 16.4 (1993), pp. 554–79; Sachiko Kusukowa, *Picturing the Book of Nature: Image, Text, and Argument in Sixteenth-Century Human Anatomy and Medical Botany* (Chicago: University of Chicago Press, 2012), pp. 8–19; Barbara Stolz, "Das Bild-Druckverfahren in der Frühen Neuzeit," *Marburger Jahrbuch für Kunstwissenschaft* 39 (2012), pp. 93–117, esp. pp. 107–108.

8. E.g., Strauss, *The German Single-Leaf Woodcut*, vol. 1, pp. 195, 202, 204.

9. I am indebted to Shira Brisman for this phrasing. See, further, Brisman, "A Matter of Choice: Printed Design Proposals and the Nature of Selection, 1470–1610," *Renaissance Quarterly* 71.1 (Spring 2018), pp. 114–64.

10. Here I follow Vanita Seth's *Europe's Indians, 1500–1800* (Durham: Duke University Press, 2010), pp. 12–13. On the broader intellectual dynamic between New World exploration and the Protestant Reformation, see Kim Siebenhüner, "Luthers unbekannt Welten: Objekte der frühe Globalisiering im 'Zeitalter' der Reformation," in Thomas Eser (ed.), *Luther, Kolumbus, und die Folgen* (Nuremberg: Germanisches Nationalmuseum, 2018), pp. 29–35.

11. Ariana Hernàndez-Reguant, "The Columbus Quaternary and the Politics of the Encounter," *American Indian Culture and Research Journal* 17.1 (1993), pp. 17–35.

12. John Stow, *The Chronicles of England: from Brute vnto this present yeare of Christ. 1580. Collected by Iohn Stow citizen of London* (London: Henry Bynnyman, 1580), p. 875.

13. Richard Hakluyt, *The principal navigations, voiages, traffiques and discoueries of the English nation* (London: George Bishop, Ralph Newberie, and Robert Barker, 1600), p. 461; Eric H. Ash, "'A Note and a Caveat for the Merchant': Mercantile Advisors in Elizabethan England," *Sixteenth Century Journal* 33.1 (2002), p. 17.

14. See Richard Hennig, *Terrae Incognitae: Eine Zusammenstellung und kritische Bewertung der wichtigsten vorkolumbischen Entdeckungsreisen an Hand der darüber vorliegenden Original-berichte* (Leiden: Brill, 1936), vol. 2, pp. 302–306, on Adam. For the various versions of the tale, and on similar giftings to English and Denmark, see T. J. Oleson, "Polar Bears in the middle ages," *Canadian Historical Review* 31 (1950), pp. 47–55.

15. E.g., *Beschreibung seiner Schifffahrt aus Engeilandt in die Gegendt West und Nordwest i. J. 1577 . . .* (Nürnberg, n.p, 1580). The narwhal appears in George Best, "The second Voyage," p. 15, in *A True Discourse of the late voyages of discoverie, for the finding of a passage to Cathaya, by the Northvveast, vnder the conduct of Martin Frobisher Generall deuided into three books* (London: Henry Bynnyman, 1578). On the more general bibliographic specifics of the many Frobisher accounts, see Elizabeth Heale, "'Accidentall Restraints': Straits and Passages in Richard Hakluyt's *The principal navigations*," in Daniel Carey and Claire Jowitt (eds.), *Richard Hakluyt and Travel Writing in Early Modern Europe* (Aldershot: Ashgate, 2012), pp. 271–81.

16. Elisabeth Scheicher, *Die Kunst- und Wunderkammern der Habsburger* (Vienna: Molden, 1979), pp. 81 and 85–115.

17. Most are lost, but extant examples (a craft now in Frankfurt, for example) date from as early as 1663. See Gert Nooter, *Old Kayaks in the Netherlands* (Leiden: Brill, 1971), pp. 5–7 and 43–44.

18. Christian F. Feest, "North America in the European Wunderkammer before 1750," *Archiv für Völkerkunde* 46 (1992), pp. 63–69; Nooter, *Old Kayaks in the Netherlands*, pp. 5–7.

19. Feest, "North America in the European Wunderkammer before 1750," p. 64.

20. The original reads: "Ein calecutisch tärtschlein, von einer fischhaut gemacht, und zween handschuh zu ihren fechten." Hans Rupprich, *Dürer Schriftlicher Nachlass*, 3 vols. (Berlin: Deutscher Verein für Kunstwissenschaft, 1956), vol. 1, p. 166; Jean Michel Massing, "Albrecht Dürer's Irish Warriors and Peasants," *Irish Arts Review* 10 (1994), p. 223.

21. Susi Colin, *Das Bild des Indianers im 16. Jahrhundert* (Idstein: Schulz-Kirchner, 1988), pp. 186–87.

22. Stephanie Leitch, "Burgkmair's Peoples of Africa and India (1508) and the Origins of Ethnography in Print," *Art Bulletin* 101.2 (June 2009), pp. 134–59.

23. British Library, London, 1750 C.2 (6). Glaser apprenticed with his father, also a painter named Hans, and published both copies of Dürer's devotional woodcuts. See Strauss, *The German Single-Leaf Woodcut*, vol. 1, p. 333. The painter here was likely Niklas Stoer (active 1532 to 1562), who often worked with Glaser and whose father would author a perspective treaty in 1567. See Jeffrey Chipps Smith, *Nuremberg: A Renaissance City* (Austin: University of Texas Press, 1983), cat. no. 171, pp. 263–64.

24. Hildegard Frübis, *Die Wirklichkeit des Fremden: Die Darstellung Der Neuen Welt Im 16. Jahrhundert* (Berlin: Reimer, 1995), pp. 110–13.

25. Manfred Fuhrmann, "Einige Dokumente zur Rezeption der taciteischen 'Germania,'" *Der altsprachliche Unterricht* 21.1 (1978), pp. 39–49.

26. On Augsburg's wild-man tradition, see Richard Bernheimer, *Wild Men in the Middle Ages: A Study in Art, Sentiment, and Demonology* (Cambridge, MA: Harvard University Press, 1952), p. 120.

27. Hans Ulrich Roller, *Der Nürnberger Schembartlauf: Studien Zum Fest- und Maskenwesen Des Späten Mittelalters* (Tübingen: Tübinger Vereinigung Für Volkskunde, 1965), pp. 78–99.

28. Leonard Wilson Forster (ed.), *Selections from Conrad Celtis, 1458–1508* (Cambridge: Cambridge University Press, 1948), pp. 39 and 43.

29. Albertus Magnus, *De animalibus*, quoted in Shirin A. Khanmohamadi, *In Light of Another's Word: European Ethnography in the Middle Ages* (Philadelphia: University of Pennsylvania Press, 2014), p. 24; see also Gregory Velazco y Trianosky, "Savages, Wild Men, Monstrous Races: The Social Construction of Race in the Early Modern Era," in Peg Zeglin Brand (ed.), *Beauty Unlimited* (Bloomington: Indiana University Press, 2013), p. 57.

30. Between 1250 and 1500 CE, European population growth, agriculture, and the need for fuel in cities in North Europe brought about wide-scale clearing of the forests. In 900 CE, around 5 percent of land has been cleared as fields; by 1500, that number was closer to 40 percent. See Michael Williams, "Dark Ages and Dark Areas: Global Deforestation in the Deep Past," *Journal of Historical Geography* 26.1 (2000), pp. 28–46. On the broader response to European "wildernesses" being transformed into cultural "landscapes," see Dirk Johannsen, "Crossing the Ecotone: On the Narrative Representation of Nature as 'Wild'" in Bojan Borstner et al (eds.), *Historicizing Religion: Critical Approaches to Contemporary Concerns* (Pisa: Edizioni Plus, 2010), pp. 233–48.

31. See, for example, *Extract, Auß eines Erbarn Raths der Statt Nůrmberg* (Nuremberg: Balthasar Scherffen, 1621), fols. C2v–E3r, which cites older edicts specifying how and when separate kinds of trees could be cut down in the Nuremberg *Wald*.

32. Erzsébet Stróbl, "The Figure of the Wild Man in the Entertainments of Elizabeth I," in Zsolt Almási and Mike Pincombe (eds.), *Writing the Other: Humanism versus Barbarism in Tudor England* (Cambridge: Scholars Publishing, 2003), pp. 59–78, esp. p. 61.

33. Stow, *The Chronicles of England*, p. 875.

34. Mary Floyd-Wilson, *English Ethnicity and Race in Early Modern Drama* (Cambridge: Cambridge University Press, 2003), p. 2.

35. Aristotle, *Politics* 1327b.

36. Jean Bodin, *Six Books of the Commonwealth*, trans. and abridged by Jean Tooley (Oxford: Basil Blackwell, 1967), p. 155.

37. Richard Eden, transcribed in *The First Three English Books on America* (London: Archibald Constable, 1895), p. 307

38. Martin W. Leews and Kären E. Wigen, *The Myth of Continents: A Critique of Meta-geography* (Berkeley: University of California Press, 1997), esp. pp. 2–19 and 183–86.

39. Joseph Hall, *Mundus alter et idem: siue Terra Australis ante hac semper incognita longis itineribus peregrini academici nupeprrime lustrata* (Frankfurt, n.d. [1605?]), translated as *Another World and Yet the Same, Bishop Joseph Hall's Mundus Alter et Idem*, trans. John Millar Wands (New Haven: Yale University Press, 1981), p. 114. See John Wands, "The Theory of Climate in the English Renaissance and *Mundus Alter et Idem*" in I. D. McFarlane, *Actus Conventus Neo-Latini Sanctandreani: Proceedings of the Fifth International Congress of Neo-Latin Studies* (Binghamton: Medieval and Renaissance Texts, 1986), pp. 523–24.

40. Hall, *Mundus alter et idem*, p. 144.

41. Daryl W. Palmer, "Hamlet's Northern Lineage: Masculinity, Climate, and the Mechanician in Early Modern Britain," *Renaissance Drama* 35 (2006), p. 5 n. 13.

42. Hayden White, "The Forms of Wildness: Archaeology of an Idea," in Edward Dudley and Maximilian Novak (eds.), *The Wild Man Within: An Image in Western Thought from the Renaissance to Romanticism* (Pittsburgh: University of Pittsburgh Press, 1972), pp. 3–38.

43. Florike Egmond and Peter Mason, "'These Are People Who Eat Raw Fish': Countours of the Ethnographic Imagination in the Sixteenth Century," *Viator* 31 (2000), pp. 312–13.

44. George Best, "A true reporte of such things as hapned in the second voyage of Captayne Frobysher . . . ," in *A True Discourse of the late voyages of discoverie, for the finding of a passage to Cathaya, by the Northvveast, vnder the conduct of Martin Frobisher Generall deuided into three books* (London: Henry Bynnyman, 1578), pp. 61–68.

45. Goropius Becanus [Jan Gerartsen van Gorp], *Origins Antwerpianae . . .* (Antwerp: Christoffel Plaintin, 1569), p. 1046.

46. Henry Percival Biggar (ed.), *The Precursors of Jacques Cartier, 1497–1534, A Collection of Documents Relating to the Early History of the Dominion of Canada* (Ottawa: Government Printing Bureau, 1911), p. 64.

47. See David B. Quinn, *Sources for the Ethnography of Northeastern North America to 1611* (Ottawa: National Museums of Canada, 1981), p. 47, no. 40.

48. Public Record Office, London, Document SP 91/1,13, quoted in Quinn, "La femme et l'enfant Inuit de Nuremberg, 1566," pp. 312–13. The document dates from January 1579.

49. Anthony Grafton, *New Worlds, Ancient Texts: The Power of Tradition and the Shock of Discovery* (Cambridge, MA: Harvard University Press, 1992), pp. 210–11.

50. Jacques Cartier, *Voyages en Nouvelle-France: Texte remise en français modern part Robert Lahaise et Marie Couturier* (Quebec: Hurtubise, 1977), p. 60.

51. Antoine de Montchrestien, *Traicte* (1615), quoted in Geoffroy Atkinson, *Les nouveaux horizons de la Renaissance francaise* (Paris: Droz, 1935), p. 352.

52. Best, *A True Discourse of the late voyages of discoverie*, epilogue.

53. Hernán Cortés, *Letters from Mexico*, trans. and ed. Anthony Pagden (New Haven: Yale University Press, 1971), pp. 100–101.

54. Peter Arnade, *Beggars, Iconoclasts, and Civic Patriots* (Ithaca: Cornell University Press, 2008), pp. 142–45.

55. In the colossal literature on Antwerp iconoclasm in 1566, see, specifically, Guido Marnef, *Antwerpen in de Tijd van de Reformatie* (Amsterdam: Meulenhoff, 1996), pp. 127–46; Alistair Duke, "De Calvinisten en de 'paapse beeldendienst': De denkwereld van de beeldenstormers in 1566," in M. Bruggeman, et al. (eds), *Mensen van de Nieuwe Tijd: Een liber amicorum voor A. Th. Van Deursen* (Amsterdam: Berk Bakker, 1996), pp. 29–45.

56. Arnade, Beggars, *Iconoclasts, and Civic Patriots*, p. 113.

57. H. van Alfen (ed.), *Kroniek eener Kloosterzuster van het voormalig Bossche Klooster . . .* (s'Hertogenbosch: Provinciaal Genootschap van Kunsten en Wetenschappen in Noord-Brabant, 1931), pp. 5–6.

58. Edmond de Coussemaker (ed.), *Troubles religieux du XVIe siècle dans la Flandre Maritime, 1560–1570: Documents originaux*, 4 vols. (Bruges: de Zuttere, 1876), vol. 2, p. 246.

59. Arnade, *Beggars, Iconoclasts, and Civic Patriots*, p. 124, and more broadly Alastair Duke, *Dissident identities in the early modern Low Countries* (Farnham, UK: Ashgate, 2009).

60. On Coenen, see Florike Egmond, *Een bekende Scheveninger: Adriaen Coenen en zijn Visboeck van 1578* (The Hague: Centrum voor Familiegeschiedenis van Scheveningen, 1997).

61. Adriaen Coenen, *Een Visboek*, Adriaen Coenen MSS, Koninklijke Bibliotheek, The Hague, 78E54, fol. 40r: "In den tijden Als men alhier In hollant die beelde stormighe ded door / die Goesen soe hebbe ic Andriaen Coenenzoon ghesien een Wilt Wijf met / een kint ende men sagh se om gelt dese vrouwe was mede gecleet Aldus da- / nich faetsoen van cleedighe als desen wilde man met zeehonts vellen of / robbe vellen dat Ruych buten ende dat kint was mede aldusdanigh gecleet zij en hadde geen sprake over haer oft en wolde niet spreken. Item van dese vrowue / hebbe ic gesien in scravenhage in der herbergh van den molen daer dese vrouwe / haer meesters die se liet besien tuis lagen to weten al dit dat die waerdinne / genaemt Anna pouwels Tot dat wilde wijf sprac ende wees haer op en deel /

beelden die somige vergult waren somighe geverwet" (alsoe haer man hooft man was van sint Antonis Outaer daer om die beelde daer gevlucht waren ende geberecht). / En Anno powels wees ende seyde siet lecht u hande samen dit is u heer / u godt ende so wijsende op de beelde Waer op die wilde vrouwe haer hooft / scudde ende slooch haer hooft om hoge ende leyde aldaer haer hant te. / samen Aldus dat daer wel an haer scheen dat zij kennis hadde van Godt van hemelrijcke Al sic an dit wel an haer bemerckte Aldus kent Godt almachtich wel den zijnen ende den zijnen hem hem zij lof / Amen."

62. For another instance of New World captives made to "perform" before a European public, see the case of Tupinamba in Rouen in 1550 in Rebecca Zorach, "'Taken by night from its tomb': Triumph, Dissent, and Danse Macabre in Sixteenth-Century France," in Elina Gertsman (ed.), *Visualizing Medieval Performance: Perspectives, Histories, Contexts* (New York: Routledge, 2008), pp. 223–46.

63. The full text is in Strauss, *The German Single-Leaf Woodcut, 1550–1600*, vol. 1, p. 376: "lasst uns Gott dem allmechtigen dancken für seine Wolthat / das er uns in seinem Wort erleucht hat / das wir nicht so gar wilde Leut und Menschen fresser sein / wie in dieser Landschaft sein / das die Weib gefangen und heraus gebracht worden / den sie gar nichts von dem rechten waren Gott wissen / sondern schier erger den das Vihe leben / Gott wolle sie auch zu seinem erkenntnis beteren / Amen."

64. Adriaen Coenen, quoted in Quinn, "This New Prey," p. 134: "ende noch meer ander die te lanck souden zijn / om al int particuliere te varhalen."

65. Heinrich Bullinger, *Second Helvetic Confession, quoted in Stuart Clark, Vanities of the Eye* (Oxford: Oxford University Press, 2007), p. 167.

66. Arnade, *Beggars, Iconoclasts, and Civic Patriots*, p. 117.

67. Brian Cummings, "Iconoclasm and Bibliophilia in the English Reformation, 1521–1558" in Jeremy Dimmick, James Simpson, and Nicolette Zeeman (eds.), *Images, Idolatry, and Iconoclasm in Late Medieval England: Textuality and the Visual Image* (Oxford: Oxford University Press, 2002), p. 194.

68. Jean Céard, *La nature et les prodigies: L'insolite au XVIe siècle* (Geneva: Droz, 1977), pp. 365–71; Lorraine Daston, "How Nature Became the Other: Anthropomorphism and Anthropocentrism in Early Modern Natural Philosophy," in Sabine Maasen et al. (eds.), *Biology as Society, Society as Biology: Metaphors* (Dordrecht: Kluwer Academic, 1995), pp. 37–56.

69. Frank Lestringant, "Calvinistes et cannibales: Les écrits protestantes sur le Brésil français (1555–1560)," in Lestringant, *L'expérience huguenote au Nouveau Monde: XVIe siècle* (Geneva: Librarie Droz, 1996), pp. 77–118.

70. Zentralbibliothek, Zürich, XXV 1396 (4). See Cécile Dupeux, Peter Jezler, and Gabriele Keck (eds.), *Bildersturm: Wahnsinn Oder Gottes Wille?* exh. cat., Bern/Strasbourg, 2001 (Zürich: NZZ Verlag, 2001), no. 135.

71. Michel de Montaigne, *The Essays of Montaigne*, trans. E. J. Trechmann, 2 vols. (Oxford: Oxford University Press, 1946), vol. 1, p. 210.

72. p. C. Hooft, *Neederlandsche histoorien, sedert de ooverdraght der heerschappye van kaizar Karel den Vyfden, op kooning Philips zynen zoon* (Amsterdam: Elzevier, 1642), p. 279.

73. Herodotus, *The Histories* 4.106.1.

74. Dionyse Settle, *A true reporte of the laste voyage into the west and northwest regions, &c. 1577. worthily atchieued by Capteine Frobisher* (London: Henrie Middleton, 1577), fols. Cvr–Dv.

75. Becanus, *Origines Antwerpianae*, p. 1046: "Vidi hic Antwerpiae feminam una cu prole illinc abreptam: quae, cum putaret Christianos cundem, quem sui carnis humanae deuorandae ritum habere, tam solicite semper prolem suam, quae quinque vel sex paulo plus minus annorum erat, custodiebar; ut aegerrime ferret, si quis contingeret, metuens nimirum, ne ad epulandum raperetur." See Egmond and Mason, "'These Are People Who Eat Raw Fish,'" pp. 312–13.

76. Jean Bodin, quoted in Frank Lestringant, "Rage, fureur, folie cannibales le Scythe et le Brésilien," in Jean Céard (ed.), *La folie et le corps* (Paris: Presses de l'École Normale Supérieure, 1985), pp. 49–80.

77. Miya Tokumitsu, "The Migrating Cannibal: Anthropophagy at Home and at the Edge of the World," in Bret Rothstein (ed.), *The Anthropomorphic Lens: Anthropomorphism, Microcosm and Analogy in Early Modern Thought and Visual Arts* (Leiden: Brill, 2015), pp. 93–116.

78. Thomas Cummins, "The Golden Calf in America," in Michael W. Cole and Rebecca E. Zorach (eds.), *The Idol in the Age of Art: Objects, Devotions and the Early Modern World* (Farnham: Ashgate, 2009.), p. 87.

79. Quoted in *ibid.*, p. 87 n. 26.

80. Nicholas M. Beasley, "Wars of Religion in the Circum-Caribbean," in Margaret Cormack (ed.), *Saints and Their Cults in the Atlantic World* (Columbia: University of South Carolina Press, 2007), p. 160.

81. Irene Wright (ed.), *Documents Concerning English Voyages to the Spanish Main 1569–1580* (London: Hakluyt Society, 1932), cited in Beasley, "Wars of Religion in the Circum-Caribbean," pp. 157 and 159.

82. Susan Juster, "Iconoclasm without Icons," in Linda Gregerson and Susan Juster (eds.), *Empires of God: Religious Encounters in the Early Modern Atlantic* (Philadelphia: University of Pennsylvania Press, 2001), pp. 223–24.

83. *Ibid.*, p. 229.

84. Folger Library, Washington, DC, shelfmark L.a.987. See Rachel Doggett, with Monique Hulvey and Julie Ainsworth (eds.), *New World of Wonders: European Images of the Americas, 1492–1700*, exh. cat. (Washington, DC: Folger Shakespeare Library, 1992), cat. 4, pp. 38–39.

85. Michael Lok, quoted in Quinn, "This New Prey," p. 71.

86. Nicole Blackwood, "Meta Incognita: Some Hypotheses on Cornelis Ketel's Lost English and Iunk Portraits," *Nederlands Kunsthistorisch Jaarboek* 66 (2016), p. 37.

87. Th. M. Chotzen, and Maartje Draak (eds.), *Beschrijving Der Britsche Eilanden: Een Geillustered Geschrift Uit Zijn Engelsche Ballingschap* (Amsterdam: de Sikkel, 1938), pp. 72–75.

88. Settle, *A true reporte of the laste voyage into the west and northwest regions*, p. 19.

89. Paul Hulton, *America 1585: The Complete Drawings of John White* (Chapel Hill: University of North Carolina Press, 1984), p. 29.

90. Public Record Office, London, MS no. SP12/118: "Doctor Doddyngs Reporte of the Sicknesse and Death of the Man at Bristoll which Capt. Frobisher brought from the North-West." See the transcription in Neil Cheshire, et al., "Frobisher's Eskimos in England" *Archivaria* 10 (Summer 1980), pp. 40–42.

91. Alden T. Vaughn, "Trinculo's Indian: American Natives in Shakespeare's England," in Peter Hulme (ed.), *"The Tempest" and Its Travels* (Philadelphia: University of Pennsylvania Press, 2000), p. 59.

92. *Ibid.*, p. 30. See also Franz Obermeier, "Canadian Iunk in 16th Century European Illustrations," in Wolfgang Klooss (ed.), *Narratives of Exploration and Discovery* (Trier: Wissensschaftlicher Verlag, 2005), pp. 159–75.

93. The visitor was Frederick, Duke of Wittenberg. See "A True and Faithful Narrative of the Bathing Excursion" (1602), quoted in William Benchley Rye (ed.), *England as Seen by Foreigners* (New York: Benjamin Blom, 1865), p. 18.

94. Best, *A True Discourse of the late voyages of discoverie*, fol. 124. On the passage, see Christian Kiening, *Das wilde Subjekt: Kleine Poetik der Neuen Welt* (Göttingen: Vandenhoek & Ruprecht, 2006), pp. 174–75.

95. *Annals of Great Britain under Queen Elizabeth* (London, 1577), in Kim Sloan (ed.), *A New World: England's First View of America* (Chapel Hill: University of North Carolina Press, 2007), p. 168.

96. For the list of expenses paid by the Cathay Company for the second Frobisher voyage, see Blackwood, "Meta Incognita," p. 26.

97. George Best, "A true reporte of such things as hapned in the second voyage of

Captayne Frobysher," 19r. The printed margin gloss in the original printing (London: British Library copy, C13a9[1]) reads: "The Savage captive amazed at his countreyman's picture." From British Library copy; original printing C13 a.9 (1), fol. 19r.

98. Randall C. Davis, "Early Anglo-American Attitudes to Native American Languages," in Carmen G. Biase (ed.), *Travel and Translation in the Early Modern Period* (Amsterdam: Rodopi, 2006), pp. 229–38.

99. Stephen Greenblatt, *Marvelous Possessions*, pp. 114–16. On Best's possible sources, see Cassander L. Smith, "'For They Are Naturally Born': Quandaries of Racial Representation in George Best's *A True Discourse*," *Studies in Travel Writing* 17.3 (2013), pp. 233–49.

100. But Greenblatt's quotation curiously elides the term; see *Marvelous Possessions*, pp. 114–15.

101. "Jam expressiones viventium vultuum, quae contrafacta nunc vocant, quam similes conficiebat, quam infallibiles, quam veras? (What images of living faces [Dürer] was already producing, which they are now calling *contrafacta*, how faultless, how real!)," in Rupprich, *Dürer Schriftlicher Nachlass*, vol. 1, p. 309. On Camerarius's invocation of the novelty of the term, see Jeffrey Ashcroft, *Albrecht Dürer: Documentary Biography*, 2 vols. (New Haven: Yale University Press, 2017), vol. 2, p. 955 n. 16 (doc. no. 299).

102. Josua Maaler, *Die teütsch spraach; alle wörter, namen, un arten zů reden in hochteütscher spraach* (Zurich: Christopher Froschauer, 1561), fol. 1v: "Abcontrafehen. Effingere / Abmachen / abmaalen. Ein lädlich Abcontrafehen / oder eigenlich abmallen. Exprimere tabella alicuius effigiem."

103. Woodcut, 35.7 x 28.4 cms., Zurich, Zentralbibliothek, VII 102 PAS II 15/32; Wolfgang Harms and Michael Schilling (eds.), *Die Sammlung der Zentralbibliothek Zürich: Kommentierte Ausgabe*, 2 vols. (Tübingen: Max Niemeyer, 1997), vol. 2, pp. 204–205. The Strasbourg edition was published by Fischart, the Augsburg by Michael Manger, and the Nuremberg edition by Leonhard Heussler.

104. See the transcription in Quinn, "This New Prey," p. 138.

105. Bruno Weber, "'Die Welt begeret allezeit Wunder': Versuch einer Bibliographie der Einblattdrucke von Bernhard Jobin in Strassburg," *Gutenberg-Jahrbuch* (1976), p. 273, n. 12.

106. There is a record of Aldee, a London printer, registering a title with the Stationers' Company called "A description of the purtrayture and Shape of those strange kinde of people whiche the worthie master Martin Fourbosier brought into England in Anno 1576, and 1577." No copies survive, but the numerous drawn versions of the design (and the incorporation into sheets like Glaser's) suggest that exemplars must have found their way

to mainland Europe. See Edward Arber (ed.), *A Transcript of the Registers of the Company of Stationers of London 1554–1604*, 5 vols. (London: privately printed, 1875), vol. 2, p. 145.

107. Michael Gaudio, "'Counterfeited According to the Truth': John White, Lucas de Heere, and the Truth in Clothing," in Kim Sloan (ed.), *European Visions: American Voices* (London: British Museum, 2009), pp. 24–32.

108. Hans Glaser, designer of the Nuremberg sheet, also published versions of Dürer workshop compositions, including a chiaroscuro *St. Anne With the Holy Family* (Geisberg 770).

109. Tattooed chin and cheek lines (*tamlughun*) also remain traditional markers of social maturity for Inuit, Alaskan Yupic, and Eastern Siberian women, statements of the ability to withstand pain. Such lines also functioned as gender-specific marks in warfare; because Eskimo intertribal conflict often took place in near or total darkness among heavily clothed males, the chin tattoo allowed women to be identified as noncombatants and their lives, ostensibly, to be spared. See H. Kapel, et al., "Tattooing," in J. Hansen, et al. (eds), *Greenland Mummies* (Montreal: McGill–Queen's University Press, 1991), pp. 102–15, and Renée Fossett, *In Order to Live Untroubled: Iunk of the Central Arctic, 1550–1940* (Winnipeg: Manitoba University Press, 2001), p. 47. I am extremely grateful to Norman Vorano for his guidance on the topic. In fact, in the London exemplar of the broadsheet, the faces of the captives are colored brown, their lips touched in red, the ground painted in green, the tattoos in deep blue.

110. Alfred Gell, *Wrapping in Images: Tattooing in Polynesia* (Oxford: Oxford University Press, 1996), pp. 108 and 110. Lars Krutak, "Of Human Skin and Ivory Spirits: Tattooing and Carving in Bering Strait," in William W. Fitzhugh, Julie Holowell, and Aron Crowell (eds.), *Gifts from the Ancestors: Ancient Ivories of Bering Strait* (New Haven: Yale University Press, 2009), pp. 190–203.

111. Krutak, "Of Human Skin and Ivory Spirits," in Fitzhugh, Holowell, and Crowell (eds.), *Gifts from the Ancestors*, pp. 190–203.

112. Juliet Fleming, *Graffiti and the Writing Arts of Early Modern England* (London: Reaktion, 2001), p. 87.

113. On the bifurcated "marking" relationship between New World tattooing and print, see Michael Gaudio, *Engraving the Savage: The New World and Techniques of Civilization* (Minneapolis: University of Minnesota Press, 2008), pp. 2–6 and 21–23.

114. Neil L. Whitehead, introduction to Hans Staden, *Hans Staden's True History: An Account of Cannibal Captivity in Brazil*, trans. Neil L. Whitehead and Michael Harbsmeier (Durham: Duke University Press, 2008), p. 72.

115. Hal Foster, "Artist as Ethnographer," in George E. Marcus and Fred R. Myers (eds.),

The Traffic in Culture: Refiguring Art and Anthropology (Berkeley: University of California Press, 1995), pp. 302–309.

116. Claude Lévi-Strauss, "Sur Jean de Léry," in Jean de Léry, *Histoire d'un voyage faict en la terre du Brésil* (Paris: Flammarion, 1994), p. 13.

117. Claude Lévi-Strauss, *The Savage Mind* (London: Weidenfeld and Nicolson, 1966), pp. 16–22.

118. Franz Boas, introduction to James Teit, *Traditions of the Thompson River Indians of British Columbia* (Boston: Houghton Mifflin, 1898), p. 18. While pursuing a doctorate in physics at Kiel, Boas had participated in expeditions to Baffin Island, where he actually collected specimens (among them mittens, spears, and dolls) later donated to the Royal Museum in Berlin; see Franz Boas, "Sammlung aus Baffin-Land," *Original-Mittheilungen aus der Ethnologischen Abtheilung der Königlichen Museen zu Berlin* 1.2–3 (1886), pp. 131–33.

119. Friedrich Winkler, *Die Zeichnungen Albrecht Dürers*, 4 vols. (Berlin: Deutsches Verein für Kunstwissenschaft, 1939), vol. 4, no. 823.

120. Natalie Dupêcher, "Seeing and Believing Albrecht Dürer's Walrus," unpublished seminar paper, Princeton University Department of Art and Archaeology, 2014, p. 10.

121. "1521 / Das dosig thÿr van dem jch do das hawbt / contrefett hab ist gefangen worden / jn die niderlendischen see." On the contested translations of "dosig thÿr," see Ashcroft, *Albrecht Dürer*, no. 163.26, vol. 1, p. 636.

122. Dupêcher, "Seeing and Believing Albrecht Dürer's Walrus," p. 10.

123. Walkendorf had actually sent a letter to Rome along with the walrus, describing its "stiff and messy beard" and then offering a poem in the creature's own voice:

The Bishop of Trondheim

Had me stabbed on the shore

And sent my head to Pope Leo in Rome

So that many people might see me.

Quoted in Brian W. Ogilvie, *The Science of Describing: Natural History in Renaissance Europe* (Chicago: University of Chicago Press, 2006), p. 233.

124. Kirsten A. Seaver, "'A Very Common and Usuall Trade': The Relationship between Cartographic Perceptions and 'Fishing' in the Davis Strait circa 1500–1550," in Karen Severud Cook (ed.), *Images and Icons of the New World: Essays on American Cartography* (London: British Library, 1996), p. 11.

125. Such fishermen are recorded sailing Northeast of Iceland as early as 1517. See Jean-Pierre Proulx, *Basque Whaling in Labrador in the Sixteenth Century* (Ottawa: Natural History Park Service, 1993), p. 12.

126. Fritz Koreny, *Albrecht Dürer und die Tier- und Pflanzenstudien der Rensaissance* (Munich: Prestel, 1985), p. 14.

127. Valentin Kiparsky, "L'histoire du morse," *Annales Academiae Scientarium Fennicae* 73, series B (1952), pp. 46–48.

128. On the trade in walrus ivory between the Norse and Northern Europe, see Karin M. Frei, et al., "Was It for Walrus? Viking Age Settlement and Medieval Walrus Ivory Trade in Iceland and Greenland," *World Archaeology* 47.3 (2015), pp. 439–66.

129. Winkler, *Die Zeichnungen Albrecht Dürers*, vol. 4, no. 855.

130. Colin Eisler, *Dürer's Animals* (Washington: Smithsonian Institution Press, 1991), p. 275.

131. Caroline Walker Bynum, "Wonder," *American Historical Review* 102.1 (February 1997), p. 14.

132. René Descartes, quoted in Lorraine Daston and Katherine Park, *Wonders and the Order of Nature, 1150–1750* (New York: Zone Books, 1998), p. 13.

133. Darcy G. Grigsby, *Extremities: Painting Empire in Post-Revolutionary France* (New Haven: Yale University Press, 2002), p. 168.

134. Valentin Groebner, "*Complexio* / Complexion: Categorizing Individual Natures, 1250–1600," in Lorraine Daston and Fernando Vidal (eds.), *The Moral Authority of Nature* (Chicago: University of Chicago Press, 2004), pp. 361–83. The quotation appears on pp. 364–65. On the construction of "Arctic" identity, see Patrizia Isabelle Duda, "Arcticness: In the Making of the Beholder," in Ilan Kelman (ed.), *Arcticness: Power and Voice from the North* (London: UCL Press, 2017), pp. 40–48.

135. Martin A. Berger, *Sight Unseen: Whiteness and American Culture* (Berkeley: University of California Press, 2005); Toni Morrison, "Romancing the Shadow," in Morrison, *Playing in the Dark: Whiteness and the Literary Imagination* (Cambridge, MA: Harvard University Press, 1992), pp. 31–59. More specifically, on the early modern North American context, see Wendy Harding, *The Myth of Emptiness and the New American Literature of Place* (Iowa City: University of Iowa Press, 2014), esp. pp. 27–48.

136. Claude Lévi-Strauss, *Tristes Tropiques*, trans. John Weightman and Doreen Weightman (New York: Atheneum, 1975), p. 1.

137. Sophie Lemercier-Goddard and Frédéric Regard, "Introduction: The Northwest Passage and the Imperial Myth: Project, History, Ideology, Myth" in Frédéric Regard (ed.), *The Quest for the Northwest Passage: Knowledge, Nation, and Empire, 1576–1806* (London: Pickering and Chatto, 2012), pp. 1–54.

138. Homi K. Bhabha, "Signs Taken for Wonders," *Critical Inquiry* 12 (1985), pp. 144–65, esp. pp. 153–54.

CHAPTER FIVE : A ROMAN INTERRUPTION

1. Olaus Magnus, *Historia de gentibus septentrionalibus* (Rome: Giovanni Viotto, 1555), p. 37. (Hereafter *Hg.*) All quotations (and page numbers) are from this edition, and the translations are based (with occasional alterations) on Olaus Magnus, *Description of the Northern Peoples*, ed. Peter Foote, trans. Peter Fisher and Humphrey Higgens, with annotations derived from the commentary by John Granlund (London: Hakluyt Society, 1996), 3 vols. (Hereafter *OM.*) The snowflake passage appears in *OM*, p. 53.

2. On the circumstances of the book's illustrations, see Elena Balzamo, "Olaus Magnus savait-il dessiner?' *Proxima Thulé* 6 (2010), pp. 121–41; Peter Gillgren, "The Artist Olaus Magnus: Vision and Illustration," in Carlo Santini (ed.), *I Fratelli Giovanni e Olao Magno* (Rome: il Calmo, 1999), pp. 147–55. For Viotto in Rome, see G. Ludovico Masetti Zannini, *Stampatori e librai a Roma nella II metà del Cinquecento* (Rome: Palombi, 1980), p. 100.

3. *Hg*, p. 36; *OM*, p. 53.

4. See, for example, Harry B. Weiss, "Olaus Magnus, Credulous Zoologist, and Archbishop of the Sixteenth Century," *Journal of the New York Entomological Society* 38.1 (1930), pp. 35–37; Jakob Otnes, "Swedish Influence on Norwegian Hydrology Prior to 1814," *Geografiska Annaler. Series A, Physical Geography* 63.3–4 (1981), pp. 119–25. On Olaus as folklorist, see Wolfgang Seegrün's review of a 1972 German edition of the *Historia*, in *Historische Zeitschrift* 219.2 (1974), pp. 479–80.

5. For an overview of Olaus's project and biography (with original documents reproduced), see Kurt Johannesson, *Renaissance of the Goths: Johannes and Olaus Magnus as Politicians and Historians*, trans. James Larson (Berkeley: University of California Press, 1991), esp. pp. 139–206. On the political circumstances in Sweden, see Johannes Nordström, *Johannes Magnus och den götiska romantiken* (Stockholm: Almqvist & Wiksell, 1975).

6. P. F. Grendler, *The Roman Inquisition and the Venetian Press, 1540–1605* (Princeton: Princeton University Press, 1975), pp. 52 and 57.

7. Hubert Jedin, *A History of the Council of Trent*, trans. Ernest Graf, 2 vols. (St. Louis: Herder, 1961), vol. 2, p. 477.

8. *Hg*, pp. 1–2; *OM* dedication, pp. 1–2.

9. *Hg*, p. 4; *OM* dedication, p. 2.

10. Edward H. Landon (ed.), *A Manual of Councils of the Holy Catholic Church* (Edinburgh: John Grant, 1909), pp. 180–96.

11. *Hg*, pp. 1–2; *OM* dedication, pp. 1–2.

12. Unabridged translations of the tract appeared relatively quickly: French (1561), Dutch (1562), Italian (1565), German (1567), and English (1658). See Elena Bolzamo, "La

fortune littéraire des frères Johannes et Olaus Magnus ou les enjeux de la traduction," *Proxima Thulé 5* (2006), pp. 135–37.

13. Jorge Luis Borges, "Olaus Magnus," in Borges, *La moneda de hierro* (Buenos Aires: Emecé, 1976), p. 23.

14. *Hg*, p. ii; *OM*, p. 2.

15. *Hg*, p. 471; *OM*, p. 668.

16. *Hg*, p. 547; *OM*, p. 796.

17. *Hg*, p. 454; *OM*, pp. 384–85.

18. Jakob Ziegler, *Schondia* (Augsburg: Opilionis, 1532); Augsburg: Staatsbibliothek, 2Gs 915, fol. 95r.

19. On this passage, see Rune Blix Hagen, s.v. "Olaus Magnus," *The Encyclopedia of Witchcraft: The Western Tradition* (Santa Barbara: ABC-CLIO, 2006). More generally, on the idea of a haunted Arctic, see Monique Mund-Dopchie, "Imaginaire des îles de l'Extrême-Nord dans la littérature géographique de la Renaissance," in Éric Schnakenbourg (ed.), *Figures du Nord: Scandinavie, Groenland et Sibérie. Perceptions et représentations des espaces septentrionaux du Moyen Âge au XVIIIe siècle* (Rennes: Presses universitaires de Rennes, 2012), pp. 85–102.

20. Carlo Santini, "Strategie della communicazione nella Historia di Olao Magno," in Santini (ed.), *I Fratelli Giovanni e Olao Magno*, pp. 309–31. Various Olaus translations often sanitized the original Latin content: a French edition of 1560 printed in Antwerp, for example, expunged dozens of woodcuts about church liturgy; Olaus's screeds against "monstrous" Lutheran pictures quietly vanished from the first English translation (London, 1668).

21. *Hg*, p. 57; *OM*, p. 77.

22. *OM*, added note, vol. 1, p. 90.

23. *Hg*, p. 58; *OM*, p. 78.

24. *Hg*, p. 50; *OM*, p. 67.

25. *Hg*, p. 49; *OM*, p. 67.

26. *Hg*, p. 1; *OM*, p. 65.

27. Johannes Trithemius, *Polygraphiae libri sex* (Oppenheim: Haselberg, 1518), fol. P7r.

28. For example, *Hg*, book 1, chapter 34; book 5, chapter 4; book 8, chapter 1; book 13, chapter 35.

29. Georges Didi-Huberman, "The Aporia of the Detail," in Didi-Huberman, *Confronting Images: Questioning the Ends of a Certain History of Art* (University Park: Pennsylvania State University Press, 2004), p. 230: "Contrary to the fragment whose relationship to the whole only puts it into question, posits it as an absence or enigma or lost memory, the

detail in this sense imposes the whole, its legitimate presence, its value as response and point of reference, even as hegemony."

30. Jennifer Raab, *Frederic Church: The Art and Science of Detail* (New Haven: Yale University Press, 2015), p. 5.

31. *Hg*, p. 33; *OM*, pp. 47–48

32. *Hg*, p. 33; *OM*, p. 47. See M, P. Charlesworth, "Arctic Travel and Warfare in the Sixteenth Century," *Polar Record* 4.26 (1943), pp. 52–60.

33. *Hg*, pp. 33–34; *OM*, p. 47. For Magnus's isolation of cold within the context of his broader ethnographic project, see Barbara Sjoholm, "'Things to Be Marveled at Rather Than Examined': Olaus Magnus and *A Description of the Northern Peoples*," *Antioch Review* 62.2 (Spring 2004), pp. 245–54.

34. Cotton Mather, *The Christian Philosopher: A Collection of the Best Discoveries in Nature, With Religious Improvements* (Charlestown: J. McKown, 1815), p. 214.

35. Robert Burton, *Anatomy of Melancholy* (New York: New York Review of Books, 2001), p. 191.

CHAPTER SIX : ARCTIC INK

1. The earliest mention of the pulp appears in: Johan Karel de Jonge, *Nova Zembla: De voorwerpen door de Nederlandsche zeevaarders na hunne overwintering aldaar in 1597 achtergelaten en in 1871 door Kapitein Carlsen teruggevonden, beschreven en toegelicht*, 2nd ed. (The Hague: Nijhoff, 1873), no. 75.

2. J. Braat, J. P. Filedt Kok, J. H. Hofenk de Graff, and P. Poldervaart, "Restauratie, conservatie, en onderzoek van de op Nova Zembla gevonden zestiende-eeuwse prenten" *Bulletin van het Rijksmuseum* 28.2, pp. 43–79.

3. On the history of the voyage and the archaeology of the find, see the introductory matter to S. P. L'Honoré Naber (ed.), *Reizen van Willem Barents, Jacob van Heemskerck, Jan Conelisz: Rijp en anderen naar het Noorden (1594–1597)*, 2 vols. (The Hague: Nijhoff, 1917), vol. 1; J. Braat, et al. (eds.), *Behouden uit het Behouden Huys: Catalogus van de voorwerpen van de Barentsexpeditie (1596), gevonden op Nova Zembla. De Rijksmuseumcollectie, aangevuld met Russische en Noorse vondsten*, exh. cat. (Amsterdam: De Bataafsche Leeuw, 1998); Jaap Jan Zeeberg, *Into the Ice Sea: Barents' Wintering on Novaya Zemlya* (Amsterdam: Rozenberg, 2005).

4. Donald F. Lach and Edwin J. van Kley, *Asia in the Making of Europe, Volume 3: A Century of Advance* (Chicago: University of Chicago Press, 1998), pp. 516–57.

5. John. F. Richards, *The Unending Frontier: An Environmental History of the Early Modern World* (Berkeley: University of California Press, 2003), p. 590.

6. Sarah M. Nutt, "The Arctic Voyages of William Barents in Probable Relation to Certain of Shakespeare's Plays," *Studies in Philology* 39 (1942), pp. 254–60.

7. Daryl M. Palmer, *Writing Russia in the Age of Shakespeare* (Aldershot: Ashgate, 2004), pp. 167–68.

8. See B. van Selm, *Een menighte treffelijcke Boecken Nederlandse boekhandelscatalogi in het begin van de zeventiende eeuw* (Utrecht: HES, 1987), pp. 225 and 304–305; J. P. Filedt Kok, "Gravures" in J. Braat, et al. (eds.), *Behouden uit het Behouden Huys*, pp. 170–71.

9. J. W. Ijzerman, "Hollandsche Prenten als Handelsartikel te Patani in 1602," in *Gedenkschrift Uitgegeven ter Gelegenheid van het 75-Jarig Bestaan op 4 Juni 1926 (Koninklijk Instituut voor de Taal-l, Land- en Volkenkunde van Nederlandsch-Indië)* (The Hague: Nijhoff, 1926), pp. 84–109.

10. Dick Walda, *Gevangen in Het Ijs: De Overwintering van Willem Barents op Nova Zembla* (Houten: Fibula, 1996), pp. 121–26.

11. Jan Braat, "Dutch Activities in the North and the Arctic during the Sixteenth and Seventeenth Centuries," *Arctic* 37.4 (December 1984), pp. 473–80.

12. Jan Huygen van Linschoten, 1601, quoted in Jaap Jan Zeeberg, *Climate and Glacial History of the Novaya Zemlya Archipelago, Russian Arctic: With Notes on the Region's History of Exploration* (Amsterdam: Rozenberg, 2002), p. 56.

13. J. C. A. de Meij, "Oorlogsvaart, kaapvaart en zeeroof," in G. Asaert, J. van Beylen, and H. P. H. Jansen (eds.), *Maritieme geschiedenis der Nederlanden*, 4 vols. (Bussum: De Boer Maritiem, 1976), vol. 1, pp. 309–10.

14. J. M. Kleiboer, "Scheepsklok, in 1597 door J. Heemskerck en W. Barendsz op Nova-Zembla achtergelaten," *Oud Holland* 46 (1929), pp. 67–72.

15. On Plancius, see J. Keuning, *Petrus Plancius: Theoloog en Geograaf 1552–1622* (Amsterdam: P. N. van Kampen & Zoon, 1946); on his theory of an ice-free Northwest Passage, see pp. 108–19.

16. Gerrit de Veer, *Waerachtighe beschryvinghe van drie seylagien, ter werelt noyt soo vreemt ghehoort . . . deur de Hollandtsche ende Zeelandtsche schepen by noorden Noorweghen, Moscovia ende Tartaria na de coninckrijcken van Cathay ende China . . .* (Amsterdam: Cornelis Claesz, 1598), fol. 24r. For a useful English translation, see Gerrit de Veer, *A true description of three voyages by the north-east towards Cathay and China: undertaken by the Dutch in the years 1594, 1595, and 1596*, ed. Charles T. Beke and William Phillip (London: Hakluyt Society, 1853), p. 105. The publisher of the first de Veer edition, Cornelis Claesz, also owned the print shop that produced all of the engravings lost on Nova Zembla.

17. De Veer, *Waerachtighe beschryvinghe*, fol. 25r–25v.

18. Gerrit de Veer, *Om de Noord: De tochten van Willem Barentsz en Jacob van Heemskerck en de overwintering op Nova Zembla, zoals opgetekend door Gerrit de Veer*, ed. V. D. Roeper and G. J. D. Wildeman (Nijmegen: Sun, 1996), p. 105.

19. Margaret Cohen, *The Novel and the Sea* (Princeton: Princeton University Press, 2010), pp. 22–23.

20. Margaret Schotte, "Expert Records: Nautical Logbooks from Columbus to Cook," *Information and Culture* 48.3 (2013), p. 287.

21. David Waters, *The Art of Navigation in England in Elizabethan and Early Stuart Times* (New Haven: Yale University Press, 1958), pp. 83–86.

22. Adriaen Veen, *Tractaet vant Zee-bouck-houden*... (Amsterdam: B. Andriaenszoon, 1597); see Schotte, "Expert Records," p. 312 n. 32.

23. John Gatonbe, *Journal of a Voyage for the Discovery of a North-West Passage*, in John Churchill, *Collection of Voyages and Travels: Some Now First Printed from Original Manuscripts, others translated out of foreign languages and now first publish'd in English, to which are added some few that have formerly appear'd in English, but do now for their excellency and scarceness deserve to be reprinted*, 6 vols. (London: Churchill, 1732), vol. 6, p. 248.

24. De Veer, *Waerachtighe beschryvinghe*, fol 28r: "zy conden uyt haer ooghen niet sien, ende waren daer duer by naest verdwaelt vanden rechten wech."

25. *Ibid.*, fol. 36v.

26. *Ibid.*, fol. 34v–35r. The occurrence thus described was in fact a real geophysical phenomenon, the "Nova Zembla effect," in which the sun's reflection deceptively precedes itself on the horizon, a situation extant only in the Arctic. See Siebren van der Werf, "Astronomical Observations during Willem Barents's Third Voyage to the North (1596–97)," *Arctic* 51.2 (1998), pp. 142–54.

27. De Veer, *Waerachtighe beschryvinghe*, fol. 30r.

28. Zeeberg, *Climate and Glacial History of the Novaya Zemlya Archipelago, Russian Arctic*, pp. 139–42. On the island's atomic history, see Anatoly M Matushchenko, "Some Characteristics of Atmospheric Nuclear Tests at the U.S.S.R. Test Sites (1949–62)," in Charles S. Schapiro (ed.), *Atmospheric Nuclear Tests: Environmental and Human Consequences* (New York: Springer, 1998), pp. 63–68.

29. Anne Goldgar, "Time and Space in the Early Modern Arctic," lecture at RSA Boston, April 2016. Goldgar is preparing a book-length study of the Barents voyages, which she kindly discussed with me.

30. De Veer, *Waerachtighe beschryvinghe*, fol. 44v–45r: "wy met alle man ghelijcker handt heen met bylen, houweelen ende allerley ghereetschap daer toe diende om den wech wat

te effenen, daer deur wy de schuyten naet water souden sleepen, lancks den wech die vol ys ende ys-berghen lach, daer wy grooten arbeyt deden, met houwen, smyten, schoppen, graven ende wechwerpen."

31. *Ibid.*, fol. 32r.

32. J. Braat, et al. "Restauratie, conservatie, en onderzoek" pp. 46–51.

33. Joel Fischer, "The Suddenness of Place: Siân Bowen and Nova Zembla," in Siân Bowen (ed.), *Siân Bowen and Nova Zembla: Suspending the Ephemeral*, exh. cat. (Sheffield: RGAP, 2012), p. 93.

34. On the chemistry of the process, see Pia C. DeSantis, "Some Observations on the Use of Enzymes in Paper Conservation," *Journal of the American Institute for Conservation* 23.1 (1983), pp. 7–27.

35. Sarah Reidell, head of paper conservation at the Kislak Center for Special Collections at the University of Pennsylvania Libraries, personal correspondence, March 31, 2017.

36. Peter Poldervaart, quoted in *Siân Bowen and Nova Zembla*, p. 117.

37. As in, say, Dürer woodcuts from the Kaiser Friedrich Museum stowed in Bavarian salt mines during the Second World War. See Petra Winter, "'Zwillingsmuseen' im geteilten Berlin: Zur Nachkriegsgeschichte der Staatlichen Museen zu Berlin 1945 bis 1958," *Jahrbuch Der Berliner Museen* 50 (2008), pp. 16–20.

38. Listed in the inventory of the 1871 Carlsen expedition (and there identified as by Hendrick Goltzius); see the introduction to Gerrit de Veer, *The three voyages of William Barents to the Arctic regions (1594, 1595, and 1596)*, 2nd ed. (London: Hakluyt Society, 1876), p. lviii.

39. Siân Bowen, "Bringing It Together," https://bowenatrijksmuseum.wordpress .com/2012/01/21/bringing-it-together.

40. Shira Brisman, *Albrecht Dürer and the Epistolary Mode of Address* (Chicago: University of Chicago Press, 2016), pp. 45–74; on "communicative capitalism," see Jodi Dean, *The Communist Horizon* (New York: Verso, 2012), pp. 122–56. And on the important idea of the printed page as the opposite of the icon, see Joseph Koerner, "On monuments," *Res* 67/68 (2016/2017), pp. 5–6.

41. "Iure gentium quibusvis ad quosvis liberam esse navigationem." Hugo Grotius, *Mare Liberum* (Leiden: Elzvier, 1609), fol. A1r. 25. On the famous passage in relation to the broader history of international piracy, see Daniel Heller-Roazen, *The Enemy of All: Piracy and the Law of Nations* (New York: Zone Books, 2009), pp. 120–22.

42. Hugo Grotius, *The Free Sea, Translated by Richard Hakluyt*, ed. David Armitage (Indianapolis, Liberty Fund, 2004), p. 25.

43. Martine Julia van Ittersum, "Hugo Grotius in Context: Van Heemskerck's Capture of the Santa Caterina and Its Justification in De Jure Praedae (1604–6)," *Asian Journal of Social Science* 31.3 (2003), pp. 511–48.

44. Jean Lévesque de Burigny, *The Life of the Truly Eminent and Learned Hugo Grotius*, 7 vols. (London: A Millar, 1754), vol. 1, pp. 30–31.

45. Hugo Grotius, "Defense of Chapter V of the Mare Liberum," reprinted in *The Free Sea*, p. 70.

46. Christopher Connery, "Ideologies of Land and Sea: Alfred Thayer Mahan, Carl Schmitt, and the Shaping of Global Myth Elements," *boundary 2* 28.2 (2001), p. 178.

47. On this issue, see Adriana Craciun, "The Frozen Ocean," *PMLA* 125.3 (May 2010), p. 694.

48. Hugo Grotius, quoted in A. M. Meijerman, *Hollandse Winters* (Antwerp: Standaard, 1967), p. 59.

49. Issak Beeckman, quoted in Adriaan M. J. de Kraker, "The Little Ice Age," in Pieter Roelofs (ed.), *Hendrick Avercamp: Master of the Ice Scene* (Amsterdam: Rijksmuseum 2009), p. 27.

50. Hartmut Lehmann, "Frömmigkeitsgeschichtliche Auswirkungen der 'Kleinen Eiszeit'," in Wolfgang Schieder (ed.), *Volksreligiosität in der modernen Sozialgeschichte* (*Geschichte und Gesellschaft, Sonderheft* 11) (Göttingen: Vandenhoeck & Ruprecht, 1986), p. 37. On Schaller, see also Philipp Blom, *Die Welt aus den Angeln* (Munich: Carl Hanser, 2017), pp. 34–35, 52.

51. *Vber die grossen und erschrecklichen Zeichen am Himmel vnd auff Erden . . .* (Leipzig: n.p, 1562), fol. A2r: "Ein grosse Kalte die volgt hernach / Und viel ein gros gewaltig schnee / Die kelt tbet manchem arm man wehe." Munich, BSB P.o. germ 2104f.

52. Renward Cysat, *Collectanea chronica und denkwürdige Sachen pro chronica Lucernensi et Helvetiae*, vol. 1, pt. 2, p. 946, quoted in Martin Hille, "Mensch und Klima in der frühen Neuzeit: Die Anfänge regelmäßiger Wetterbeobachtung. 'Kleine Eiszeit' und ihre Wahrnehmung bei Renward Cysat (1545–1614)," *Archiv für Kulturgeschichte* 83 (2001), p. 84.

53. Wolfgang Behringer, "'Kleine Eiszeit' und Frühe Neuzeit," in Wolfgang Behringer, Hartmut Lehmann, and Christian Pfister, *Kulturelle Konsequenzen der "Kleinen Eiszeit,"* (*Veröffentlichungen des Max-Planck-Instituts für Geschichte* 212) (Göttingen: Vandenhoeck & Ruprecht, 2005), pp. 415–508.

54. A useful comparison here might be more recent attempts to "understand the active role of human agency not only in the *construction* of facts, but also in the very *existence* of the phenomena those facts are trying to document," as Bruno Latour puts it. See Latour, "Agency at the Time of the Anthropocene," *New Literary History* 45 (2014), p. 2.

55. The painting seems to have been commissioned for the Delft town hall. See P. J. J. van Thiel, "De Schilderijen van Het K.O.G," *Leids Kunsthistorisch Jaarboek* 10 (1995), p. 55, no. 1078.

56. "Ao 1565, den 2 Januarii namiddach met die vloet in eeen groet quartier uers is een ysgeberecht ghecomen op 't hoeft tot Delfshaven, hoegh wesende 23 roe voet ende langh 17 roeten." See Evert van Straaten, *Koud Tot op Het Bot: De Verbeelding van de Winter in de Zestiende en Zeventiende Eeuw in de Nederlanden* (The Hague: Staatsdrukerij, 1977), p. 76. On the problematics of relating meteorology and early modern art in general, see Christian-Dietrich Schönwiese, "Europäische Klimageschichte und ihre Verbindungen zur Kunst, insbesondere Malerei," in Werner Wehry and Franz Ossing (eds.), *Wolken, Malerei, Klima in Geschichte und Gegenwart* (Berlin: Deutsche Meterologische Gesellschaft, 1997), pp. 39–58.

57. Alistair Fowler, "Bruegel's Hunters in the Snow," *Source: Notes in the History of Art* 36.1 (Fall 2014), pp. 9–15; Claire Billen and Chloé Deligne, "Bruegels Winterszenen" in Tine Luk Meganck and Sabine van Sprang (eds.), *Bruegels Winterlandschaften: Historiker und Kunsthistoriker im Dialog* (Stuttgart: Hatje Cantz, 2018), pp. 130–149.

58. Marx and Engels, in fact, described chill as the atmosphere of capitalism, the "icy water of egotistical calculation" that submerged the religious fervor of an earlier era. Karl Marx and Friedrich Engels, *The Communist Manifesto*, trans. Samuel Moore (London: Penguin, 2002), p. 222.

59. P. S. Allen, and H M. Allen (eds.), *Opus Epistolarum Des. Erasmi Roterodami, Volume 4* (Oxford University Press, 1926), p. 392, no. 174.

60. John Calvin, *Institutes*, book 1, ch. 16.

61. Franziska Hilfiker, "Negotiating Arctic Waters: John Davis's The Worldes Hydrographical Description," in Susanna Burghartz, et al. (eds.), *Sites of Mediation: Connected Histories of Places, Processes, and Objects in Europe and Beyond* (Leiden: Brill, 2016), pp. 353–72.

62. John Davis, *The Worldes Hydrographical Description* (London: Thomas Dawson, 1595), fol. C1v.

63. Robert Boyle, *New experiments and observations touching cold, or, An experimental history of cold begun: to which are added an examen of antiperistasis and an examen of Mr. Hobs's doctrine about cold* (London: John Crook, 1665), p. 522.

64. *Ibid.*, pp. 234, 300, 393.

65. Edward Pellham, *God's power and providence shewed, in the miraculous preservation and deliverance of eight englishmen . . .* (London: John Partridge, 1631), p. 11.

66. Letter of Giovanni Michiel to the doge and the senate, 1555, quoted in R. Brown (ed.), *Calendar of State Papers and manuscripts relating to English Affairs existing in the archives and collection of Venice*, 38 vols. (London: Stationer's Office, 1877), vol. 6, no. 269.

67. Jens Munk, quoted in C. C. A. Gosch, *Danish Arctic Expeditions 1605 to 1620: In Two Books* (London: Hakluyt Society, 1897), p. 6.

68. Gosch, *Danish Arctic Expeditions*, book 2, pp. cvi–cvii. Sections of Munk's account were later republished in Issac La Peyrère, *Relation du Groenland* (Paris: Augustin Courbe, 1647).

69. Richard Hakluyt, *The principal navigations, voiages, traffiques and discoueries of the English nation* (London: George Bishop, Ralph Newberie, and Robert Barker, 1600), p. 692.

70. Stephen Parmenius was born in Buda between 1555 and 1560 and was brought up a Calvinist in the Turkish sector the city. He studied in Heidelberg, then at Oxford, where he seems to have shared rooms with Richard Hakluyt at Christ Church College. Sailing to North America with Gilbert in summer 1583, Parmenius spent two weeks exploring the shore near St. Johns, during which he dispatched various letters back to England, carried on surviving vessels of the expedition. See David B. Quinn and Neil M. Cheshire, *The New Found Land of Stephen Parmenius* (Toronto: Toronto University Press, 1972), esp. pp. 58–66.

71. British Library, London, Cotton MS Otho E. VIII, fol. 78r.

72. Braat et al. (eds.), *Behouden uit het Behouden Huys*, p. 158.

73. On Pet and Jackson, see Robert Baldwin, "John Dee's Interest in the Application of Nautical Science, Mathematics, and Law to English Naval Affairs," in Stephen Clucas (ed.), *John Dee: Interdisciplinary Studies in English Renaissance Thought* (Dordrecht: Springer, 2006), pp. 97–130, and Helen Wallis, "England's Search for the Northwest Passages in the Sixteenth and Early Seventeenth Centuries," *Arctic* 37.4 (December 1984), p. 457. A curious report from 1584 by a factor to the Muscovy Company was quoted in Samuel Purchas's vast collection of travel stories: "Your people have bin at the said River of Obs mouth with a Ship, and there was made shipwrecke, and your people were slaine by the Somoeds, which thought that they came to rob and subdue them." See T. E. Armstrong, "The Arctic," in David B. Quinn (ed.), *The Hakluyt Handbook*, 2 vols. (London: Hakluyt Society, 1974), vol. 1, p. 257 n. 2.

74. Pellham, *God's Power and Providence*, p. 11.

75. Hans Blumenberg, *Shipwreck with Spectator: Paradigm of a Metaphor for Existence* (Cambridge, MA: MIT Press, 1997), pp. 7–79.

76. François Rabelais, *Le Quart livre des faicts et dicts héroïques du noble Pantagruel* (Lyon: Baltasar Aleman, 1552), p. 488.

77. *Ibid.*, ch. 55.

78. Arthur Tilley, "Rabelais and Geographical Discovery, II," *Modern Language Review* 3.3 (April 1908), pp. 209–17; Abel Lefranc, *Les navigations de Pantagruel: étude sur la géographie Rabelaisienne* (Paris: H. Leclerc, 1905), pp. 59–60.

79. Elcie Eduard Léon Mellema, *Dictionaire ou promptuaire françoys-flameng, très-ample et très-copieux* (Antwerp: J. Waesbergue, 1589). See Braat, Behouden Huys, p. 304, no. 10.1.17.

80. Eric M. MacPhail, *Dancing around the Well: The Circulation of Commonplaces in Renaissance Humanism* (Brill's studies in intellectual history, vol. 232) (Leiden: Brill, 2014), pp. 44–45.

81. Joseph Addison, "Frozen Voices," *Tatler* 254 (November 23, 1710), in George Aiken (ed.), *The Tatler, Edited with Introduction and Notes* (London: Duckworth, 1899), pp. 287–92.

82. André Thevet, *Cosmographie universelle*, fol. 674r, quoted in Frank Lestringant, *Mapping the Renaissance World: The Geographical Imagination in the Age of Discovery* (Cambridge: Polity, 1994), p. 153 n. 15.

83. Elizabeth L. Eisenstein, *The Printing Press as an Agent of Change: Communications and Cultural Transformations in Early Modern Europe*, 2 vols. (Cambridge: Cambridge University Press, 1980), vol. 1, pp. 113–28.

84. Alois Riegl, "Oströmische Beiträge," in *Beiträge zur Kunstgeschichte: Franz Wickhoff gewidmet von einem Kreise von Freunden und Schülern* (Vienna: A. Schroll, 1903), pp. 1–11; Riegl, *Spätrömische Kunstindustrie* (Vienna; Staatsdruckerei, 1927), p. 181.

85. Quoted in Weiland Schmied, *Caspar David Friedrich* (Cologne: DuMont, 1975), p. 102.

86. Peter Rautmann, *C. D. Friedrich: Das Eismeer: Durch Tod zu neuem Leben* (Frankfurt: Fischer, 1991), p. 19.

87. See the exhibition history in Helmut Börsch-Supan and Karl Friedrich Jähnig, *Caspar David Friedrich: Gemalde, Druckgraphik, und bildmässige Zeichnungen* (Munich: Prestel, 1973), p. 387.

88. Johannes Grave, *Caspar David Friedrich und die Theorie des Erhabenen* (Weimar: VDG, 2001), pp. 22–23.

89. On the specifics of the oil sketches, see Werner Sumowski, *Caspar David Friedrich: Studien* (Wiesbaden: Franz Steiner Verlag, 1970), pp. 172 and 174.

90. Schmied, *Caspar David Friedrich*, p. 102.

91. Andriana Craciun, *Writing Arctic Disaster: Authorship and Exploration* (Cambridge: Cambridge University Press, 2016), esp. pp. 204–209.

92. George Best, *A True Discourse of the late voyages of discoverie, for the finding of a passage to Cathaya, by the Northvveast, vnder the conduct of Martin Frobisher Generall deuided into three books* (London: Henry Bynnyman, 1578), p. 13. To this day, Nova Zembla itself is properly classified not as in island, but as an archipelago.

93. Best, *A True Discourse of the late voyages of discoverie*, quoted in James McDermott,

"Frobisher's 1578 Voyage: Early Eyewitness Accounts of English Ships in Arctic Seas," *Polar Record* 32.183 (1996), p. 235.

94. Best, *A True Discourse of the late voyages of discoverie*, quoted in Hilfiker, "Negotiating Arctic Waters," p. 355.

95. Rosalind Krauss, "Grids," *October* 9 (1979), pp. 52 and 59.

96. W. Miklenitsch, "Die Arbeit der Macht an den Leben: Opferökonomie und Opfer-politiken — Am Leitfaden von Bataille, Adorno, and Foucault," in Peter Sloterdijk and Otto Kallscheuer (eds.), *Peter Sloterdijks "Kritik der zynischen Vernunft"* (Frankfurt am Main: Suhrkamp, 1987), pp. 299–51.

97. Theodor W. Adorno, "Education after Auschwitz," in *Critical Models: Interventions and Catchwords*, trans. Henry W. Pickford (New York: Columbia University Press, 2005), p. 201.

98. Theodor W. Adorno, *Negative Dialectics*, trans. E. B. Ashton (New York: Continuum, 1973), p. 347.

99. See the excellent essay by Simon Mussell, "'Pervaded by a Chill': The Dialectic of Coldness in Adorno's Social Theory," *Thesis Eleven* 117.1 (2013), pp. 55–67. More generally on Adorno's coldness, see J. M. Bernstein, *Adorno: Disenchantment and Ethics* (Cambridge: Cambridge University Press, 2001), pp. 396–414.

100. Theodor W. Adorno, *Prisms*, trans. Samuel and Shierry Weber (Cambridge, MA: MIT Press, 1981), p. 158.

101. Theodor W, Adorno, *Minima Moralia: Reflections from Damaged Life*, trans. E. F. N. Jephcott (New York: Verso, 1974), p. 163. Original: ". . . zur verzweifelten Isolierung Verge-sellschafteten nach Miteinandersein hungern und zu kalten Haufen sich zusammenrot-ten," in Adorno, *Gesammelte Schriften*, ed. Rolf Tiedemann et al., 20 vols. (Frankfurt am Main: Suhrkamp, 2003), vol. 4, p. 186.

102. Adorno, *Negative Dialectics*, p. 191, emphasis added.

103. Blumenberg, *Shipwreck with Spectator*, p. 7.

CHAPTER SEVEN: THERE ARE NO FORTRESSES

1. *SSSR na stroike*, 1934, no. 10, pp. 4–5. On USSR in Construction as a serial, see Erika Wolf, "USSR in Construction: From Avant-Garde to Socialist Realist Practice," Ph.D. diss., University of Michigan, 1999, and Katerina Romanenko, "Photomontage for the Masses: The Soviet Periodical Press of the 1930s," *Design Issues* 26.1 (2010), pp. 29–39. On Lissitzky's involvement, see Victor Margolin, *The Struggle for Utopia: Rodchenko, Lissitzky, Moholy-Nagy* (Chicago: University of Chicago Press, 1997), pp. 181–83.

2. In the vast literature on the *Chelyuskin* adventure, see T. E. Armstrong, *The Northern*

Sea Route: Soviet Exploitation of the Northeast Passage (Cambridge: Cambridge University Press, 1952), Katerina Clark, "Little Heroes and Big Deeds: Literature Responds to the First-Five Year Plan," in Sheila Fitzpatrick (ed.), *Cultural Revolution in Russia, 1928–1931* (Bloomington: Indiana University Press, 1978).

3. Maxim Gorky, "Piercing the Arctic," *Literary Digest* 2 (May 1936), p. 15.

4. John McCannon, *Red Arctic* (Oxford: Oxford University Press, 1998), pp. 110–34; Rosalinde Sartorti, "Stalinism and Carnival," in Hans Gunther (ed.), *The Culture of the Stalin Period* (London: Palgrave, 1990), pp. 44–65. Veniamin Kaverin's *Two Captains*, written between 1938 and 1945, told the story of Russian polar explorers before the Revolution, winning the Stalin Prize in Arts in 1946. The book was reissued no fewer than forty-two times over the next quarter century.

5. Pier Horensma, *The Soviet Arctic* (London: Routledge, 1991), p. 32.

6. Robert Service, *Stalin: A Biography* (Cambridge, MA: Harvard University Press, 2005), pp. 105–106.

7. *SSSR na stroike*, 1933, no. 12, p. 7.

8. James Forsyth, *A History of the Peoples of Siberia, Russia's North Asian Colony, 1581–1990* (Cambridge: Cambridge University Press, 1992), pp. 1–27.

9. Michael Murrin, *Trade and Romance* (Chicago: University of Chicago Press, 2013), p. 236.

10. Horensma, *The Soviet Arctic*, p. 59.

11. Russian expansion into Siberia, Soviet doctrine held, was peacefully different from what had occurred in the West. It "took place not by the expulsion of aboriginals, much less their extermination, but by the assimilation of vacant expanses by new-comers 'floating around' the dwelling-places of the indigenous peoples," as an official Russian history was to put it in the 1970s. Quoted in Forsyth, *A History of the Peoples of Siberia*, p. 110. The story was, obviously, somewhat more complex: see Yuri Slezkine, *Arctic Mirrors: Russia and the Small Peoples of the North* (Ithaca: Cornell University Press, 1996), pp. 265–311. Solzhenitsyn's metaphor of the gulag as an archipelago has its own precedents; see Natalia Pervukhin, "The 'Experiment in Literary Investigation' (Čexov's Saxalin and Solženicyn's Gulag)," *The Slavic and East European Journal* 35.4 (1991), pp. 489–502.

12. Lissitzky later claimed: "I would go so far as to say that the work involved in the presentation of an issue of the periodical, for instance, 'Chelyuskin': or 'The Constitution of the USSR' requires no less effort than a painting. And it makes no less of an impact on the public." Quoted in Sophie Lissitzky-Küppers, *El Lissitzky: Life, Letters, Texts*, trans. Helene Aldwinckle (London: Thames and Hudson, 1968), p. 387.

13. *SSR na stroike*, 1934, no. 10, p. 4. See E. Widdis, "Russia as Space," in Simon Franklin and Emma Widdis (eds.), *National Identity in Russian Culture: An Introduction* (Cambridge: Cambridge University Press, 2004), pp. 30–49.

14. See the locations listed in David J. Dallin and Boris I. Nicolaevsky, *Forced Labor in Soviet Russia* (New Haven: Yale University Press, 1947), pp. 51–62. On the importance of the gulag to the development of the Russian Arctic, see Paul R. Josephson, *The Conquest of the Russian Arctic* (Cambridge, MA: Harvard University Press, 2014), pp. 115–69. On the grim fluidity of settlement/camp/prison/town/city situations in the Soviet Arctic (with curious resonances for North America today), see Allen Barenberg, "Prisoners without Borders: Zazonniki and the Transformation of Vorkuta after Stalin," *Jahrbücher für Geschichte Osteuropas* 57.4 (2009), pp. 513–34.

15. This remains in dispute. See Dallin and Nicolaevsky, *Forced Labor in Soviet Russia*, p. 128.

16. Loren R. Graham, *Science in Russia and the Soviet Union* (Cambridge: Cambridge University Press, 1993), pp. 173–96.

17. Stephen Brain, "Stalin's Environmentalism," *Russian Review* 69 (January 2010), pp. 93–118; Yuri Schkloenko, "Environmental Considerations," *Soviet Life*, October 1977, pp. 41–45. On the broader Soviet Arctic research approach, see Vladas Stanka, *Institutions of the USSR Active in Arctic Research and Development* (Washington: Arctic Institute of North America, 1958), and, more generally, James T. Andrews, *Science for the Masses: The Bolshevik State, Public Science, and the Popular Imagination in Soviet Russia, 1917–1934* (College Station: Texas A&M University Press, 2003), esp. pp. 154–69.

18. Ruth Gruber, *I Went to the Soviet Arctic* (New York, Simon and Schuster, 1939), p. 204.

19. The survey literature on such practices is already extensive. For a sample, see Nicola Triscott, "Critical Art and Intervention in Technologies of the Arctic," in Michael Bravo and Nicola Triscott (eds.), *Arctic Geopolitics and Autonomy* (Berlin: Hatje Cantz, 2010), pp. 19–36, and the introduction to Julie Decker and Kirsten J. Anderson (eds.), *Up Here: The North at the Center of the World* (Seattle: University of Washington Press, 2016).

20. Benjamin Morgan, "After the Arctic Sublime," *New Literary History* 47.1 (Winter 2016), p. 2. Longyearbyen on Spitsbergen, home to the "doomsday" Svalbard Seed Vault, has recently begun an artist's residency program.

21. Maggie Cao, "Entropic History" in Christopher P. Heuer and Rebecca Zorach (eds.), *Ecologies, Agents, Terrains* (New Haven: Yale University Press, 2018), pp. 266–91.

22. Eliasson's comments appeared on the various versions of www.icewatch.com. On the problematics of the idea of "action" herein summoned with regard to the environment,

see T. J. Demos, *Against the Anthropocene: Visual Culture and Environment Today* (Berlin: Sternberg Press, 2017).

23. Artists 4 Climate, "Olafur Eliasson & Minik Rosing," http://www.artists4climate .com/en/artists/olafur-eliasson.

24. Quoted in Cynthia Zarin, "The Artist Who Is Bringing Icebergs to Paris," *New Yorker*, December 5, 2015, https://www.newyorker.com/culture/culture-desk/ the-artist -who-is-bringing-icebergs-to-paris.

25. David Balzer, "The Carbon Footprint of Art," *Canadian Art*, February 20, 2017.

26. Jason W. Moore, "The Capitalocene, Part I: On the Nature and Origins of Our Ecological Crisis," *Journal of Peasant Studies* 44 (2017), pp. 594–630.

27. "A Questionnaire on Materialisms," *October* 155 (Winter 2016), p. 3.

28. Lucy R. Lippard, "Art within the Arctic Circle," *Hudson Review* 22.4 (Winter 1969– 1970), p. 669.

29. *Ibid.*, p. 666.

30. For a related example of research-based Arctic practices, see Charles Stankievech, *Loveland* (Berlin: K. Verlag, 2011), pp. 197–212. 31. The label "activist" began as a slur in the 1930s, leveled against leftist protesters by reactionary forces of capital; "organizer," by contrast, is a word self-applied in trade union and labor circles during the same decade. See Astra Taylor, "Against Activism," *Baffler* 30 (2016), pp. 123–31, esp. p. 127.

32. Matthew Coolidge, quoted in Kate Haug, "The Human/Land Dialectic: Anthropic Landscapes of the Center for Land Use Interpretation," *Afterimage* 25.2 (September–October 1997), pp. 3–5. On CLUI's "tactical thinking," see Stephanie Lemenager, "The Center for Lands Use Interpretation," *English Studies in Canada* 414 (2014), p. 20.

33. Cornelia Butler, "The Catalogue of Robert Smithson's Library," in Eugenie Tsai (ed.), *Robert Smithson*, exh. cat. (Los Angeles: Museum of Contemporary Art, 2004), p. 237.

34. Michael Ned Holte, "The Administrative Sublime or the Center for Land Use Interpretation at the Circumference," *Afterall* 13 (Spring–Summer 2006), p. 25.

35. Kazimir Malevich, "Suprematism," in John Bowlt (ed.), *Russian Art of the Avant-Garde: Theory and Criticism 1902–1934* (New York: Viking Press, 1976), pp. 144–45.

36. Aleksandra Shatskikh, *Black Square: Malevich and the Origin of Suprematism* (New Haven: Yale University Press, 2012), pp. 251–71.

37. Kazimir Malevich, "Non-Objective Creation and Suprematism" (1919), quoted in Troels Andersen (ed.), *K. S. Malevich: Essays on Art 1915–1928* (Copenhagen: Borgen, 1968), p. 122.

38. *Ibid.* The original was reprinted in *Sovietskoye iskusstvo za 15 let* (Moscow: Izogiz, 1933): "Я прорвал синий абажур цветных ограничений, вышел в белое, за мной, товарищи авиаторы, плывите в бездну."

39. Kazimir Malevich to Alexandre Benois, May 1916, quoted in Irina A. Vakar and Tatiana N. Mikhienko (eds.), *Kazimir Malevich: Letters, Documents, Memoirs, Criticism*, 2 vols. (London: Tate 2015), vol. 1, p. 86.

40. Pieter Bruegel, *Adoration of the Magi in the Snow* (1567), Winterthur, Collection Oskar Reinhart. On the painting's snow as whitewash, see Joseph Leo Koerner, *Bosch and Bruegel: Parallel Worlds* (Princeton: Princeton University Press, 2016), p. 286.

41. Olga Klyonova, "Features of Malevich's Painting Technique Revealed in the Process of the Restoration of His Works," in Yevgenia Petrova (ed.), *Kazimir Malevich in the Russian Museum* (St. Petersburg: Palace Editions, 2000), pp. 32–34.

42. This phrasing is from T. J. Clark, *Farewell to an Idea: Episodes from a History of Modernism* (New Haven: Yale University Press, 1999), p. 271. 43. Quoted in John McCannon, *Red Arctic: Polar Exploration and the Myth of the North in the Soviet Union* (Oxford: Oxford University Press, 1997), p. 88.

44. Among the horrors of the gulag experience most familiar to the West are interminable rail journeys to Siberia. And yet many of the camps in the Arctic (roughly 10 percent of all those extant in the USSR by the 1940s, according to one estimate) were serviced solely by boat.

45. Horensma, *The Soviet Arctic*, p. 52.

46. Amy K. Powell's brilliant *Depositions: Scenes from the Late Medieval Church and the Modern Museum* (New York: Zone Books, 2012), esp. pp. 120–23, is the most important study in this vein.

47. Hito Steyerl, "In Defense of the Poor Image," in Steyerl, *The Wretched of the Screen* (Berlin: Sternberg Press, 2012), p. 32.

48. Robin Kelsey, "Landscape as Not Belonging," in James Elkins and Rachael Z. DeLue (eds.), *Landscape Theory* (London: Routledge, 2010), pp. 203–12.

49. On the assumption, shared by both post-1970s environmental activists and climat-echange deniers, the idea of nature as other (for humans to, by turns, live in "balance" with or exploit), see Timothy Morton, *Hyperobjects: Philosophy and Ecology after the End of the World* (Minneapolis: University of Minnesota Press, 2013), pp. 99–133. For the full story on Alaska, see Peter Coates, *The Trans-Alaska Pipeline Controversy: Technology, Conservation, and the Frontier* (Fairbanks, AK: University of Alaska Press, 1993), pp. 162–74 and, more polemically, Sam Hall, *The Fourth World* (New York: Vintage, 1987).

50. See Alan C. Braddock and Christopher Irmscher (eds.), *A Keener Perception: Ecocritical Studies in American Art History* (Tuscaloosa: The University of Alabama Press, 2009).

51. Eric Naiman, introduction to Evgeny Dobrenko and Eric Naiman (eds.), *The Landscape of Stalinism: The Art and Ideology of Soviet Space* (Seattle: University of Washington Press, 2003), pp. 11–17. On the idea of blindness as real sight, vital still is Paul de Man, *Blindness and Insight: Essays on the Rhetoric of Contemporary Criticism* (New York: Oxford University Press, 1971), esp. pp. 102–41.

52. John E. Kutzbach, "Simulated Climatic Changes: Results of the COHMAP Climate-Model Experiments," in H. E. Wright, Jr., et al. (eds.), *Global Climates since the Last Glacial Maximum* (Minneapolis: University of Minnesota Press, 1993), pp. 136–69; D. G. Vaughan, et al., "Observations: Cryosphere," in Thomas F. Stocker, et al. (eds.), *Climate Change 2013: The Physical Science Basis. Contribution of Working Group I to the Fifth Assessment Report of the Intergovernmental Panel on Climate Change* (Cambridge: Cambridge University Press, 2013), pp. 323–29.

53. Rob Nixon, *Slow Violence and the Environmentalism of the Poor* (Cambridge, MA: Harvard University Press, 2013), esp. pp. 7–14.

54. "Ice and Fire: Large Blaze Burns in Greenland for Two Weeks," *Guardian*, August 19, 2017, https://www.theguardian.com/world/2017/aug/20/ice-and-fire-large-blaze-burns-in-greenland-for-two-weeks.

Image Credits

1.1	The Huntington Library Collection
1.2	The Carnegie Museum of Art
1.3	National Gallery of Art, Washington
2.1	University of Toronto
2.2	John Carter Brown Library at Brown University
2.3	bpk Bildagentur/Kupferstichkabinett, Staatliche Museen, Berlin/ Volker-H. Schneider/Art Resource, NY
2.4	© National Gallery, London/Art Resource, NY
2.5	© National Gallery, London/Art Resource, NY
2.6	Royal Danish Library
2.7	Getty Research Institute Open Content Program
2.8	Munich Bayerische Staatsbibliothek
2.9	The Stapleton Collection/Bridgeman Images
3.1	British Library/Granger. All Rights Reserved
3.2	Harvard University
3.3	The Huntington Library Collection
3.4	© Lawerence Weiner, courtesy of the Marian Goodman Gallery. Photo Harvard Library
3.5	Library of Congress, Rare Book and Special Collections Division
3.6	Canadian Museum of History
3.7	The John Carter Brown Library at Brown University
3.8	The John Carter Brown Library at Brown University
3.9	Getty Research Institute Open Content Program
3.10	Reproduced by courtesy of the Marquess of Salisbury

4.1   Zentralbibliothek Zurich, Department of Prints and Drawings/Photo Archive

4.2   British Library/Granger. All Rights Reserved

4.3   Getty Research Institute Open Content Program

4.4   The New York Public Library

4.5   British Library/Granger. All Rights Reserved

4.6   © The Trustees of the British Museum/Art Resource, NY

4.7   Rijksmuseum, Amsterdam

4.8   © Museum Mayer van den Bergh

4.9   Munich Bayerische Staatsbibliothek

4.10 Ghent University Library

4.11 © The Trustees of the British Museum/Art Resource, NY

4.12 Zentralbibliothek Zurich/Wikipedia

4.13 Smithsonian Institution

4.14 © The Trustees of the British Museum/Art Resource, NY

4.15 www.metmuseum.org

4.16 © RMN-Grand Palais/René-Gabriel Ojéda/Art Resource, NY

5.1   National Library, Norway

5.2   National Library, Norway

5.3   archive.org

5.4   National Library, Norway

5.5   National Library, Norway

5.6   Library of Congress, Rare Book and Special Collections Division

6.1   Christopher Heuer, Courtesy Rijksmuseum, Amsterdam

6.2   Rijksmuseum, Amsterdam

6.3   Rijksmuseum, Amsterdam

6.4   Rijksmuseum, Amsterdam

6.5   Rijksmuseum, Amsterdam

6.6   www.metmuseum.org

6.7   Rijksmuseum, Amsterdam

6.8   Harvard University

6.9   Harvard University

6.10 British Library/Granger. All Rights Reserved

6.11 © Siân Bowen. Photo courtesy of the artist

6.12 www.museumrotterdam.nl

6.13 Erich Lessing/Art Resource, NY

Index

Zone Books series design by Bruce Mau
Typesetting by Meighan Gale
Image placement and production by Julie Fry
Printed and bound by Maple Press